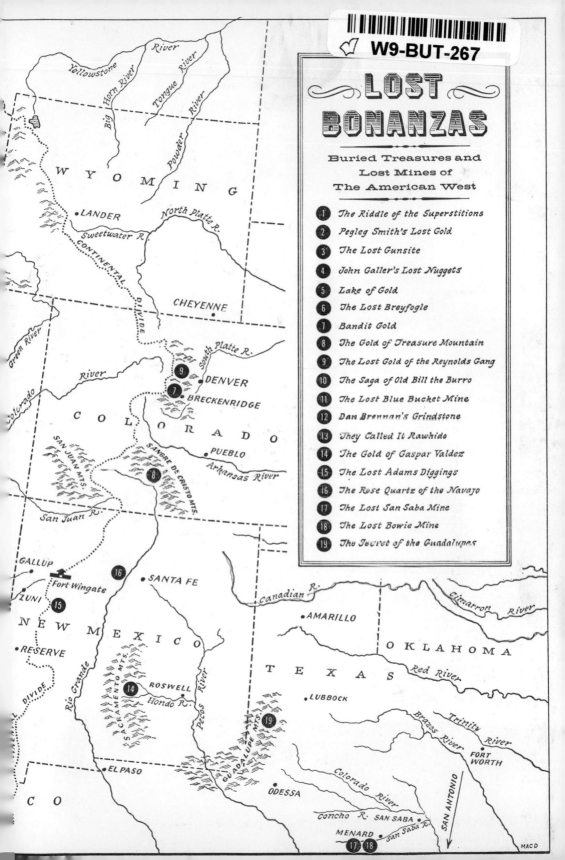

LOST BONANZAS

Buried Treasures and
Lost Mines of
The American West

1. The Riddle of the Superstitions
2. Pegleg Smith's Lost Gold
3. The Lost Gunsite
4. John Galler's Lost Nuggets
5. Lake of Gold
6. The Lost Breyfogle
7. Bandit Gold
8. The Gold of Treasure Mountain
9. The Lost Gold of the Reynolds Gang
10. The Saga of Old Bill the Burro
11. The Lost Blue Bucket Mine
12. Dan Brennan's Grindstone
13. They Called It Rawhide
14. The Gold of Gaspar Valdez
15. The Lost Adams Diggings
16. The Rose Quartz of the Navajo
17. The Lost San Saba Mine
18. The Lost Bowie Mine
19. The Secret of the Guadalupes

LOST BONANZAS

Also by Harry Sinclair Drago

GREAT AMERICAN CATTLE TRAILS

OUTLAWS ON HORSEBACK

RED RIVER VALLEY

WILD, WOOLLY AND WICKED

WHERE THE LOON CALLS

FOLLOWING THE GRASS

MONTANA ROAD

THE WILD BUNCH

BUCKSKIN EMPIRE

STAGECOACH KINGDOM

RIVER OF GOLD

LOST BONANZAS

Tales of the Legendary Lost Mines of the
American West

By HARRY SINCLAIR DRAGO

DODD, MEAD & COMPANY

NEW YORK

Printed in the United States of America
by The Cornwall Press, Inc., Cornwall, N. Y.

The author acknowledges with gratitude, permission from William Morrow
and Company, Inc. to quote from *The Lost Dutchman Mine* by Sims Ely,
Copyright 1953 by Sims Ely; permission from The Naylor Company, San
Antonio, Texas, to quote from *Lost Mines and Hidden Treasure* by Leland Lovelace, Copyright © 1961 by The Naylor Company; permission
from The Frontier Book Company, Toyahvale, Texas, to quote from *The
Golden Crescent* by Jesse Ed Rascoe, Copyright © 1962 by Edward Ells-
worth Bartholomew, *Western Treasures Lost and Found* by Jesse Ed Rascoe and *More Western Treasures Lost and Found* by Jesse Ed Rascoe,
Copyright © 1962 by Ed Bartholomew.

For

Malcolm Decker
"South Pass Pete"

a good man to have across
campfire or table

Introduction

Tales of lost mines and buried treasure are not indigenous to the United States. The world around, wherever gold and silver were taken from the earth in quantity, they sprang into existence and quickly became current in the spoken and written lore of the country in which they originated.

They go back far into antiquity. In China, for example, in the early T'ang Dynasty, gold was discovered in Shantung Province. With no law to protect their property rights, other than the armed guards they hired and maintained themselves, it followed that the owners were often murdered. In turn, the usurpers were likely to meet the same fate. Or, with his own safety in mind, a man might make a strike and, instead of declaring it, cover it up in the hope of concealing it until the Imperial government brought a semblance of law and order to Shantung. Often that was so long in coming that many prospectors died of old age, taking their secret to the grave. Naturally it became a part of local folklore that many mines had been lost.

The great trade routes to Bokhara and the west, with their rich camel caravans, were preyed on by bandit gangs, both coming and going. The merchants, returning with gold coin for their wares, often buried their treasure in the sands of Turkestan to save it and were unable to return to it.

But it is with the Spaniards that our American tales of lost mines and buried treasures of gold, jewels, and costly church vessels and ornaments are principally concerned, and it is that section of the United States, the Southwest including California, over which Spain, and later Mexico, once held sovereignty, that has been the most prolific producer of these accounts of great wealth, found and lost.

In the New World there has been a peculiar affinity between the Spaniard and precious metal from his first coming to the Americas. The avarice that sight of the silver of Montezuma and the Aztecs and the gold of the Incas aroused in him, and the depths of brutality to which he resorted to get possession of it, are too well-known to call for comment.

Having gained riches beyond their dreaming made them credulous to the point of absurdity and explains their readiness to accept any tale of even greater riches *más allá*—farther on. Their credulity reached its extremes in the expedition of four hundred Spaniards and thousands of Indians organized by Nuño de Guzmán, the Governor of New Spain, in 1529, who marched up the Pacific Coast in search of the fabled Seven Cities of Gold. They were gone two years, but all they found were the many-storied mud houses of the Zuni.

Six years later Antonio de Mendoza, the first Viceroy of New Spain, inspired by the fabulous stories of Cabeza de Vaca, one of the few survivors of a Spanish invasion of Florida, who spent several years wandering across the continent to the Pacific, outfitted a second expedition to find the Seven Cities and explore the allegedly even greater riches of a land called Quivira, both of which were nonexistent. This was the famous expedition led by Coronada.

There was gold in Arizona and New Mexico, and the Spaniards found it. Their mining operations became extensive and formed the basis for the legendary as well as real tales of their lost mines and cached treasure. The Spaniards were regarded by all Indians as their traditional enemy, and in what is now the United States they were hated and despised by the Apache, who waged incessant war on them. When a free and independent Mexico became the ruling government there was no lessening of that bitterness; they hated the Mexican less but despised him more.

With the coming of the Americans the old enmity reached new heights of savage fury, for in the Anglo-Saxon the Apache tribes and the Comanches, those wild, free rovers of the plains, recognized a sterner foe than the Spaniard and the Mexican, whose avowed purpose was to subjugate them, take possession of their ancestral homelands, and coop them up on reservations. If their fight to retain what was theirs was bloody, merciless, cruel, it was also heroic. They asked no quarter and gave none. Even when they were finally forced to submit, their spirit was not broken, and half a century was to pass before the prospector and the ranchman could consider themselves safe.

In present-day New Mexico and Arizona, four hundred years of strife, Indian revolts (other than Apache), the driving out of all Spaniards in the great Pueblo revolt of 1680, the sacking and burning of churches, the slaying of Franciscan missionaries, and the capture by bandits of hundreds of jack loads of treasure bound for Mexico City provide a fertile field for the countless tales of lost mines and cached plants of silver and gold. It is the same in California and Texas.

The lower Rio Grande and the Pecos River valleys are hallowed ground with lost treasure seekers. Other Texas rivers— the Nueces, San Saba, and Llano—are hardly less fruitful sources for tales of hidden or lost wealth. Every community has its own legends and its variations of them. Almost without exception they are based on the recollection of an aged Mexican, preferably one who was captured as a lad by the Comanches or Apaches and grew to manhood among them before being given his freedom. He has seen the mine from which they got their gold or silver. Being an excellent storyteller, which is required of all "old" Mexicans in such circumstances, he describes the mine in great detail. He is sure he can find it. But his sudden death, or some calamity, invariably occurs to prevent him from locating the rich ledge or outcrop. It doesn't keep other men from searching for it.

Ninety percent of such legends have no more foundation in fact than Coronado's Seven Cities of Gold. The tales gathered here are of another kind with the validity of history behind them. If they disagree with or contradict previously published accounts it is because it has not been my purpose to write for entertainment alone. The so-called literature of lost mines and buried treasures is a vast one. It contains more trash than will be found in any other category of writing. For forty years I have been writing about the West in one form or another, discarding what I believed to be spurious and false. I trust the reader will find some reason to believe that my time has not been wasted.

I have had something to say about the part animals have played in the discovery of silver and gold. Perhaps I should have included the experience of the Bolivian goatherd who in order to pull himself over a ledge caught hold of a bush. It came out by the roots, strewing the ground with a shower of silver. In such fashion were the world-famous silver mines of Potosi discovered. As the late J. Frank Dobie has said, the story of mineral wealth is largely the story of accident.

HARRY SINCLAIR DRAGO

Contents

Contents

ARIZONA

1

The Mythical Peraltas
and the Lost Dutchman

Had the Lost Dutchman been called the Lost German, and the mountains in which it is located been named the *Sierra de la Espuma*, rather than the Superstitions, which could have been done with equal justification, it would probably not have become the most-storied of all lost mines. But that combination of Lost Dutchman and Superstitions titillated the imagination and has given the mine enduring fame.

More men have sought it, more books and articles have been written about it, than any other "lost" mine. Myths and legends that are genuine as well as those that imagination has manufactured color the memorabilia of the Lost Dutchman. These fanciful tales not only disagree and contradict one another, but in them factual history is either ignored or twisted into convenient fiction. One thing, however, they have in common—a blind dependence on the ubiquitous Peralta Land Grant.

Unquestionably the Spanish-Mexican Peralta family was a large one, with numerous members living in California and Arizona. It is of record that in 1872, Miguel and Jesus Peralta, brothers, were engaged in mining at Wickenburg in Arizona, men of little education and very limited circumstances. At the same time, at Black Canyon, southeast of Prescott, the territorial capital, there were other Peraltas, the head of that clan being another Miguel Peralta, an elderly man, given the honorary title of Don by his fellow Mexicans.

There were still other Miguel Peraltas, among them Don Peralta's son; all keep turning up in confusing fashion in the unraveling of the great Peralta Land Grant. Don Miguel Peralta of Black Rock claimed to be the owner of the grant given him by the Mexican government prior to the Gadsden Purchase; and under the arrangement entered into between the United States and Mexico to honor authentic grants of land, it was, presumably, valuable.

He had documents, including a *cedula* on parchment, substantiating his title to an unknown number of ancient *varas* of land. To Black Canyon came George M. Willing, Jr., familiarly known as Doc Willing, whose only visible means of support was buying and selling mining claims. For as little as three hundred dollars, it was later disclosed, he bought the Peralta grant with money supplied by James Addison Reavis, of St. Louis, Missouri, the future so-called Red Baron of Arizona. This little transaction supplied the spirit for the great Peralta Land Grant swindle that was to bedevil Arizona Territory for more than two decades and all but succeed.

The fantastic Peralta Land Grant hoax, which was born in the real estate office of James A. Reavis, in St. Louis, in 1872, was a closely guarded, behind-the-scenes operation for ten years, in the course of which hundreds of ancient documents were forged and others reposing in the archives of Guadalajara, Mexico, and Mexico City were surreptitiously altered. Later, Reavis was to go to Spain, where, with the help of the American minister, he was given the freedom of the Royal Archives in Seville, into which he inserted documents to strengthen his case and removed others that were damaging.

In the gallery of ingenious American adventurers James Reavis and his Barony of Arizona must be regarded as one of the boldest. His story is so closely interwoven with the Lost Dutchman Mine that, in part, it must be examined. The threads are easily discovered.

When Doc Willing had satisfied himself that the senior Don Miguel Peralta's land grant was genuine, he bought it, as before mentioned, the papers being signed by both the old Don and his son. Willing's home was in St. Louis. He returned there at once, hoping to raise funds with which to exploit the grant. That brought him to Reavis eventually.

Reavis was prosperous. He owned several farms, city real estate, and a thousand feet of valuable river frontage. He and Willing entered into an agreement, the details of which were never made known, other than that Reavis agreed to go to Mexico and settle some debts Willing had hanging over him, contracted in California. The latter returned to Prescott, Reavis agreeing to join him there a few weeks later.

Doc Willing made the mistake of talking too much about the Peralta grant. As soon as the federal government recognized the validity of the grant, no one occupying land within its borders would have title to it until they bought a quitclaim deed from the Peralta Land and Development Company.

The extent of the Peralta grant, about which Willing spoke so glibly, had become astronomical in size. Phoenix was inside its west boundary; eastward, it extended past the line that divides today's Arizona from New Mexico and just missed embracing Silver City, New Mexico, and the famous Santa Rita copper mines. To the south, it ran in a straight line about twenty-five miles north of Tucson. It was seventy miles from that imaginary line to its northern confines. Within that principality lay Phoenix, Maricopa, Casa Grande, Mesa, Florence, Safford, Globe,

Clifton, and a dozen other towns or camps. Through it flowed the Gila River, precious beyond price in a parched land where water spelled the difference between life and death. Included along with the Gila was the greater part of the Salt River Valley and the marvelously rich Silver King Mine, which already had produced better than twenty million dollars in ore. And, of course, the Superstition Mountains. This was no ordinary land grant that Doc Willing was talking about. Geographically, Prescott was not involved, but it was still a rugged, frontier town of pioneers who had cast their lot with their fellow Arizonans. They didn't like what they had heard, and they warned Willing that if he went through with his scheme to seize the homes and ranches of their friends he would very likely be hanged from some convenient pine tree.

Doc went to the Yavapai County Courthouse in Prescott and recorded a deed conveying "a certain grant of land from a Miguel Peralta." The following morning he was found at the lodging house of R. E. Elliott lying face down on his bed—dead!

Commenting on Doc's end, the *Prescott Miner* speculated that his death had been "brought on by exposure and privation." Prescott hastily accepted that conclusion; Willing was buried and his passing forgotten.

Reavis reached San Francisco by boat from Mexico, and there learned of his partner's death. The information seems not to have disturbed him. He communicated with Mary Ann Willing, the widow, and offered her thirty thousand dollars for her late husband's estate. Mrs. Willing, living in near poverty, eagerly assented. Of the thirty thousand, there is no record of her having received more than the initial payment of three hundred dollars.

Reavis was now the sole owner of the Peralta grant, but the only evidence he had of its existence was the deed that Doc Willing had recorded in Yavapai County before his death. Will-

ing had carried with him to Prescott all the carefully manufactured "documents" that Reavis had put together, at great
expense, in St. Louis. These would seem to have been of vital
importance to him, and he might well have hastened to Prescott, determined to locate them.

Far from doing so, he remained in California for two years.
Donald M. Powell, in his carefully documented *The Peralta
Grant,* says in explanation:

His [Reavis'] health was poor for some months, and he was low
on funds. In 1875 and 1876 he taught school in Downey, California.
After this he drifted to the northern part of the state, where he tried
his hand at journalism. He was more successful as a journalist than
as a teacher. In words he found an outlet for his energies and
imagination, and . . . he was a correspondent for the San Francisco
Examiner and for the San Francisco *Call.*

In the years that followed it was revealed that his sojourn in
California had not been devoted solely to writing for the newspapers. He had, in fact, applied himself to gathering evidence,
or purported evidence, to substantiate the colossal hoax on
which he was about to embark. No one has been able to account for the sudden change in his fortunes that occurred early
in 1880 which enabled him to begin his travels. He arrived in
Phoenix in style, in the spring of that year, for, as Powell puts
it, "his first good look at Arizona." He took the stage to Prescott at once, and there, miraculously, in the attic of Judge
Henry W. Fleury's house, where they had been gathering dust
for over two years, he found Doc Willing's belongings and the
precious "documents."

He remained in Arizona only several days, and then proceeded across the continent to Washington to "inspect certain
papers," he testified later. From Washington he went to Guadalajara, in the state of Jalisco, where, posing as an American
journalist, he was given access to the archives. When he was
finished there, he journeyed on to Mexico City where, spending

money with a free hand, he ingratiated himself with government officials and in return was permitted to examine bundles of ancient royal documents dating back to the time of Philip V of Spain.

When Reavis returned to the United States, he was prepared to prove that the great Peralta grant was originally a gift from the Spanish Monarch, Philip V, to Don Miguel Nemecio Silva de Peralta de la Cordoba, the First Baron de Arizonac, and from him descended to his son Jesus Miguel Silva de Peralta de Cordoba, the second Baron, the date of recognition of the grant being set down as January 3, 1758, fourteen years after the original promulgation of the royal decree.

Down through sons, grandsons, and great-grandsons, Reavis had traced the title to his own era—and not to the Peraltas of Black Canyon. The little floating land grant they had once owned, but which was now his, no longer interested him, for he had found a direct descendant of the fabled second Baron of Arizonac, beautiful Sophia Loreta Micaela Peralta, and made her his wife. He was at last ready to make his bid for empire, and it was an impressive array of *expedientes* (copies) of documents which he filed with the U.S. Surveyor General of Arizona in Tucson.

Reavis was thirty-nine at the time, and his young wife had not yet celebrated her twentieth birthday. In appearing before the U.S. Surveyor General of Arizona and depositing with him certain "maps, cedulas, and *expedientes*" he was only making his claim to the Peralta grant a matter of official record. Although it proved nothing, it was immensely valuable to him. The timid began buying his quitclaim deeds. But he was after bigger game. In New York City in 1885 John W. Mackay, the Comstock Lode millionaire, dazzled by Reavis' prospects, entered into an agreement to advance him five hundred dollars a month for expenses while he continued his searching in Spain and Mexico for some still missing Peralta papers. What Mackay was to receive in return was not disclosed.

Previous to that, he had received much more important backing from the Southern Pacific Railroad Company. The Southern Pacific was then building eastward across Arizona, and the Texas and Pacific was reaching westward for California. Years later, Reavis testified under oath that he had received $50,000 from the Pacific Improvement Company, a Southern Pacific subsidiary, for a free right-of-way across the Peralta grant, in addition to which he was to refuse to make any accommodation with the Texas Pacific.

Reavis was not doing business with the office boy, but with Charlie Crocker himself, one of the fabled "Big Four" who had built the Central Pacific and the Southern Pacific, and by no one's reckoning a fool. He proved it by demanding and getting from Reavis a secret agreement that when title to the grant had finally been approved by the United States he (Crocker) was to have a 50 percent interest in the land.

Back in Arizona, James M. Barney, the millionaire owner of the great Silver King Mine, paid Reavis $5,000 for a quitclaim to his property. It sent a chill down the spine of the small fry; if men of the stature of Charlie Crocker, John Mackay, and Jim Barney were convinced that the United States would have to declare the Peralta grant valid, perhaps it was time for lesser men to fall in line. Not only were figures of great wealth backing Reavis, but he was employing the most famous lawyers in the country to represent him. Among them were Robert G. Ingersoll and Roscoe Conkling, as well as several others of almost equal fame.

Reavis was full of schemes, such as the Casa Grande Improvement Company, the Salt River Valley Irrigation Company, and others—all on paper and none of which ever materialized. It has been said that from his manipulations he received as much as half a million dollars, which seems a gross exaggeration. Two hundred thousand is a more believable estimate. Whatever it was, the Peralta grant was by now casting a dark and menacing cloud over that part of Arizona lying within its prescribed boundaries. And it would not go away. Even those newspapers which attacked it most virulently as a monstrous hoax and gigantic fraud could not be sure of their ground.

The only way in which a land grant claim could be either validated or invalidated was by the slow and devious procedures directed in the act of Congress of 1854 for settling the legality of grants of land made by Spanish or Mexican governments in territory subsequently ceded to the United States, all such cases being under the jurisdiction of the Department of the Interior. The surveyor general of the proper area was instructed to gather data, examine the records, and pass on the information thus gathered to the Surveyor General of the United States. It then was the duty of the secretary to study the supporting documents and make his report to the Congress, with any recommendations he cared to make.

How time-consuming and unsatisfactory this arrangement was may be gathered from a statement made in 1880 by Secretary of the Interior Carl Schurz: "After a lapse of nearly thirty years more than one thousand claims have been filed with the Surveyor General, of which less than one hundred and fifty have been reported to the Congress, and of the number so reported, Congress has finally acted upon only seventy-one." Of the law itself, he continued: "Its operation has been a failure, amounting to a denial of justice, both to the claimants and to the United States."

Since that was the path the Peralta grant had to take, who could say when or what disposition of it would be made? Obviously it was going to take years. As a matter of record, it was to take fifteen years to accomplish the downfall of James A. Reavis and his amazing collection of forged documents and perjured witnesses. It began fittingly in Santa Fe, City of the Holy Faith, when Reavis appeared to press his claim to the Peralta grant before the recently established U.S. Court of Private Land Claims, Chief Justice Reed presiding, on June 3, 1895.

Reavis got off to a bad start when he offered in evidence his beautifully embellished "ancient documents," bearing the lead seals of the Spanish Crown. Experts retained by the government pointed out that certain alterations could not have been made with a steel pen a century before the steel pen came into use.

On June 26, a week after the trial ended, the court reassembled, and Chief Justice Reed read the devastating decision:

The Court finds from the evidence that said grant or claim is not entitled to confirmation in the name of the alleged original grantee nor in the name of any one else claiming an interest therein. That the claim is wholly fictitious and fraudulent and the various documents on which the same is based are each and all of them forged, manufactured, and have been surreptitiously introduced into the records and archives at Madrid and Seville and into the records and archives in the City of Guadalajara . . . And the Court further finds that no such person as Don Miguel Nemecio Silva de Peralta de la Cordoba ever existed . . . that the plaintiff Sophia Loreta Peralta and her husband and co-plaintiff James Addison Reavis, are not in anywise related to or connected with said alleged grantee . . . but that they and each of them are fraudulent and fictitious claimants for said property.
It is therefore ordered, adjudged and decreed that the claim to property which is commonly known and called the Peralta grant . . . is hereby rejected and the petition dismissed.

Some legal verbiage has been trimmed away; otherwise, the decision is in full. Consider how sweeping it was: no first Baron of Arizonac; hence no second Baron; Sophia Loreta revealed not to be a Peralta but the daughter of one John A. Treadway, of Sherwood Valley, California, born of an Indian woman and presumably illegitimate; the Peralta grant found to be non-existent.

Reavis was placed under arrest, charged with conspiring to defraud the government. That appeared to be the end of his grandiose scheme. But it wasn't. He fought back. And so did the government. After a year of legal wrangling, he was brought to trial. On June 30, 1896, he was found guilty as charged, and two weeks later was sentenced to serve two years in the federal penitentiary and fined $5,000.

His wealthy associates had deserted him, and although he continued to talk big, he had reached the end of the road. Arizona could breath easier. James Addison Reavis could now be forgotten, but not the fabled Peralta grant. Over the years it had become so interwoven with the legends and folklore of Arizona that the mythical Peraltas, not the real ones, color all the tales of the Lost Dutchman Mine.

Convenient stepping-stones bridge the gap from fact to fantasy. In the days of the *Californios,* long before the United States laid claim to any part of the Southwest, Mexicans from Sonora were working the placers and potholes along the lower Colorado. They were not molested by the peaceful Yumas (or Quechans, as they called themselves) who built their villages along the river and farmed the bottomlands. The situation changed rapidly when Padre Francisco Garcés and three other Franciscan missionaries, accompanied by "twenty soldiers and their families, and twenty colonists and their families, and twelve laborers" arrived from Sonora and established two mission-pueblos near the junction of the Gila and the Colorado rivers: Purisima Concepción on the hill where Fort Yuma was later to stand, and San Pedro y San Pablo de Bicuñer, a short distance up the Colorado.

As so often happened when Spanish colonists were dealing with Indians, the latter, in this instance the Quechans, were driven to forced labor by their new masters, not only in building the missions but in the placering for gold. In increasing sullenness they saw the newcomers appropriating the best of the bottomlands. On July 17, 1787, the Quechans revolted. The priests, most of the soldiers, and many of the male colonists were beaten to death. Bicuñer and Purisima were destroyed. Those who survived were ransomed several months later to a military expedition commanded by Lieutenant Colonel Pedro Fages.

No further attempt was made to colonize the Colorado River valley. But it was believed, of course, that a great quantity of gold had been stored in the vaults of the Mission San Pedro y San Pablo de Bicuñer. Spaniards, Mexicans, and Americans searched for it in vain. For half a century they tunneled around and under the old walls until they collapsed. Always the Quechans told them they were looking for what was not there; that following the uprising, they had found the gold and thrown it into the river—which was believable, for gold meant as little to them as it did to the Apaches.

But gold was found in the potholes and in the sands at Laguna, Gila Bend, and on the Hassayampa. Why not in the inhospitable Superstitions that rise in spectacular fashion out of the desert, forty miles east of Phoenix? Experienced prospectors who ventured into their tangled canyons failed to find gold, but they discovered ancient mine workings of such a scale as to convince them that at some time in the unrecorded past of the Superstitions, hundreds of men had toiled there with pick and shovel. Spaniards? Mexicans? It didn't matter which; both races were natural miners.

Old muleshoes and an anvil of Mexican origin were found near Weaver's Needle, named for Pauline Weaver, the famous mountain man and frontiersman. No doubt about it; gold in quantity had been taken out of the Superstitions! Had those old mines been exhausted, or so covered up by an avalanche, cloudburst, or some upheaval of the earth's crust that they couldn't be found? And what about the Apaches? In the minds of men who were still alive those savage warriors had made the Superstitions forbidden ground for the white man. Perhaps that had not always been so.

Legends that survive must have some basis in fact. The legend of the mines in the Superstitions qualified. There is no record of who supplied the missing pieces that put together the folklore tale that has been so widely accepted, in some measure at least, by all who have written about the so-called Lost Dutchman. The tale has received many minor variations, but it always stems back to another Peralta grant that is as mythical as the one created in the fertile imagination of James A. Reavis. It introduces still another Don Enrico Miguel Peralta—the old Don —and his son Don Miguel Peralta, rich, landed *haciendados* of Sonora. Just where this grant lay in that vast land of open deserts, fertile valleys, and forbidding mountains between the Sierra Madre and the Gulf of California was never pinpointed. And perhaps with good reason, for in all the years since the story of these Peraltas became popular not a shred of evidence has been produced to prove that they ever existed.

Using the Peralta name in connection with the provable early mining that had been done in the Superstitions before Mexico won her independence from Spain undoubtedly lent an air of authenticity to the tale and helped to make it acceptable, for no name connected with mining in the Territory was so well-known. Then, as now, the way from Sonora into what was to become Arizona Territory was wide open. From the Mission of San Xavier del Bac, south of where Tucson was later to stand, it was less than a hundred miles to the Superstitions, most of the distance down the valley of the Rio Santa Cruz.

The New World goal of the three great religious orders—the Dominicans, Jesuits, and Franciscans—was to convert the Indians to Christianity, a pursuit in which the Franciscans of Spanish America were notably more successful than the martyred Jesuits of French Canada. And yet their zeal for the Cross did not keep them from employing their neophytes to lead them to vast treasures of gold and silver. Often they were compelled to work the mines in a kind of religious slavery. It was with impressed Indian labor that the padres took millions of dollars in silver from the group of mines known as the Lost Tayopa, in the Sierra Madre, to name but one source, and transported it on muleback to Vera Cruz and from there to Spain.

It was through the isolated missions of the north that information regarding mining possibilities was gathered and forwarded to Mexico City. We are told that it was by such means that Don Peralta and his son were informed that gold in great quantity might very likely be found in the Superstitions. The Peraltas were interested enough to dispatch a small party of trained prospectors to investigate. Their report was so favorable that the following spring the Peraltas outfitted an expedition of several hundred of their peons and, accompanied by a long train of lumbering, wooden-wheeled *carretas,* set out for the Superstitions.

Fact catches up with fiction here, for an expedition of great size did move into the Superstitions, reaching the mountains from the south, by way of where old Pinal was to stand, which itself long ago became a forgotten ghost town—though the evidence to support it was not found until 1911, when a natural corral, several square miles in extent, well grassed and with several pools of living water, was discovered on the flat top of Bluff Spring Mountain. It was not only a corral but a fortress, for it was so located that half a dozen men armed with rifles could have slaughtered any band of prowling Apaches.

Bluff Spring Mountain rises abruptly on all sides, and for years it was believed that no trail led to the top. More by accident than design, in 1911 Jim Anderson, a cowboy employed on the Bark ranch, in pursuit of a bull, broke through the dense brush that clothed the lower slope and came upon an ancient trail, washed out and badly gullied but presenting unmistakable evidence that it once had been heavily used. Anderson reported his find to Jim Bark and Sims Ely, the two most intelligent and persistent searchers for the lost mines in what the Spanish called the *Sierra de la Espuma* (Mountains of Foam), so named because of the horizontal white limestone formation that marks the crest of the Superstitions for miles.

Bark and Ely, accompanied by Anderson, explored the trail and Bluff Spring Mountain. At the top, they found easily identifiable mounds of mule bones and iron Mexican artifacts. In places the trail was worn too deep to have been the result of erosion alone. They reasoned that mules, hundreds of them, had been driven over it time after time. But to what purpose? Obviously it had something to do with mining, and since heavy timbers were required for tunneling, the most reasonable explanation was that the mules had been used to drag them over the almost impassable mountains, work that was calculated to break down any animal. Mexicans were notoriously cruel in their treatment of horses and mules, which tended to account for the piles of bones that had been found.

The Superstitions are almost treeless, save for the few cottonwoods in Fish Creek canyon. Even mesquite, large enough for timbering, is not easily come by. Bark and Ely had never been able to explain the forty acres of mesquite stumps they had found on a plateau some ten miles northeast of the Bark ranch. The stumps measured from six to ten inches in diameter. They could not have been cut for firewood, since green mesquite will not burn. To have snaked the dressed trunks over the mountains to a mine pit would have been murderous work. But it could have been done. Once they had reached their destination and served their purpose, the timbers could have been used to cover up the workings.

The tales differ as to how long the first so-called Peralta Expedition remained in the Superstitions. Presumably it arrived in the late spring of one year, when the weather was favorable, and left in the autumn of the next. Legend says that a great battle with an overwhelming number of Apaches occurred as the train was leaving the mountains, in which "Peralta," the father, and a number of his peons were killed. The rest, under the command of the old Don's son, made their way back to Mexico with an undisclosed amount of gold.

From evidence uncovered on the apron of volcanic tufa that stretches out from the western wall of the Superstitions, some three miles east of the old mining camp of Goldfield, in 1909–10, it can be accepted as fact that a sanguinary battle between the Mexicans and Apaches, lasting several days, occurred. The rest is conjecture. If the hardy leader of the expedition was killed, as he well might have been, his name was not Don Miguel Peralta.

But some legends die hard, particularly that of the mythical Peraltas and the Lost Dutchman.

2

The Riddle of the Superstitions

Gold may be where you find it, but do not look for it in volcanic tufa. That's exactly what a six-foot-five Scandinavian who went by the name of Silverlock (his real name was Peterson) and his German partner, Peter Malm, did. When they pitched camp in the shadow of the Superstition wall and went to work in 1907, they were promptly dubbed "the crazy men." For nearly three years, they pocked the rocky plain with numerous holes, none more than four or five feet deep. It was taken for granted that they were looking for gold, but opening a hole for a few feet and then moving on to one new location after another was hardly what men would do in opening a mine.

The big Swede and his partner were secretive and unfriendly. They bought their supplies from the Mormon cooperative in the little town of Mesa, and the only person who ever got any information from them was the man who ran it, for he was also the express company agent, and made shipments for them, presumably gold. After the first year there were no more shipments. Silverlock and Malm were soon in rags and would have starved to death but for the generosity of Jim Bark, the ranchman who with Ely and Anderson had explored Bluff Spring Mountain.

Once, in a sudden burst of confidence, Silverlock told him that the gold they had picked up had not been washed down from Black Mountain, which reared up behind them. He said that in Denver, Malm and he had purchased a waybill to the place from an old Mexican who had lived most of his life with the Apaches, and that here a great battle between the Apaches and several hundred Mexicans, who were returning home with forty muleloads of gold, had been fought and that the victorious Indians had slashed the leather *aparejos* (pack saddles) to ribbons and dumped their contents on the ground.

It seemed to confirm the old story of the slaughtering of the so-called Peralta Expedition, and it added fuel to Bark's determination to find the Lost Dutchman, an ambition that was never to be fulfilled. According to his friend Ely, it was Bark who in 1893 named the Lost Dutchman after Jacob Waltz.

Silverlock ended his days in the territorial hospital for the insane, and Malm died at the Maricopa County poor farm. Their end was in keeping with the pattern of defeat, disaster, and death that so many seekers of the gold of the Superstitions found.

Turn back now from 1910 to 1864–65 and the two doctors on whom hangs much of the storied history of these mountains and the then little-known surrounding region. First, there was Dr. Abraham D. Thorne, a native of Nauvoo, Illinois, and a graduate of the Rush Medical College of Philadelphia. Armed with a diploma that had cost him twenty dollars and testified to the fact that he had been given a degree in medicine, he set out for the West to establish a practice. The War between the States had begun. The government had withdrawn the regulars from the frontier posts and manned them instead with volunteers from what was known as the California Column. In Taos, New Mexico, Dr. Thorne became acquainted with Colonel Kit

Carson, the famous scout, who was not only U.S. Indian Agent for the Territory, but colonel of a regiment of volunteer cavalry. Carson advised him to join one of the frontier garrisons if he wanted to get into practice at once. Thorne accepted this advice and was sent to the military post at Lemitar, New Mexico, on the Rio Grande, where he served for a year as contract surgeon and doctor.

In spite of his lack of experience, he must have acquitted himself creditably. His acquaintance with Carson ripened. The latter ordered him to Fort McDowell, on the Verde River, thirty-two miles northeast of a settlement just coming into being that called itself Phoenix. Thorne had demonstrated a marked ability for getting along with Indians and winning their respect. It was more as a mediator than as a doctor that he was sent to Fort McDowell. Specifically, his task was to curb the growing unrest among the Verde River (Tonto) Apaches and keep the peace.

Being careful never to seek precedence over the tribal medicine men, consulting with them frequently, he soon was moving among the Apache villages in perfect safety, successfully treating the old and the very young. Apaches were not supposed to know the meaning of gratitude, but they were so grateful for what he had done for them that when, a year later, he announced that he was leaving, they took him blindfolded into the mountains and showed him a pile of gold ore—not a mine, just a pile of hand-picked ore—and told him to fill a buckskin *aparejo*. Before the blindfold was replaced, he had a quick look around and was satisfied that he would recognize the canyon if ever he returned.

Thorne's father and his brothers were in business in San Jose, California. He journeyed there and turned his Apache ore into currency. Accounts differ as to how much he received for it— seven thousand or eight thousand dollars. Some months later he returned to Lemitar to make his permanent home there. His practice became large enough to allow him to live in comfort and putter in his extensive garden. The years went by but he neither talked about the gold the Apaches had given him nor felt any urge to find the canyon to which they had taken him.

After his father died, his eldest brother came to New Mexico and insisted that they try to find the secret bonanza. The two brothers went to Fort McDowell, but the Verde River Apaches had been removed to the San Carlos Reservation. It is hard to believe that Dr. Thorne expected to get any help from them, for he knew no Apache would show a mine to a white man, no matter how much they might admire him. He and his brother searched in vain, not once but twice. Of one thing he now was certain: the peak he had seen so briefly was Weaver's Needle! It was exasperating to realize that somewhere within a five-mile circle, of which Weaver's Needle was the center, were untold riches and to be unable to find them.

Dr. Thorne was deaf to his brother's proposal that they try again as soon as he could find money to finance a real expedition. But in 1883, eighteen years after his experience with the Verde River Apaches, Dr. Abraham Thorne, on funds supplied by his brother, outfitted an expedition at Pinal for another assault on the secret of the Superstitions. This was to take its place in Lost Dutchman lore as the Groom-Thorne Expedition. That Dr. Thorne had been persuaded to try again, and that a rich miner of Bob Groom's stature had become his partner, were due to several events that had occurred at Pinal in 1880 and 1881.

In the summer of 1880, three years prior to the Groom-Thorne Expedition, two young soldiers whose enlistment had expired came over the mountains on foot from Fort McDowell. They were to become important figures in the story of the Lost Dutchman. History gives them no names, and all we know about them is contained in the account by Aaron Mason, the general manager of the great Silver King Mine.

The Silver King had a mill at Pinal, where its ores were reduced. Mason was manager of the mill as well as the mine and was often in Pinal. The two young men had come to Pinal in the hope of getting work at the Silver King. They were directed to Mason's office where, in the presence of Bob Bowen, the superintendent at the Silver King, and Colonel A. J. Doran, one of the Territory's leading citizens, they told how, to save time, they had crossed the Superstitions on foot, rather than using government transportation the long way around through Phoenix. They had no outfit, but it was summer and they slept wherever night overtook them. They showed Mason and his friends some specimens of ore they had picked up on the dump of what appeared to be a long-abandoned mine.

Mason, Bowen, and Doran saw at once that it was very rich. The boys had a bag full. They dumped it on Mason's desk and were amazed when told that it would assay up to seven hundred dollars.

But this little was nothing; they said they had seen enough to fill a wagon. They couldn't describe the place where they had found the gold, other than that it was high up in terribly rough country. They were positive, however, that they could find their way back to it.

Aaron Mason was interested, but he couldn't believe that the men who had been working the mine would have disappeared and left a fortune lying on the dump, unless they had been killed by Apaches. He advised the boys to outfit themselves and return to the old mine at once. They knew nothing about mining law. He instructed them as to the monuments and notices they would have to put up and the papers that would have to be filed on their return.

The following morning he paid them a little better than seven hundred dollars for their ore and advised them to keep their plans to themselves. Between the money he paid them and the wages they had saved, they had upward of a thousand dollars. They spent several hundred for burros and supplies. After dark, they left Pinal and disappeared into the mountains. They were never seen again.

Their understanding with Mason was that they were to be back in ten days. Some time later, a search party organized by Mason found the body of one. The following day, the body of the other was discovered. Both had been slain by gunfire and stripped of all clothing, in the Apache fashion. Their outfit was never located.

The strong presumption, at first, was that they had been killed by Indians. But doubt was cast on this when Pinal recollected that a club-footed derelict, who supported himself by doing menial work for the saloons, had been absent from town at the time the two soldiers were gone and that he now was mysteriously supplied with money. The suspicion grew that he was the murderer. He was questioned and his story that he had been in Florence and had won money gambling was soon proved false. There was no question but he had heard about the two young soldiers and the gold they had sold to Mason. Mining was the life of Pinal. Nothing connected with it could be kept secret.

The belief became widespread that the saloon handyman had followed the two boys into the mountains and murdered them—not for the old mine they believed they had discovered but for the few hundred dollars they had on them—then turned the burros loose to join those that were running wild, burned or buried the camp gear, and hastened back to Pinal. In keeping with what passed for "frontier justice," the cry was raised that the man be hanged forthwith and no questions asked. So-called cooler heads prevailed, however, and it was decided to deport him. Learning what was in store for him, the suspected murderer stopped the Florence stage outside the town that evening and drifted out of the Territory. He was later reported in Alaska, but no positive identification was made. But what occurred at Pinal, in July, 1880, can be documented, and it must be accepted as further proof that at some unknown time, gold in quantity had been mined in the close vicinity of Weaver's Needle.

Following on the heels of the killing of the young soldiers and the tale they had told Aaron Mason, a young man named Joseph Dearing projected himself into the tragic and often fantastic search for the lost gold in the Superstitions. Dearing was not in Pinal when the story of the two boys was being widely talked about. But he heard it and set out to find the abandoned mine they claimed to have discovered. A year passed between the finding of their bodies and Dearing's arrival at the Silver King, in August of 1881. In the intervening twelve months, other men had tried to locate the mine and failed. Dearing was confident he had found it.

He was broke, and he had come to the Silver King looking for a job. It was his intention to work for a couple of months, which would give him money enough to outfit himself and a friend from his home in California, who was to join him in September. Dearing had worked in mines in Arizona and Colorado. Superintendent Bowen, seeing that he knew his business, put him to work after a short delay while new timbers were being installed in several of the Silver King tunnels.

Dearing did not do any talking, but his secret was too good to keep, and after he struck up a friendship with John Chewing, his shift boss, a man considerably older than himself, he took him into his confidence. Though he wouldn't say where the mine was located, he described it—a funnel-shaped hole, twenty feet deep, half-filled with the debris of the years, and down the slope there was the walled-up portal of a tunnel leading to the bottom of the pit.

Chewing had heard many such tales and was skeptical until Dearing showed him some specimens of rich ore. In his youthful enthusiasm Dearing was counting the days until he could take to the hills with his partner and claim the fortune that awaited them, when the tunnel in which he and half a dozen men were working caved in, snuffing out his life.

Chewing left the Silver King and took up the hunt for Dearing's mine. He told his friends at Tortilla Flat that he was going to devote a year to finding it. But his one year became two and then three, with always another canyon to be explored. Eventually he lost count of the passing years. Until failing health stopped him, he pursued his fruitless search for the funnel-shaped pit that haunted his dreams.

Turn back now to the Groom-Thorne Expedition that was being organized at Pinal. But for the soldier boys and the Joe Dearing incidents, it is to be doubted that Bob Groom would ever have "thrown in," as the old saying had it, with Dr. Thorne. Groom was an experienced mining man. From the Groom placers on Groom Creek (named for him) he had garnered a comfortable fortune. Dr. Thorne wisely turned over the leadership of the expedition to him and let him hire the men who were to accompany them into the Superstitions. Groom selected six men, two of them camp tenders. Including himself and Dr. Thorne, that made eight, and all were to go in well armed, for the Apaches were on the prowl again.

The expedition left Pinal in September, the best time of the year as regarded grass and water. It was Groom's intention to explore Needle Canyon, LeBarge Canyon, and West Boulder, and be gone a month.

He was convinced that the ore the two soldiers had sold Aaron Mason and the specimen Joe Dearing had shown John Chewing had come from the same mine. In some way Chewing had got possession of Dearing's sample. Groom asked Mason to examine it. Mason compared it with a piece of the soldiers' gold he had placed in his specimen cabinet and pronounced them identical. Groom was also of the opinion that the gold the Apaches had given Dr. Thorne had come from the same mine.

He was too hardheaded, too practical a man, to believe, as many did, that old, abandoned gold mines were sprinkled around in the Superstitions. "One mine!" he told himself.

Without question the Groom-Thorne Expedition was the best led and most thorough attempt ever made to find the Lost Dutchman. In LeBarge Canyon they found a circular wall of rocks that could have been built as a fortification or to wall in a spring that once flowed there. It was in LeBarge Canyon that Thorne thought he had found the place to which the Apaches had led him. Weaver's Needle could be seen four or five miles off to the southwest. With redoubled zeal they searched the vicinity without being rewarded.

The rougher the country, the more carefully they searched. Beneath towering cliffs they examined the draws and side canyons. In one, they found where an earth tremor had sliced off the whole side of a mountain and spilled it over the canyon floor. The exposed face of rock had weathered enough to make it impossible to say when the fall had occurred—two or three years or a hundred. If the old mine was in that canyon, it was buried forever.

Groom led his party over the high ridge into West Boulder. Time was running out on them, supplies were getting low; but with dogged determination they continued to search, until the evening came, as they sat around the fire, when he said they would have to get out.

Defeated, dispirited, they made their way back to Pinal. Groom suggested to Thorne that they might have another try at it sometime. Thorne shook his head and said no; he had had enough. And this time he meant it.

In 1865, the year following Dr. Abraham Thorne's generous treatment by the Verde River Apaches, another doctor, John D. Walker, took his place as one of the most important figures in the sometimes confusing history of the Superstitions. Like Thorne, he was from Illinois and had migrated to California, where he had finished his medical education and become a licensed physician and surgeon. His color and strong facial features revealed the strain of Indian blood in him, very likely Sauk or Winnebago. When the California Column was organized to garrison the desert forts from which Union troops had been withdrawn for active duty in the East, he volunteered and was assigned as doctor and wagon master of the trains that were transporting flour and other supplies to the posts in what is now Arizona and New Mexico. He made his headquarters among the friendly Pimas along the Gila.

It was after a long illness that unfitted him for further immediate military duty that Walker decided to make his permanent home among the Pimas. His medical services were in demand; he learned the Pima language, was adopted into the tribe, married a Pima woman, and became their adviser in their dealings with the whites. Of the many services Walker rendered the Pimas, and the Maricopas, their neighbors but not related to them, who lived a few miles down the Gila, none was half so important as instilling in them the will to stand up and fight their hereditary enemy, the Apaches, who for a century and more had raided them at will, destroying their crops, running off their cattle and horses and mistreating their women.

The Pimas and Maricopas outnumbered the Apaches (Chiricahuas) two to one. But the latter, with the regular troops withdrawn from the frontier posts, were raiding at will and spreading terror over the Territory. Governor Godwin had received permission from the War Department to organize a regiment of citizen soldiers to take the field against the Apaches. Arizonans thought it was a good idea, but they refused to enlist. This was Dr. Walker's opportunity. After the post of captain had been refused by several men, Godwin appointed Walker. In a few weeks he had a company of four hundred Pimas and Maricopas ready to follow him. They were raw material, without arms and any conception of military discipline.

But Walker marched them to Fort McDowell, where they were given weapons and sustenance for a short campaign into the Superstitions.

Apache scouts picked up the Walker column almost at once. They dropped back, decoying the Pimas and Maricopas, for whom they had the utmost contempt, to a mountain peak on the eastern fringe of the Superstitions, where the main body of their warriors lay concealed. To their surprise, the Pimas and Maricopas did not break and run when the first shots were fired. Obeying Walker's orders, they took cover and fired only when he ordered. Slowly, then, they began to advance up the treacherous slope. Slowly the enemy gave ground, backing up until they had a sheer drop of five hundred feet at their backs. Excellent fighters, brave, reckless, they refused to acknowledge defeat, though they had suffered terrible losses.

The battle raged on until a troop of volunteer cavalry from Camp Pinal appeared. Rather than surrender, sixty or more Apaches leaped over the cliff to their death on the rocks below. That act of desperation has been preserved in the name Apache Leap.

Defeat at the hands of the despised Pimas and Maricopas had a crushing effect on the Chiricahuas. Another twenty years were to pass before they were finally subdued, but never again did they raid the Gila River tribes.

Dr. Walker continued to live with the Pimas, revered and respected. Breaking with Indian tradition, they revealed to him a ledge of silver that would have made him wealthy had he not used the money to improve their lot. For himself and his young wife, he built a comfortable four-room adobe and furnished it as the home of a white man. To it, one evening in 1871, two Pimas brought a badly wounded man who could not stand without being supported. His name was Jacob Weiser. He was the partner of Jacob Waltz (often mistakenly spelled Walz), the man for whom the Lost Dutchman was named.

3

Where Strange Trails Go Down

In 1871, Jacob Weiser was a dying man when he was brought to Dr. Walker's home. He and his partner Waltz—for some inexplicable reason he never named him—were mining in the Superstitions. A mule had destroyed most of their provisions, and Waltz had gone to the Adams' Mill on the Gila for flour and other supplies. He had been gone five days when Apaches attacked the camp. They killed the horses and mules and then attacked Weiser. He killed several of the Indians, but an Apache arrow had grazed a lung and buried itself deep in his rib cage. Unable to stand the agony, he broke the shaft and pulled out the arrow, lacerating his flesh terribly. That night he made his escape, never doubting that the Indians had previously jumped his partner and killed him.

This much of Weiser's story is believable. When he had been without food and water for days, he finally reached the Gila and was found by the Pimas. So weak that every ounce he carried was a burden, he had thrown away his rifle, pistol, ammunition, and canteen. But, it was reported, he had a small leather bag tossed over his shoulder, in which were "pieces of rich ore and a map on rawhide that was as smooth as parchment." This surely is fiction. Weiser, by his alleged account, had been to the old mine in the Superstitions at least twice and needed no map to find his way back to it. But in all tales of lost mines, a map is priceless. Few readers can resist its pull.

Much has been written about the kindly treatment Weiser received from Dr. Walker. That can be taken for granted, for the doctor had proved himself a humane man. Knowing he was dying, Weiser, friendless and without relatives, gave him the map and the mine, from which in the past several hundred thousand dollars in gold had been taken. If Weiser's story of the old mine and his long connection with it were true, then it was a priceless gift, destined to become famous in legend and history as the Lost Dutchman.

This much is known; Dr. Walker never made any attempt to find the mine. Was this because he had no faith in Weiser's story? Or was it because ever since the battle of Apache Leap he had been a marked man among the Apaches and his life would have been forfeited had he entered the Superstitions? This seems unlikely, for he was a wealthy man and could have hired experienced miners to find the Lost Dutchman if he was loath to go into the mountains himself. The fact that Dr. Walker never mentioned the disclosures Weiser made to him until 1881, ten years after the man's death, would seem to indicate that he never regarded them seriously.

Why Walker was suddenly moved to break his long silence has never been explained. Tom Weedin, the editor of the Florence *Blade*, an old friend, was paying him a periodic visit when the doctor brought out Weiser's map and told him the German's story. We have only Weedin's word for this. He was a man of character and became an important figure in the affairs of Arizona. There is no reason to question his integrity; but in his connection with the Lost Dutchman there are several things that are difficult to understand.

Walker permitted Weedin to make a tracing of this alleged

map. This tracing had disappeared mysteriously when, some years later, an effort was made to find it. The original could not be located either. It was presumed that Dr. Walker had taken it to California when he removed to his old home in Napa County, where he died in 1893. That Weedin had been interested enough to bother making a tracing of Weiser's map—granting that such a map ever existed—would indicate that he intended to do something about it. Not only did he do nothing but a silence fell on him regarding the Lost Dutchman as profound and twice as lengthy as Dr. Walker's. In fact it was not until 1911, twenty years later, that he revealed Jacob Weiser's story as it had been related to him by Dr. Walker. Some improvements had been added to the original. Tying it to the ubiquitous Peraltas was one. Whether Dr. Walker supplied the embellishment or Tom Weedin there is no way of knowing. Stripped down to its essentials, the story amounted to this:

Jacob Weiser and his partner (Jacob Waltz) had arrived in the United States from Germany in 1850 and were swept into the Gold Rush to California. Several years later, prospecting as they moved into the southern part of the state and having no luck, they crossed the border into Sonora. In some unnamed village (Arizpe, some say), they rescued a landed Mexican from a drunken mob in a small *cantina*. He repaid them by making them his partners in the expedition he was fitting out for a long and perilous journey into the wild mountains of Arizona and to the gold mine of "fabulous richness" which his father had discovered ten years previously.

The father, Don Enrico Miguel Peralta, and most of his party had been killed in a three-day battle with the Apaches. His son, Don Miguel Peralta, had recruited a number of fighting men, as well as a great number of his peons, to accompany him. Weiser and Waltz joined him and they reached the mine sometime in 1861. Though often attacked by the Apaches, they had fought them off and when they journeyed back took with them the equivalent of $60,000 in gold.

Peralta had had enough of the Superstitions, and he offered to give them his family's rights to the mine if they would forego their share of the $60,000. Weiser and Waltz knew the mine was far from being exhausted, and they gladly accepted Peralta's offer. (If this agreement was put on paper, no evidence of it has ever been produced.)

The two Germans did not rush back to the mine in the Superstitions. Years passed before they were seen in Arizona again. Weiser is quoted as saying that he and his partner enlisted in the Confederate Army for the duration of the War between the States. But even peace did not bring them back. It has been suggested that they were waiting for the Apaches to be subdued so that they could resume work at the mine in safety. If so, it was a hope that was not to be realized. But they came back, and we know from the record that it was in the spring of 1871.

Waltz was seen in Tucson in 1872 and 1873. He often disappeared for a month or two at a time. When he returned from these absences, he had gold ore that he cashed in for money. In 1874 he appeared in Phoenix. The records of Maricopa County show that at that time he filed on a quarter-section of desert land, which a few years later was incorporated in the Phoenix townsite. He was in and out of Phoenix, never staying long. For a time he was in San Francisco. He is said by some to have gone there to dispose of ore he had shipped by express from Tucson. Admittedly his movements were erratic, but after visiting San Francisco he settled down among the Pimas and lived with them for five years. Dr. Walker was gone by then. In 1889 Waltz built an adobe on his property in Phoenix, fenced off several acres and planted it with alfalfa for his chickens. There he died in October, 1891.

Among the army of Lost Dutchman buffs and its host of commentators, the latter of all shades of knowledge and prejudice, there have always been many differences of opinion regarding the long search for the fabled mine, many of which can be reconciled. But not so when it comes to Jacob Waltz. He is the rock that splits the historians into two irreconcilable camps. By his detractors he is portrayed as a fiend incarnate, murderer, thief, lecher, and drunkard. This is the role he is given in the mountain of so-called sensational, lurid trash published in newspapers and cheap magazines and labeled the "True Story of the Lost Dutchman Mine."

Because that approach has been a profitable one, it is not surprising that several noted writers, in their books and magazine pieces, are to be found among his detractors. In the replicas of frontier days that have been built in Abilene, Dodge City, and a score of Western towns, it is always the "bad men" who are featured to attract the tourist trade. Apparently it is a proved fact that the "nice guys" have no appeal for the public. Perhaps that is why The Dons of Phoenix, the very successful booster organization, joined in the attack on Jacob Waltz. Its booklet on the Lost Dutchman, written by Oren Arnold, the popular commentator on the lore of the Southwest, has sold so well that Wilson McKenney, who can look any lost mine tale in the eye with a straight face, says facetiously, "Oren Arnold . . . is probably the only man who really 'found' the famous Lost Dutchman. He earned several thousand dollars from royalties."

It does not explain why in the *Arizona State Guide*, sponsored by Arizona State Teachers College at Flagstaff, the following bit of misinformation should appear:

The Dutchman was a prospector with a long white beard, and his name was Jacob Wolz, or Walz [sic]. He had been prospecting in the Superstitions, and a band of Apaches had driven him into a part of the mountains he had never been before. He stumbled into the camp of [three] Mexican boys . . . and they told him about their mine. Wolz [sic] killed the three Mexicans and from about 1870

) 33 (

until his death the mine was his. . . . Wolz [sic] is said to have admitted killing eight men because of the mine, including his own nephew. He died in Phoenix about 1884 [sic].

That even the man's name is misspelled is the least of its errors. No one who ever knew him well enough to speak with any authority ever accused him of killing his nephew, for he had no relatives living outside Germany. As for the killing of the three (?) Mexicans, Waltz said there were only two, and that he and Weiser shot them believing they were Apaches. Aside from this double killing, the record does not show that he was accused of any other crime of violence in his lifetime. And, of course, he did not die in Phoenix "about 1884."

During the several years that he wintered in Tucson, he sometimes drank to excess, as did most of the male inhabitants of that frontier town. It hardly justifies stigmatizing him as a drunkard. Certainly as an old man, living out his life in Phoenix, he was not a frequenter of saloons. If his neighbors found him "peculiar" it was because he lived the life of a hermit. But the character the mythmakers fashioned for him, a few years after his death, seemed to take on a little verisimilitude by picturing him as a bewhiskered sot, bountifully supplied with gold, throwing his money away in the saloons of Florence and Tucson.

The greatest absurdity, and the cruelest, fastened on him was the name of lecher. Probably no one knows how old Jacob Waltz was when he became acquainted with Helena Thomas. Certainly he was an old man and well beyond the time when his lecherous proclivities are of any moment. Mrs. Thomas herself was past middle-age when she came to Phoenix from Denver in the summer of 1888, with her husband Charlie, a shiftless character who subsequently deserted her, and her foster son, German-born Reinhardt Petrasch, a boy of about sixteen.

To support herself and the boy, Helena Thomas opened a family bakery. She was successful enough to partition off the

front of her shop and add ice cream and soft drinks to her bread
and rolls. She needed eggs in quantity and became Jacob
Waltz's best customer. It brought him to her place several times
a week and was the beginning of a friendship that lasted as
long as he lived. In his relations with Helena he was both kind
and generous, nothing more; but without a shred of documentation his vilifiers accuse him of having made her his mistress
and say that she used his infatuation with her to wheedle out
of him the secret of the Lost Dutchman. This is as absurd as
the often-repeated charge that he shot Jacob Weiser, when it
is well known that an Apache arrow was responsible for the
man's death.

Unmistakably Waltz was a troubled, psychotic weakling in
many ways, obsessed for the last twenty years of his life with
the thought that he was responsible for the death of his partner.
He had left Weiser alone in camp when he went out to buy
flour at Adams' mill. He was to be back in three days. Five days
passed before he returned to find the camp destroyed and
Weiser missing. On discovering a blood-stained shirt, he became convinced that his partner had been carried off by the
Indians to be tortured to death. "If I had got back as I promised, the two of us might have held them off," he is said to have
told Helena Thomas. "I wasted a day waiting for my horse to
be shod. I can't forgive myself. It cost Jacob his life."

Several writers have stated that Waltz never learned that
Jacob Weiser had been taken to Walker's home and had received competent medical care. This verges on the incredible.
Dr. Walker had left the Pimas' village some time before Waltz
settled among them. But surely some of the Pimas spoke enough
English, or cowpen Spanish, to be able to communicate with
him. Many were still living who had been there when Weiser
died. Once having learned that Waltz had done some mining
in the Superstitions, it seems they would have told him about
Weiser. They probably told him, although he kept it secret,

even in his last years when he was unburdening himself to Helena and young Reiney Petrasch. The youngster spoke German, and that helped to unlock the old man's tongue.

Piecing together Waltz's disclosures and measuring them against Weiser's story, one finds them in singular agreement. The sequence of events that brought them out of Sonora to the mine in the Superstitions as related by one is echoed by the other. It is from Waltz, however, that we learn that he and his partner made it a practice to cache their high-grade ore in three different places, some distance from the mine, so that if they were attacked and run out they wouldn't lose everything. Waltz said he had returned to the mine alone, in 1872, the year following Weiser's death, and had taken the gold from what he called "one of the little caches." Several times after that he made his way into the Superstitions but turned back when he discovered that he was being followed.

If it is true that he brought gold out of the mountains on only one occasion, it must have been a considerable amount, for in 1890 he loaned Helena Thomas $1,500 when her creditors were about to seize her business. This sum was in high-grade gold ore, not cash, contained in a number of sealed tin cans. Again, in his last hours, he told Helena that there was a box of gold under his bed, and he wanted her to have it. Young Petrasch found the box and took it to Helena's place and transferred the contents to a clean box. Apparently they weren't the only ones who knew what it contained, for when they returned from the funeral they found their box empty.

There can be little doubt that Waltz gave Helena his mine, with explicit directions for finding it and the untouched caches of ore. Ironically, this was the third time the Lost Dutchman was given away; previously, the rich Mexican (Peralta or whatever his name) had given it to Weiser and Waltz, and Weiser had given it to Dr. Walker. It was a gift that brought only failure and poverty to Helena Thomas. As long as her money lasted, she and Reiney searched in vain for the mine and the caches of gold. When they could go on no longer, Reiney's father and uncle, experienced miners, came from Colorado to look for it. They were equally unsuccessful. "The Curse of the Superstitions" became a popular saying when Reiney Petrasch commited suicide and Helena Thomas died a pauper and had to be buried at the town's expense.

Curse or not, failure and tragedy continued to be the portion of those who sought the Lost Dutchman, even long after the turn of the century. Of all those whose names are part of the lore of those frowning, mysterious mountains, none was so physically unfit to seek the mine as Adolph Ruth. He was a frail, educated man of sixty, so crippled that he could not walk without a cane. Years before, he had fallen down the shaft of an old Spanish mine in California and broken his hip. It had been pinned together with a silver plate, but left him lame for the rest of his life. He had been in government service in Washington for many years. His son, Dr. Erwin C. Ruth, was also a government employee, in the Bureau of Animal Husbandry, and had been stationed on the Texas-Mexico border for several years, inspecting cattle that were being brought into the United States. Through Mexican friends he had come into possession of maps and documents purporting to show the way to several rich mines in the Superstitions.

It was under such circumstances that Adolph Ruth arrived at W. A. (Tex) Barkley's Quarter-Circle-U ranch in June, 1931. This ranch, known as the Bark ranch, on the western fringe of the mountains, and previously mentioned, was purchased by James E. Bark in 1930, but he apparently had not yet taken possession when Adolph Ruth put in an appearance. In addition to Barkley (not to be confused with Jim Bark) and his cowboys, several prospectors were always to be found there. The old man talked freely about his plans and his maps—too freely it would seem.

He told Barkley where he wanted to set up his base camp, and from the description he gave, Tex knew it was in West Boulder Canyon. He informed the old man that the easiest way to get there from the ranch was up Willow Creek Canyon to its summit, overlooking Weaver's Needle, and then down into West Boulder, where there was sure to be water. He was amazed when Ruth told him he meant to go in alone and wanted to hire two of Barkley's men to pack in his outfit.

Barkley did his best to dissuade him from such a dangerous undertaking, but Ruth was adamant. Reluctantly he agreed to wait three days, until Barkley got back from a business trip to Phoenix, when Barkley himself would pack him in.

Tex had been gone only a day when Ruth induced two prospectors to take him in. On returning to the ranch, the two men reported that they had gone in by way of First Water, a Quarter-Circle-U line camp, and had seen Ruth comfortably camped in West Boulder. They were gone by the time Barkley got back from Phoenix. "I had a hunch somethin' was wrong," he was afterward quoted as saying. Taking one of his cowboys, he left for West Boulder at once to see for himself how "comfortable" Adolph Ruth was. He found Ruth's camp without difficulty, but Ruth was not there. His boots were, which meant that wherever he was he was wearing light shoes, totally unsuited for that rocky country.

There were signs about camp that told Barkley that Ruth had been absent for twenty-four hours, perhaps longer. It convinced him that the man had met with an accident or foul play. The steep, treeless walls of the canyon made it unnecessary to look for him there. He had to be lower down. Barkley began shouting and firing his pistol at intervals. There was no response.

Returning to the ranch, he telephoned the sheriffs of both Maricopa County and Pinal County, since the imaginary line between the two counties ran through West Boulder Canyon.

Deputies from both offices were on hand the following morning. It marked the beginning of a search that was prosecuted off and on for six months, in which many men took part, before a search party sent out by a Phoenix newspaper solved the mystery of Adolph Ruth's disappearance. They had dogs with them. In the thick brush of West Boulder Canyon the dogs found a skull that had been pierced by two bullet holes.

The skull was sent to Washington, where positive identification was made by Ruth's dentist. A month later Tex Barkley and Deputy Sheriff Jeff Adams of Phoenix discovered the scattered bones of a skeleton in West Boulder. The silver plate in the hip was evidence enough that they were the bones of Adolph Ruth. In the pockets of the dead man's coat they found his notebook and several trinkets, but no sign of the Spanish "documents" and map.

In Washington, Dr. Ales Hrdlicka, the noted anthropologist, examined the skull at Dr. Erwin Ruth's request and reported that the bullets that had pierced it had been fired at an angle that ruled out the possibility of their having been self-inflicted.

It was murder, for which no one has ever been brought to justice. The motive? Can there be any doubt that it was committed to gain possession of the map Adolph Ruth had shown so freely at the Bark ranch?

Much has been made of the three words in Latin, found scrawled in Ruth's notebook, *"Veni, vidi, vici,"* which translate into "I came, I saw, I conquered," and the equally cryptic line at the bottom of the page: "about two hundred feet across from cave—" Does it mean that he had found the mine before he was killed? If so, after the crime was forgotten, wouldn't the guilty man, who shared his secret, have returned to West Boulder to help himself to his fortune? Of course, death may have overtaken him somewhere far from the Superstitions and prevented his return. Such ironies of fate are common.

Tex Barkley and Deputy Sheriff Adams were convinced after

studying the surrounding terrain that Adolph Ruth had been killed some distance from where they found his bones, and his body dragged to that spot and dumped in the deep brush for concealment. Similarly, sixteen years later, in 1947, on the finding of the body of missing James A. Cravey, Pinal County Sheriff Lynn Early declared that it had been dragged some distance from where the killing occurred. There was another similarity: both men had been beheaded.

In his way, Cravey was more naïve than Adolph Ruth, just as stubborn, and the prey of his unwarranted, tenderfoot self-confidence. By profession he was a retired commercial photographer. When he settled in Phoenix the previous year, he gave his age as sixty-three. A rather stocky man, apparently in good health, he shunned publicity and kept his plans so much to himself that it was not until newspaper headlines reported him missing in the Superstitions that his acquaintances realized that he had come to Phoenix to search for the Lost Dutchman.

In 1947, Arizona was no longer the sprawling, sparsely populated land of its territorial days. Phoenix and Tucson were on their way to becoming big cities. Great government dams and miles of irrigated canals had turned the Salt River Valley into a rich, fertile wonderland. Paved highways crisscrossed the state, and dude ranches and posh motels, with their beach umbrellas and swimming pools, seemed to sprout into being overnight. America had discovered a new and exciting winter playground in Arizona. Airplanes winged their way across its skies. The stagecoach and the buckboard were gone, and the wealthy rancher now drove to town in his private plane. But the gold of the Superstitions had lost none of its lure.

No one had yet attempted to get into them by air, but as Cravey watched the helicopter operated by the Southern Arizona Airways hovering over town, he became convinced that with skillful handling it could set him down where he wanted to go. He visited the heliport on several occasions and talked with Ed Montgomery, who operated the service. Montgomery recalled later that Cravey told him he had some definite information about the lost "Spanish mine," and was certain he could find it. The upshot of these conversations was that on June 16, Montgomery and two of his pilots picked up Cravey and his outfit at his home in Phoenix and drove him out to the heliport, several miles east of town. The material was weighed and lashed onto the helicopter. The whole party then proceeded down the highway to the vicinity of Apache Junction, the helicopter perched on a low trailer behind Montgomery's Jeep.

Chuck Marthens, an experienced pilot, made the flight with Cravey. Later, in a statement made to the sheriff of Maricopa County, he said he first landed on a barren peak to give Cravey an opportunity to get his bearings, and that the latter had pointed out a canyon where he wanted to be set down. This was done, and there Marthens left him, supplied with food and water enough to last him for ten days, the spot within ten miles of the Apache Trail Highway. So far as known, he was the last man to see Cravey alive.

How did the man know exactly where he wanted to be set down? Several of his neighbors recalled his saying from time to time that he had had considerable mining experience. This may be doubted, for he never gave any details and no substantiating evidence has ever been forthcoming. If he had a map to guide him, he never said so, and no one ever saw it. This doesn't prove that he didn't have one. If he did, was it by any chance the missing Adolph Ruth map? All we know for certain is that when he was found there was no map among his personal effects. But again this proves nothing, for his light-caliber rifle, mining pick, and canteen were also missing. True enough, he was killed in LeBarge Canyon and Ruth in West Boulder; but could not Cravey have become confused and mistaken one for the other?

Cravey had been flown into the mountains on June 16. On July 3, friends of the missing man appealed to Sheriff Boies to investigate his disappearance. As soon as it was learned that he had last been seen in Pinal County, Sheriff Early led a search party into the Superstitions. They failed to find Cravey, and on July 6, Montgomery and Marthens volunteered to look for him from the air. They found his camp without difficulty, but although they flew low enough to skim the brush as they worked LeBarge Canyon, they failed to find a clue to his fate. By now it was obvious that he could no longer be alive, and his disappearance was written off as just another in the long list of mysterious tragedies associated with the Lost Dutchman Mine.

So it remained until February 21, 1948, when the morning *Arizona Republic,* of Phoenix, printed the following dispatch from its Mesa correspondent:

Discovery of James A. Cravey, Sixty-two(?)-year-old retired photographer, 1014 West Polk Street, Phoenix, who disappeared in the rugged Superstition Mountains last June, while seeking the legendary Lost Dutchman Mine, was reported tonight by two Arizona visitors. They are Capt. R. F. Perrin, U.S. Army, retired, and Lt. Commander William F. Clements, of Chicago, guests of Sunset Trail Ranch, eleven miles east of here. The two men reported finding the skeleton of a man minus the skull, late this afternoon, two and a half miles south of Weaver's Needle, while on an all-day hike in the area. Because of the hour, they did not search for the skull, but brought the man's wallet back to Sunset Ranch. Identification was made through papers in the wallet. Sheriff Cal Boies was notified in Phoenix. Boies said Sheriff Lynn Early of Pinal County will organize a party to pick up the skeleton tomorrow morning. Cravey is the twentieth person known to have lost his life while looking for the fabled lost mine in the Superstitions.

It is of no consequence that Perrin and Clements were prospecting, rather than hiking, when they made their grisly find. What is an important error in the newspaper story is that Sheriff Early and his party found Cravey's skeleton (and later the skull) two and a half miles east of Weaver's Needle, not two and a half miles south of it. Over fairly passable country, it was upward of two miles from the foot of Bluff Spring Mountain, where the discovery was made, to the site of Cravey's camp. Keeping in mind that his supplies were limited and that the only way he could get out of the mountains was by walking out, which couldn't be done by way of Bluff Spring Mountain, one questions that he ever got that far away in that direction, and can only conclude that he was killed near his camp and the body then transported to where it was found.

The unexplained killings of Adolph Ruth and James Cravey occurred long after I became interested in the history of the Lost Dutchman Mine and further convinced me that, far from being the will-o'-the-wisp of myth and fable, it really exists. When a crime is committed, the law looks for motivation. What motivation can be suggested for these two savage murders that is not in some way connected with the secret of the Lost Dutchman? Was it possible that some madman was roaming the inner fastnesses of the Superstitions, killing to make sure that its secret should not be revealed?

Barry Storm, whose contribution to the lore of the Superstitions is not inconsiderable, describes such a character in his *Thunder Gods Gold* and relates how he barely escaped death at his hands on several occasions. When I first read it, many years ago, I must confess it was more than my credulity could take. I have since changed my mind, at least to the point of acknowledging that where the Lost Dutchman is concerned, the improbable often becomes the probable.

Back in the days when the very name Apache spelled terror to the whites, the tale was spread that their squaws had worked all of one winter covering the mine so thoroughly that no trace of it would ever be found. It was only one of the many discouraging arguments advanced to convince the prospective searcher that it would be useless to proceed. Talk of that sort fell on deaf ears; men continued to look for the Lost Dutchman; today, equipped with electronic locaters and assorted scientific gadgets, a new breed of treasure seekers continues the search. They are younger, better educated, than the old-timers, who knew little or nothing about the twin sciences of geology and mineralogy. Some are sensitive enough about what they are doing to pretend to the skeptics that looking for the lost gold of the Superstitions is only an exciting lark. One need pay no attention to that; they are in dead earnest. And who can say that they will not succeed where the others who preceded them have failed?

CALIFORNIA

4

Pegleg Smith's Lost Gold

No dedicated searcher for lost treasure ever lived who couldn't —and didn't—manipulate facts to conform with what he believed. Whenever he was confronted by an obstacle to his line of reasoning, he either ignored it or invented some plausible logic to get him around it, without changing course. That was particularly true of the burro-punching seekers of Pegleg Smith's lost mine.

If you had hunted it for years in the Borego Badlands, you brushed aside the reported discovery of black manganese-coated nuggets—Pegleg's mysterious "black gold"—and his "three hills" in the Chocolate Mountains, far to the northeast. Proving that the lost mine could not be anywhere else, you continued to push deeper into the fantastically eroded red sandstone canyons and sandhills of the Borego. Likewise, if you were prospecting in the Chocolates or the Santa Rosa Mountains, you were not stampeded by news of a discovery in the Boregos; you stayed where you were, confidant that the Lost Pegleg was there and nowhere else.

This has set the searching for Pegleg Smith's treasure apart from the tracking down of all other lost mines. There was good reason for it. Unlike the Lost Dutchman and the Adams' Diggings, it couldn't be nailed down in one region. No one was sure where it was, and men looked for it all the way from the San Ysidro Mountains in the West to the Colorado River in the east, and from the Mexican border north to the Mojave Desert.

That vast region of mountains, sand, and desert was easy to reach from the west, most of it lying within what may be loosely termed the backyard of Los Angeles. This proximity to the ever growing West Coast centers of population produced a veritable army of amateur gold seekers, whose knowledge of the Lost Pegleg was limited to the countless highly tinted newspaper stories they had read. In addition there were the pure quill prospectors, men who "knew rock." It adds up to the fact —and it is beyond question—that more men have sought the Lost Pegleg than ever searched for any other so-called lost mine.

The majority of them have been solo hunters, or have gone out in groups of two or three, seldom more. Some have not returned, for it is a grim, inhospitable land, where death walks at the side of the inexperienced and the foolhardy. The myths and legends that have grown up about Pegleg Smith are legion, and some of them are so fantastic that they need not be taken seriously. But there are others that cannot be dismissed so easily, not when you remember that men have had such faith in them that they have knowingly risked their lives seeking his fabulous mine.

In his *On the Trail of Pegleg Smith's Lost Gold*, Wilson McKenney describes Peglophiles as "those people who have been inoculated with the virus of the yarn." He divides them into three classes:

(1) Those who have sought and heard all versions of the story . . . and who maintain a simple faith in the validity of the story and the reality of the gold. (2) Those who openly and loudly spurn the yarn as pure fabrication of imagination . . . it is largely composed of

critics and debunkers, the kind who take fiendish delight in telling a four-year-old the facts about Santa Claus, and (3) Those who know the story and are vaguely fascinated by it but have had no personal experience with mining or contact with the desert.

I am afraid he will put me in his second classification—although I have never disillusioned little children about Santa Claus—but I belong squarely in the third group too, for I am more than "vaguely fascinated" by the lore that surrounds the Lost Pegleg Mine, even though it is as preposterous as it is ingenious.

If you will look beyond these fabulous tales—and tales are all they are—and turn to the records, you will find no evidence that Pegleg Tom Smith ever had a mine anywhere, at any time. The only gold he is known to have had was the rich specimens on the strength of which he induced gullible men to grubstake him on numerous occasions. If he ever had any samples of rich, gold-bearing black quartz in his possession, they had not been produced by his pick, for he was a "prospector" who never did any prospecting.

Of course, when you are dealing with lost mines, one rule takes precedence over all others; if you believe it, it's so. But of the hundreds who searched for Pegleg's mythical mine, not one found any gold. It didn't convince them, however, that they were looking for something that was as chimerical as the pot of gold at the rainbow's end. The only gold the Lost Pegleg ever produced was mined by feature story writers who long ago discovered that any story about a lost mine made good newspaper copy. But if Pegleg's mine was mythical, he was real enough himself.

Thomas L. Smith was born at Crab Orchard, Kentucky, on October 10, 1801. While still in his teens he ran away from home and headed west. In St. Louis, he worked several years for Antoine Robedoux, the fur merchant and outfitter. This was exactly the atmosphere he craved, and he became acquainted with such notables as Jim Bridger, Kit Carson, Milton Sublette, and Ceran St. Vrain. When Alexander Le Grand organized his first expedition to Santa Fe, Smith went with him. It introduced him to the wild, free life of the plains, and having got a taste of it, he wanted no other. He trapped with Sublette and others, "married" a Shoshone woman, and settled down with the Indians on Green River. During those years, the late 1820's, he seems to have acted as agent for the St. Louis Fur Company. He spoke several Indian languages and gained some prestige by leading the Shoshones to victory in a minor engagement against the Utes.

William Caruthers says in his excellent *Loafing Along Death Valley Trails:*

While trapping for beaver with St. Vrain (and a large party) on the Platte, Smith was shot by an Indian, the bullet shattering the bones in his leg just above the ankle. He was talking with St. Vrain at the moment and after a look at the injury, begged those about to amputate his leg. Having no experience, his companions refused. He then asked the camp cook to bring him a butcher knife and amputated it himself, with minor assistance from the noted Milton Sublette.

Smith was then carried on a stretcher to his winter quarters on the Green River. While the wound was healing he discovered some bones protruding. Sublette pulled them out with a pair of bullet molds. Indian remedies procured by his squaws (he had three by now) healed the stump and in the following spring of 1828 he made a rough wooden leg. Thereafter he was called Pegleg by the whites and We-he-to-ca by all Indians.

A wooden socket was fitted into the stirrup of his saddle and with this he could ride as skillfully as before.

He was not yet thirty, his vigor unimpaired, but the loss of his leg must have curtailed his range as a trapper, at least temporarily, for presently he began trading whisky to the Shoshones, the Snakes, and the Utahs, with whom he had cemented relations by marrying into each of the three tribes. As a whisky trader he did not lose face with his wide circle of acquaintance among mountain men, many of whom had engaged in the business themselves.

In 1829, he was with a large party of trappers under the leadership of the noted Ewing Young, who was to play a leading role in the settling of Oregon some years later, on the Virgin River near its junction with the Colorado. They were so successful that when the season was half over, Ewing Young dispatched Pegleg and Maurice LeDuc to Santa Fe, the nearest market, with a load of peltries. Instead of making their way to Santa Fe or Salt Lake, as they were ordered to do, Pegleg and LeDuc crossed the Colorado at the future site of Fort Yuma and headed westward for Los Angeles.

Up to this point the worst that can be said against Tom Smith is that he was grossly immoral and the slave of his appetite for whisky—rather universal failings, his time and place considered. But here he stands revealed as unfaithful to his trust, a liar and a cheat. Certainly it was his intention, when he left Ewing Young and the others at the mouth of the Virgin, to abscond with the furs that had been entrusted to him—which he proceeded to do. It was the turning point of his rather remarkable career and put on him a stigma from which he never recovered.

Much effort has been expended in trying to trace the route LeDuc and Smith took in crossing the Colorado Desert. Mounted on mules and leading their pack animals, they entered an unknown land of sandhills and drifting sand about which they knew nothing. It was waterless, treeless, and trailless. Of necessity they must have passed through the weird, frightening Algodones sand dunes west of what is now Yuma, where the furnace-like heat sucks the moisture out of a man's body. The consensus is that they turned northwest in the vicinity of the Cargo Muchacho Mountains, keeping the sandhills to their left and the Chocolate Range to their right.

It was in that region, according to Smith, that they cached part of the furs, in order to travel faster. It was also there that he claimed he saw his "three golden hills" and picked up his nuggets of "black gold." For more than a century and a quarter the "three golden hills" and the "nuggets of black gold" have been the foundation on which the Lost Pegleg legend has rested. Some dedicated Peglophiles believe they have located the "three golden hills"; but no one has found any "black nuggets." In fact, a careful sifting of the evidence bares no proof that anyone ever saw them.

In 1829, the *Pueblo de Nuestra Senora la de los Angeles* was still a small Spanish-Mexican town. There Smith and LeDuc disposed of their furs to a sea captain for the China trade. If they returned to the furs they had cached and brought them in, it has escaped the record. Plentifully supplied with money, Smith went on a protracted drunk. He was belligerent even when sober. When inflamed with liquor his violent temper plunged him into one fight after another. After wrecking several *cantinas,* he beat up the proprietor of the Bella Union Hotel, using his wooden leg to advantage in the fracas. It resulted in the *alcalde's* ordering him out of town. Smith and his partner left as directed, but as they headed east, they ran off several hundred horses and were beyond Cajon Pass before the theft was discovered. The story has it that they got through to Taos with part of the *caballado* and disposed of the animals there.

For the next twelve years Pegleg Smith had no other business than stealing California horses. On one occasion he led a hundred and fifty Utah Indians across the Sierra Nevada into southern California where they made off with three hundred horses. During this period of his life, he lived with the friendly Snakes on the Bear River in today's Idaho. To him came Old Bill Williams, the famous scout and mountain man for whom the Bill Williams River and Williams, Arizona, are named.

With Old Bill came a man equally famous, the mulatto Jim Beckwourth, trader, scout, and all-round frontiersman.

Between them they worked out a plan for a horse-stealing expedition into California that would dwarf anything that had preceded it. They arranged to rendezvous at Resting Springs. (It will be found, on a good map, about ten miles south of Shoshone, the gateway to Death Valley.) When they gathered there on May 1, 1840, they had a large band of Indians with them. They slipped over Cajon Pass undetected, and on May 14, Juan Perez, the Administrator at San Gabriel Mission, startled the authorities by announcing that every ranch in the valley from San Gabriel to San Bernardino had been stripped of its horses. Posses were organized at once, but the horse thieves beat them off, and it was not until five days later that Governor Jose Antonio Carillo and seventy-five armed men took up the trail. There was a battle near Resting Springs. A lot of ammunition was exploded and a large number of horses killed or so badly wounded that they had to be destroyed. That was the end of the chase; the *Californios* were defeated. Pegleg Smith and his associates made off with an estimated twelve hundred horses, which they sold in Utah to emigrants, traders, and ranchers.

"Smith," says Caruthers, "may be said to be the inventor of the Lost Mine, as a means of getting quick money. The credulous are still looking for mines that existed only in Pegleg's fine imagination. [He] saw in man's lust for gold, ways to get it easier than the pick and shovel method. . . . When his money ran out he always had a piece of high-grade gold quartz to lure investment in his phantom mine."

The Gold Rush of '49 passed him by. A broke, crippled old soak, he hung around San Francisco for several years, cadging drinks and begging a handout. Once he tried to organize an expedition to recover his "lost" treasure on the Colorado Desert, but it collapsed almost before it got started. Making his way back to San Francisco, he died there in the county hospital in 1866, friendless and discredited. But the Lost Pegleg lived on without him. In fact, it was not much before 1875 that it became one of the great lost mine stories of the Southwest. This suddenly reviving interest came about in a strange way; somebody "discovered" that there were two Pegleg Smiths. This complicated the situation considerably. The skeptics who had pretty well disposed of the original Pegleg were set back and had to begin all over.

The credulity of the confirmed seekers of lost mines is incalculable. They will believe what they want to believe, and when they are confronted with facts that run counter to their convictions, they will maneuver around them without changing direction. The advent of the second Pegleg necessitated some readjustments, but they were equal to it. Smith, they said, was the commonest of names, and thousands of men had lost a limb in the great War between the States. This second Pegleg had to have a beginning, as far as the lost mine was concerned, and it was soon agreed that Fort Yuma was the place.

Since he was a cripple, he could not have been a deserter from the army, as some stories had it. That version was quickly discarded, and, more plausibly, he was believed to have been just a hanger-on at Fort Yuma, perhaps a civilian employee. Soon the early tales began to mesh, and the one that has survived is well known to all Peglophiles.

Supposedly—and this is all supposition—the second Pegleg stole a wagon, loaded with provisions, and drove north along the Colorado beyond Castle Dome, where he swam his mules across the river, pulled the wagon over by a rope, and hid out at a waterhole in the treeless Chocolate Mountains. It was there that he discovered a ledge of brown, gold-bearing quartz. From time to time he sold small quantities of gold and bought supplies at San Bernardino, traveling, McKenney says, "by way of Dos Palmas and San Gorgonio Pass."

In the summer of 1871, a deserter from Fort Yuma staggered into San Bernardino clutching a small bag of gold. He was put to bed in the county hospital, and when he had recovered sufficiently to talk, he told the doctor and a fellow patient that he had found a dead man on the desert, with a bag of gold beside the body. The description of the dead man tallied with that of Pegleg Smith, and it was assumed that it was he.

The soldier could not describe the place where he had found the body. He knew no place names. But he was confident that when he recovered his health he could find his way back to it. The doctor was eager to organize a search party, hoping that after finding the body the trail to Pegleg's mine might be discovered. The soldier died in the hospital. A search was made, but neither mine nor the dead man was found.

The story of Thomas L. Smith is history, and it can be documented. The Lost Pegleg Mine is legend. And yet the search for it continues unabated. The few old-timers who are left and will never give up have been joined by hundreds of eager young rock-hounds who range far and wide in their Jeeps, a weekend on the desert being regarded by them as a thrilling and sometimes profitable experience from the standpoint of the amateur lapidarian.

But for all of the long searching and the agony and tragedy that have often been a part of it, no gold has been found. Despite all the tales of "old Spanish mines" with which southern California is said to abound, its gold production has been minimal, excluding Death Valley and the Panamints. The only gold mine of any consequence ever discovered on the Colorado Desert was at Picacho, thirty miles north of Yuma on the California side of the Colorado. This was worked intermittently for years. In 1905 a modern mill was built there and production soared, with over five hundred men being employed. To the south, some gold was mined in the Julian District, but that soon pinched out. Both were quartz mining operations. But neither Picacho nor the Julian District got much attention from the seekers of the Lost Pegleg, who have held from the first that it is a surface deposit, so that is what they have gone on looking for, year after year.

Perhaps it explains why they have devoted so much of their attention to the Borego Valley, where gold has never been found and geologists say there is no likelihood that it ever will be found.

There are many rich mines that have largely escaped public notice, while the illusory Pegleg, which never produced a dollar, is known to thousands. But the legend will not die—not so long, at least, as the dream of finding lost treasure continues to excite the imagination.

5

The Lost Gunsight

Even a hasty accounting of the lost mines of Death Valley adds up to a score and more—the Lost Johnnie Mine, the Lost Dutch Oven, the Lost Goler, the Lost Bullet, the Lost Indian Joe, the Lost Breyfogle, and the Lost Gunsight among them. The Gunsight was the first, the original lost mine of Death Valley, antedating the Breyfogle by five years. None of them were mines, of course, just "finds," discoveries, either factual or alleged.

Hundreds of men have searched for the Gunsight. Over the years many have disappeared into the void in which it is supposed to lie. How many lives the Gunsight has claimed, no one knows. But as William Caruthers says, "There are scores of sunken mounds on lonely mesas which an old-timer will explain tersely with 'He was lookin' for the Gunsight.'" Only to the Breyfogle have the historians given more space. The various accounts mesh much better than might be expected.

Sometime in October, 1849, Captain Jefferson Hunt led a long, well-provisioned wagon train out of Salt Lake City, Utah, bound down the Old Spanish Trail to California. It was composed largely of Mormons whose purpose was to colonize the San Bernardino Valley. Along with them went two parties of

Gentiles, bound for the California goldfields, who were to take their place in history as the Forty-Niners and the Jayhawkers (who included the Bennett-Arcane party), forty-six in all, with the Jayhawkers outnumbering the Forty-Niners three to one.

Why a group of men that was organized at Westport, Missouri, for the long journey across the plains to Salt Lake City, by way of the emigrant trail to Oregon and Camp Douglas, should have elected to label themselves the Jayhawkers is puzzling, for the majority of them were not from Kansas, the state with which, for better or for worse, the name has been closely associated for a century and more. It is an honored name today, but as used by Texas cattlemen, driving their herds up the trail, from 1845 to the days preceding the War between the States, it was synonomous with border ruffian. Is it possible that Jayhawker is not as indigenous to the Sunflower State as so widely believed?

By the time Captain Hunt's train reached Mountain Meadows, Utah, the gold seekers were so dissatisfied with the southerly course he was pursuing that they threatened to break away unless he changed direction and struck off to the west. That was where the goldfields were, and they wanted to get there; they were not interested in reaching southern California.

Hunt had seen Death Valley and the Panamints. He warned them of the suffering and likely disaster they would encounter if they pointed west. They knew nothing about the country through which they would have to pass, and they refused to heed his warning.

On November 1, 1849, they parted company with the caravan. They found the going so bad that in a few days some of them turned back and rejoined the train; but not the Wades, Briers, the Bennett-Arcane party, or the tough-minded Jayhawkers from Illinois, Georgia, and Mississippi. They soon found it impossible to pursue anything like a straight course. Mountains turned them aside, as did the searching for water.

But they went on. They crossed Emigrant Valley, swung south around the Spotted Mountains, and reached what was later to become known as Frenchman Flat.

Ahead of them they had the Amargosa Desert. They were suffering, but they were undaunted, believing in their ignorance that the worst was behind them. Coming off the desert, they were days getting through the bleak, forbidding Funeral Mountains (unnamed at the time) that barred the way ahead of them. But at last they looked down on the hell that Captain Hunt had warned they would have to cross—the Death Valley Sink, the lowest spot on the North American continent, a scorched, forbidding wasteland, where the swirling winds sketched weird arabesques in the sand. Beyond this glaring inferno they could see the massive, unbroken two-mile-high wall of the Panamints baring the way to the west. "There they lumbered to a halt, staring in awe and dismay at the towering peaks of the Panamints," says Harold O. Weight, the best of all Death Valley chroniclers. In that moment of awful contemplation, they no longer thought of gold. To escape from this terrible trap into which their folly had led them and get out with their lives was their only aim.

To get their wagons through the miles of sand that stretched out ahead of them was impossible. Though it meant putting themselves afoot, they burned their wagons (very likely near Stovepipe Wells), saving only their food, oxen, and other indispensables. The irony of their situation, of which they were ignorant, was that as they struggled across Death Valley in their fight for life, Jefferson Hunt's wagons were rumbling over Cajon Pass into the valley of San Bernardino.

They reached a small stream—the only running water they were to see. It was warm but palatable. Of course, this was the future Furnace Creek. Beyond it they crossed the dry wash of the underground Amargosa River. California State Mineralogist Henry G. Hanks states in the Third Annual Report for

1883, "The Amargosa River heads in Nevada—and flows southerly for a hundred miles or more. While there are channels produced by floods of great extent, and a canyon cut by the river at some former period, never within the knowledge of man has any water been known to flow into Death Valley through the old river bed, known as the Amargosa Wash." The evidence contradicts him. The Amargosa is an underground river. It has been known to come to the surface for a few yards and then suddenly disappear. Other errors occur in the Hanks report. Speaking of the Jayhawker–Forty-Niner party he says:

Those who escaped, in relating the horrors of the journey, told romantic stories of mines, gold and silver, all generally exaggerated, but which had induced others to visit the locality in search of the mythical mines described. Bennett (Ashael), one of the emigrants, drank at a running stream of clear water, on the pebbly bottom of which he said he saw lumps of glittering gold; an unlikely story, for gold is seldom if ever seen under such circumstances. Another said he found a piece of white metal, which he took with him, not knowing until he required a new gunsight that it was pure silver. This story, more absurd, if possible, than the first, has caused a number of parties to visit and explore Death Valley.

No one ever heard Ash Bennett say that he had found a stream of running water with chunks of gold at the bottom. The millions in gold and silver that the Death Valley region has produced since Henry Hanks expressed his skepticisms provides an adequate answer.

True, many harrowing, highly colored accounts have been written about the agony and despair of the combined Jayhawker–Forty-Niner party as it fought its way across the floor of Death Valley. Their ordeal was terrible enough without being embellished with the fiction that hatred and strife split them into factions. Little hint of this is found in the tales told by the survivors of the expedition; nor is any reference made to their sitting in judgment on one of their number, who was caught stealing a few drops of water from their scanty and precious supply, as pictured dramatically on a well-known Death Valley radio show.

The stories of strife and dissension undoubtedly sprang from the fact that a group of Forty-Niners, led by Captain Towne and Jim Martin, split away from the main group when they came face to face with the towering barrier of the Panamints, having resolved to take the desperate chance of climbing directly over the mountains. After three days of trying to crawl over the precipices and chasms of Tucki Mountain, the Towne-Martin party rejoined the Jayhawkers at their camp on what came to be known as White Sage Flats.

This was the last time that those who had survived the Death Valley crossing were to be together as a whole. They had come up from the desert by way of today's Emigrant Wash and proceeded through unnamed canyons to White Sage Flats. They were without water and food, having butchered and eaten the last of their oxen. Providentially, one of the Turner brothers killed a deer. The meat didn't go far, divided among so many. But they regarded it as a propitious sign; if they could find game, there was a chance that they might live to get out of the mountains and across another desert beyond. Even better fortune came to them as they rested at White Sage Flats; it began to snow. They scooped it up and melted it.

They were weak, undernourished, and on the verge of starvation. To lighten weight, they had long since stripped themselves of everything but their guns and canteens. In their condition, the best they could hope to do was three or four miles a day. Winter had come to the high places, and being without blankets, they suffered from the cold. They were spared knowing that they still had some seventy miles to go before reaching the first outposts of civilization. All they could do was to go on and hope that some of them would be spared. To better their chances, they decided to split up into little groups of twos and threes.

After the first day, they lost contact with one another. Some were lucky; others were not. Those who survived took it for granted that the others had died. As soon as they had recuperated, they began the long trek north to the Mother Lode. All through the diggings stories were told of the great wagon train of California-bound emigrants who had perished in Death Valley. If the details varied, it was because the tales were set in motion by widely separated survivors who still believed they were among the few to come out alive. As a matter of fact, the majority had come through safely. A year passed before that was fully realized. By then it no longer mattered; more momentous interests were engaging the gold-mad attention of California.

But if the Forty-Niner–Jayhawker expedition had been forgotten, White Sage Flats was not. It was there that the Lost Gunsight was born as the Forty-Niner–Jayhawker party gathered together for the last time. It chanced to be New Year's Day, 1850. They couldn't have cared less.

There are several versions of what took place. This is the one heard oftenest. After escaping death in the valley, a Jayhawker named Bennett sighted a deer. Raising his rifle to shoot, he saw that in some manner the bead sight had been lost. Picking up what he thought was a thin piece of shale, he wedged it in the sight slot and fired. Later, at White Sage Flats, he removed the makeshift sight to improve it and then discovered that it was pure silver that he could whittle with his knife. It was passed around. Half a dozen men handled it. When Bennett was asked where he had picked it up, he said: "On a mesa a bit below. The ground was black with the stuff."

Silver did not interest his listeners just then. Nor would pure gold have mattered to them, in their desperate situation. But they remembered!

Another version of the Bennett story says that he didn't discover his rifle sight was a piece of silver until he took the weapon to a gunsmith at the Mariposa Mines near today's Merced to have a new sight made. The gunsmith recognized the metal at once, and when he asked Bennett where he had picked it up, the latter is alleged to have said, "Where I picked it up there was a mountain of it."

A third version of this story names Captain Towne as the man who picked up the piece of silver, somewhere between the last camp in Death Valley, where the Towne-Martin party split away from the Jayhawkers, and White Sage Flats, where they came together again, and that while seated around the feeble fire, he whittled out a bead sight for his rifle to replace the one he had lost. When asked what the metal was, he is reputed to have said, "Why, it's silver! I could have picked up a cartload on the mesa I was crossing!"

Of course, the younger of the two Turner brothers was said to have killed the deer they ate at White Sage Flats. But such divergencies soon disappeared. The different stories merged and became one. Somewhere in the vicinity of the flats there was a great surface deposit of almost pure silver, and it didn't matter that the "ground was black with it" or that it could be "picked up by the cartload."

With such bright prospects it was inevitable that the search for the Lost Gunsight would not be long in getting under way. Within the year (1850) an expedition guided by one of the Turners made a determined effort to find it. They promptly got lost, and were not only unsuccessful but were famished when they made their way back to old Fort Tejon, north of today's Lebec, California. Three or four of their number wanted to try again. They enlisted the support of Dr. E. Darwin French. He financed the outfit, and early in September he left with them. They had an Indian to guide them. He got them as far as Darwin Falls and Darwin Wash, both later named in honor of Dr. French, and refused to go any further, asserting that this was the last water they would find. After prospecting the adjacent area, they turned back without finding the mesa that was "black with silver."

Later, Dr. Darwin French left his Fort Tejon ranch and established his home at Oroville, in northern California. But he was not finished with the Lost Gunsight. He waited ten years before he tried a second time to find it. In the meantime, it had lured a hundred others into the Panamints and the fiery furnace of Death Valley. Many left their bones to whiten where they fell; a few found outcrops of silver and started mines that made them comfortably wealthy. Their big, overall contribution was that they opened new mining districts that led to the big silver strikes in the Panamints, Slate Range, Telescope Peak, and the great borax fields. They did not find the fabulous mesa where native silver could be "picked up by the cartload."

Of all the searchers for the Lost Gunsight, Dr. Darwin French must be acclaimed the foremost. More than any other he explored the great, sun-baked sink that the Shoshone Indians called *Tomesha,* or Ground Afire, and that William Manly of the original Forty-Niners named Death Valley. Dr. French gave it many of the place names by which we know it today—Darwin Wash, Darwin Falls, Bennett's Well (named for Ashael Bennett of the Bennett-Arcane party), Towne's Pass (for Captain Towne), Furnace Creek and Panamint, both range and valley.

In Oroville, California, far-removed from the hunting grounds of the Lost Gunsight, Dr. French had long been nursing his dream of finding the mesa. When the Comstock Lode, across the line in Nevada, began disgorging its silver millions, he could hold back no longer. It is not likely that he knew anything about geology, but realizing that the incredibly rich mines of the Comstock, the Mizpah, the Gould and Curry, and the Ophir were located along a tremendous north-south fault in the earth's crust, he reasoned that the same fault could have occurred in the mountains that guarded Death Valley. Never for a moment had he doubted the existence of the Lost Gun-sight. He knew it was there—waiting to be found.

He organized an expedition that would be prepared to spend months, not weeks, searching for it. In his friend Dr. Samuel G. George he found a kindred spirit. They chose their men carefully, twelve in all, and in the early spring of 1860 they set out down the Sacramento Valley and the San Joaquin. On reaching Visalia, they turned up the South Fork of the Kern River, and then southwest to Walker's Pass. From there, they doubled back north to Indian Springs and Little Owens Lake. Their way led northeast, then to Hot Mud Springs, across the Argus Mountains, and on to what we know as Darwin Canyon and Darwin Spring. After exploring the surrounding country, they crossed the head of Panamint Valley, got over the Panamint Mountains through Towne's Pass, and descended into Death Valley as far as today's Furnace Creek.

In Dr. French's mind, it was beside the point that he located a vein of silver in Wildrose Canyon and another in the Coso Range. It was not Gunsight silver, not the great treasure that was somewhere in those mountains. He and Dr. George made a gallant effort to find it, exploring more of the Great Sink than any white man before them. Turning back, they searched the immediate region of White Sage Flats with exhausting patience. They did not find the mesa that was black with silver.

Dr. French came in again the following year. By now he was not only looking for the Lost Gunsight but trying to find the tribe of Indians who were reputed to be making their bullets out of gold. He found neither. In the meantime, on October 1, 1860, Dr. George had come back for a second try with his own expedition. He crossed Panamint Valley and reached Telescope Peak, the highest point in Death Valley. With him was a young man named Dennis Searles, who, with his older brother, John Searles, was to make considerable Death Valley history in the years to come.

Dr. George staked some claims, but as far as the Gunsight was concerned, his second try was no more successful than the first. He returned to Oroville with his followers and disappears from the lore of the Lost Gunsight. But the search was prosecuted by others. Later that same year, 1860, a third member of the medical profession, Dr. Hugh McCormack, was in Panamint Valley and is believed by some commentators to have crossed Death Valley. One is skeptical about his discovery of a "mountain seamed with silver" and the samples of wire silver he is said to have exhibited. More factual are the attempts of three of the original Forty-Niners to find the Gunsight.

Ashael Bennett led a small party in from the south portal (San Bernardino) in 1860–61, but turned back before he got fairly started. J. W. Brier, a minister, and one of the leaders of the Bennett-Arcane faction, along with a small group made a valiant effort in 1865 to find the long-lost Gunsight. In 1869, Bill Rhodes guided a group of treasure seekers to White Sage Flats. They were as unsuccessful as the expeditions that had preceded them.

William Lewis Manly, another original Forty-Niner, came back to seek the Lost Gunsight. He incorporated his experiences in his book *Death Valley in Forty-Nine,* a rambling account in which many errors occur. It is a collector's item today. Taken at his own word, he came much closer to losing his life in searching for the Lost Gunsight than in making his way across Death Valley with the Forty-Niners. "Lost and without water and beaten to my knees," he says, "I was deserted by my companions and escaped death by a miracle."

Of course, Manly did not find the Gunsight. No one has found it. If a great silver bonanza was ever there, it still is; no one has carried it away. No other so-called lost mine has fired the imagination of so many men over so long a period with no better evidence of its existence than a bead of silver— the little required to fashion a rifle sight. Or is the evidence to be found in the fact that White Sage Flats lies in the center of a highly mineralized district that has produced millions in both gold and silver? The great strikes made in the Panamints and Panamint Valley—Ballarat, Panamint City, Skidoo—were less than forty miles away. Names of a dozen other mines discovered could be listed. Would they have been found if the long hunt for the Lost Gunsight had not drawn scores of prospectors and developers into that tormented, dehydrated region where a bucket of water left in the sun will evaporate in an hour? Probably not. Certainly the Lost Gunsight hastened the discovery of Death Valley's multimillion-dollar borax industry and made it world-famous. John Searles came in to Death Valley with Dr. Darwin French's expedition in 1860 and got his first look at the country. The following year his younger brother, Dennis, came in with Dr. George's party. They returned together later and began developing some gold and silver claims in the Slate Range at a place overlooking a slimy marsh, from which they boiled water for drinking purposes. They were still there in 1880, taking a comfortable living out of the ground.

For a dozen years and more, they had often sat in front of their dugout in the evening after the day's work was done and gazed without interest at the muck-filled swamp at the bottom of the slope without suspecting that they had a fortune in their front yard. In 1875, Isadore Daunet had discovered borax in Death Valley. He did nothing about it, and it was not until Aaron Winters found borax on Furnace Creek and sold his claims for $20,000 to the Pacific Coast Borax Company that, learning of the sale, Daunet returned from Arizona, filed on a number of claims and began a refining plant that he called the Eagle Borax Works.

It was only then that John Searles began to wonder if the rim of crystals on the pots in which he and his brother boiled swamp water for drinking purposes might not be borax. Tests proved that it was. They filed mineral claims on what they named Borax Lake, which in time became Searles Lake. Things began to move rapidly after that, and they were shipping crystallized borax by wagon to Mohave two years before the Pacific Borax Company got its Harmony Works into production.

It was only the beginning. The American Potash and Chemical Company moved in and established the town of Trona (coined from natron, the scientific name of sodium carbonate) to house its processing plants. It would fill several pages to list the products, by-products, and chemical derivatives that have their origin in Searles Lake.

Like so many others, John and Dennis Searles had not found the Lost Gunsight. But they had searched for it; otherwise, it is not likely that they would ever have found themselves in the Slate Range. In a way the Lost Gunsight had paid a long-delayed dividend.

6

John Galler's Lost Nuggets

Tales of lost mines that are genuine are so few in number that one wonders why John Galler's Lost Mine, which the leading historians of the Death Valley region agree is authentic, has received so little attention from the professional and amateur treasure seekers who have combed that country for years. Perhaps the explanation lies in the fact that there were almost certainly two John Gallers—or almost, one spelling his name Galler and the other Goller—and that there has been a great deal of confusion about Galler's Wash and Goller's Canyon, one often being mistaken for the other, or the place names which they have acquired being thought of as referring to the same location, which they do not.

A map will show you Galler's Wash running down from the west side of the Panamints into the wide trough between the Panamints and the Slate Range; Goller (or Goler) Canyon lies some forty miles to the south on the southeastern face of the El Paso Mountains a little to the northwest of Randsburg.

So here are two men of almost identical name, and of the same racial background (both were German), finding gold in the same general area and once having left it, for the same reason (thirst and starvation), unable to find their way back to it. The first appeared in 1850, the second either in 1870 or several years later.

The best way to untangle this riddle is to begin with the John Galler who crossed Death Valley as a member of the original Jayhawker party. With that expedition there was another German, identified as Wolfgang Tauber. As they spoke very little English, their common language became a bond between them, and although they were strangers, it set them apart from the others.

After climbing out of Death Valley the Jayhawker–Forty-Niner party had split up. The two Germans are believed to have gone with the Towne-Martin group of Georgians which shortly became lost and broke up. Subsequently, however, the various groups were reunited at White Sage Flats on that memorable New Year's Day of 1850. It was after that rendezvous that the Jayhawker–Forty-Niner expedition divided into parties of two and three men, each trying in its own way to get out of the mountains.

Undoubtedly the two Germans—Galler and Tauber—followed the ridges of the Panamints southward until they reached Butte Valley, where they found a way open to the west and Panamint Valley by going down the wash that bears Galler's name. Relying on the statements Galler made later, that was the course they took.

William L. Manly, in his *Death Valley in Forty-Nine,* says he came down to Los Angeles in 1862, and had Galler's story firsthand. "We had been without water for three or four days and were living on grass and roots," Galler told him. "We had almost reached the bottom of the wash, when I could go no further. My partner went on a hundred yards or so, when I heard him yell 'John, come see what I found—gold!' Gold meant nothing to me; I wanted water. I made my way down to him a few minutes later and dropped to my knees at a little spring. I took only a few sips at a time. When I felt better, I looked at the nuggets he had found. They were all around the pool. It didn't mean anything to me; I wanted to get out of that country. But he filled his pockets with them and we managed to go on. We found a ranch and after we had rested a few days, we made it to Los Angeles."

The ranch has been identified as the great Camulos Rancho of Don Ignacio del Valle. Once he reached the Pueblo Los Angeles, Galler began to prosper. By trade, he was a blacksmith and wheelwright and became the first American to establish such a business in the still predominantly Spanish-Mexican town. "After convincing the Californians that his spoke-wheel wagons would function more effectively than the rounded slabs of wood, the only vehicles then used," says Caruthers, "he made a comfortable fortune and no one in the pueblo had a reputation for better character."

According to Manly, Galler and Tauber separated after reaching Los Angeles, with the latter continuing south "to the village near San Luis Rey, where he started a clothing store. Shortly afterward, he was killed." It is also said that Tauber embarked for Germany the following year and was lost at sea. In any event there is no evidence that he ever attempted to find his way back to Galler Wash and the placer gold he had discovered.

As for Galler himself, not until the memory of the ordeal he had suffered in getting out of Death Valley began to dim did he show any interest in trying to relocate the spring and its field of nuggets. For years he had kept several of these on display in his shop and made no secret of how they had been found. If he was vague about where they had been picked up it was because he was honestly uncertain of the location. He believed, however, that if he got back into the country, certain landmarks that he remembered would come into focus and he could find the wash.

By that time—it was in 1860—he was comfortably well-off. Possibly the excitement caused by Dr. Darwin French's efforts to find the Lost Gunsight and the discovery of gold in Death Valley led him to close his shop for a few weeks and try to find his way back to what we know as Galler's Wash. He was unsuccessful. But he tried again and again. His efforts always ended in failure, and in 1862 he threw up his hands in disgust and went back to making wagons. Since then, gold has been found in Galler's Wash, but it was not Galler's gold.

Ten years later, perhaps more, another German, John Goller, by name, an experienced but unsuccessful prospector, came down the Panamints. With his coming, because of the similarity of names—Galler and Goller—the confusion that has plagued latter-day treasure seekers and many commentators began, and it has not been lessened by dropping one of the l's and spelling the name Goler.

Presumably, Goler did some prospecting as he journeyed southward, without finding anything of interest. Free of the Panamints and moving down the valley, he found the passage between the Slate Range and the Argus Range, passed Scarles Lake and, with open country ahead of him, coursed southwest for Mojave, roughly the route of today's U.S. Highway 6. When a range of low mountains blocked his way, he cut through, rather than around, them. That he recognized them as the El Paso Mountains is certain, for it was to the El Paso Mountains, northwest of Randsburg, that he returned whenever he could raise a grubstake.

He was fairly well through them and was moving down a gulch, when, out of food, he stopped to drink at a spring. The sand was flecked with gold. It was the same experience Galler and his partner Tauber had. Put it down to coincidence—and coincidence is not to be treated lightly in the world of lost mines—the proverbial chance in a million that happens only to the lucky. Over the years it was to entice into the hitherto neglected El Paso Mountains a stream of prospectors, pure quill and amateur, the latter largely from Los Angeles, which by the mid-eighties was preponderantly American and growing apace.

After washing out enough gold to provide himself with some convincing samples, Goler lined out for Los Angeles. When he had crossed a narrow valley at the mouth of the gulch, he paused to make certain that he could find his way back to it. Climbing a hill, he sat down and drew a map of the surrounding country. (This map turned up many years later and was used in the reportedly successful effort to find the, by then, Lost Goler.) He claimed many times that from where he sat down to sketch the canyons and ridges he could see the mouth of the gulch in which he had found his gold. If so, his eyes were better then than later.

To make doubly sure that he could find his way back, he climbed to the crest of the hill and there drove the barrel of his Spencer rifle into the ground and left it as a landmark to guide him. A quarter of a century and more later, an old, rusted Spencer rifle was found stuck into the ground on the top of a hill. It was several miles from today's Goler's Gulch, but was unquestionably Goler's gun.

In Los Angeles John Goler had no difficulty in finding a man to grubstake him. Grant Cuddeback, a well-known rancher, had faith in him and on at least three occasions supplied the money to enable Goler to try to relocate his mine. Interest in the Lost Goler did not end with Goler's death. Long after otherwise sensible men would have written the Lost Goler off as truly lost, several showings were made in the gulch that bears Goler's name. And then, two incredible optimists struck the jackpot. It was taken for granted that John Goler's find had been re-discovered—which may, or may not, have been true. Figures that can be taken as authentic say that upward of a million dollars in gold was taken from Goler Canyon and its gulches. "Including nuggets worth up to $1,000. Those weighing five to ten ounces were common," says Ada Giddings in *Desert Magazine*.

The discovery of gold in quantity in Goler Canyon completely eclipsed the find the first John Galler and his partner had made in Galler Wash. Today, whenever the name is mentioned, it is usually in error, the speaker really referring to Goler Canyon, with which he is familiar. He well may never have heard of John Galler.

Today the El Paso Mountains and Goler Gulch are a changed country, with the steel-jacketed Los Angeles Aqueduct uncoiling over the hills and paved highways striking off across the sagebrush desert where once the big freighting outfits and the borax teams plodded through the dust. Yet, for all of its prosperity, it lives in the memory of its vanished importance.

In a region where cloudbursts are of frequent occurrence and particular violence, eroding canyons and gulches, there is little reason to doubt that the pool and gold nuggets found by Galler and Tauber were long since covered up. But what nature covers up, it sometimes uncovers. This could happen tomorrow. Yet after a century and a half and more, it is not likely. Galler's nuggets are lost and will remain lost—one of the few authentic treasure nests that might have pointed the way to a bonanza.

7

Lake of Gold

The story of Adam Lingaard's lake of gold has been told many times and in many different ways, usually with little regard for the facts. The reader will have to decide for himself whether the incredible "find" Lingaard claimed to have made addled his mind, or whether he was just a scheming, consummate liar of the first rank. A third possibility has often occurred—namely, that he found a Machiavellian pleasure in the consternation he spread over the Yuba, Yola, and American River placer diggings with his tale. To get men who were making from one to three hundred dollars a day to drop their shovels, desert their sluice-boxes, and follow him into the Sierras, he had to offer them a bonanza beyond their rosiest dreaming. This, he proceeded to do.

It was well known that many of the old volcanic blowouts in the High Sierras were at that time small lakes of varying sizes. The siren song that Lingaard whispered about in Downieville, Nevada City, Sierra City, and other camps was that he had found such a lake, the encircling shores of which were covered with nuggets of gold, in proof of which he exhibited a handful that he had picked up. He told those who would listen that this gold was only what had been washing down the mountains for centuries; that the Mother Lode was far back in the Sierras.

He asked no one to believe him. He had slipped into camp unheralded and left the same way, only to reappear somewhere else. The most skeptical said he was looking for a grubstake. They changed their tune when it became known that Lingaard had exchanged a sizable amount of gold for currency in Grass Valley. Suddenly he became the talk of the diggings, the prophet who could lead them to the promised land. He returned to Downieville and began outfitting for what those who were watching him were sure was a return to his Lake of Gold. A man named Sam Davis became their spokesman.

"No, I was not going to the lake," Lingaard told Davis. "The summer is spent now; it would be dangerous to go so far this late in the year. [It was September, 1850.] I am going no further than Yuba Pass now. Next spring I will organize an expedition and go back to the gold lake with just a few men I can trust. We will bring out so much gold we will have to be careful not to dump it on the market all at once and drive the price down."

It was talk to stagger even such hardheaded men as Sam Davis and his friends. So much gold that it might break the current market price of the precious metal!

"Lingaard, promise us we'll be the ones you'll take in with you. We'll organize the expedition—pay for everything. Just the six of us."

Lingaard nodded in agreement. "We must keep our plans to ourselves so we will not be followed."

"There'll be no loose talk," Davis assured him. "Go on your little prospecting trip and return here and spend the winter with us."

Adam Lingaard spent the winter in Downieville, living on the fat of the land. His money was no use to him; no one would take it. Of course there was talk. An expedition to a Lake of Gold! There was no keeping a secret like that. Instead of six, the company became sixty as supplies were bought and horses and mules assembled. By devious means, four or five women attached themselves to the party.

One can only wonder what Lingaard's thoughts were as the snow began to disappear and the day drew ever nearer when he would have to lead that gold-hungry mob into the Sierras. If he had spread his tales only to amuse himself, he had had his fun, and it was over now. If he had told the truth, if he had discovered a mountain lake whose shores were covered with gold, he had nothing to fear. Otherwise, he must have regarded the future with dire misgivings.

It was after the first of May when he led the way up the North Fork of the Yuba, through Yuba Pass and over Beckwourth Butte. After that he appears to have wandered back and forth over most of today's Plumas County. Going up the North Fork, a number of men had attached themselves to the expedition without being a part of it. Most of the latter turned back after a day or two.

At most, fewer than a hundred men and women followed Lingaard into the mountains. Only in the rosy expectations of those involved, not in numbers, could it rate comparison with the periodic stampedes to the gold and silver camps of Nevada in later years. And yet early-day historians (and some modern ones, too), with senseless exaggeration, have magnified it into an exodus from the diggings that brought all work to a stop and closed most of the stores for want of help to keep them open. One writer, Leland Lovelace, whose books have a wide circulation, says:

When the story of the lake of gold began to circulate, it made wildfire look like molasses in January. Every gold camp up and down California was completely demoralized. Retail stores in San Francisco, Sacramento and way stations had such a run on . . .

mining outfits and whisky as never happened before. Mules, pack-horses and burros sold for $1,000 each. The price of flour, sugar, and coffee went up so high the merchants became wealthy enough to retire in a month's time. Every man and woman not laid up in a wheel chair was making plans and buying an outfit to go up into the Sierras hunting the lake of gold. Mining in established camps came to a standstill . . . since most of the miners were on their way to stake a claim on Lingaard's golden shores. . . .

"Within a month," writes Major Horace Bell, in his *Reminiscences of a Ranger,* published in the 1860's and still highly esteemed by people who are more impressed by the fact that the author was writing about the events of his own time rather than by the accuracy of his narrative, "50,000 men were penetrating the canyons and scaling the mountains in search of the Gold Lake . . . So strong was the pull toward the lake of gold that sailors deserted their ships, soldiers deserted the army, town councils ceased to sit. . . ."

This is nonsense and worse. It is almost a word for word repetition of what had been said when gold was discovered in Johann Sutter's millrace and the great rush to the diggings took place.

When it became apparent to Lingaard's followers that he could not find the landmarks which were to lead back to his fabulous find, several small groups broke away from the main party and began searching independently. They got higher and higher into the Sierras. They found several lakes, but where their crystal clear depths lapped the shore, no sign of gold rewarded them.

Lingaard was looking for a narrow passage in a cleft mountain that would tell him where he was and open the way to his fabulous Lake of Gold. Weeks passed. At a great height, they reached a plateau from which they could see snow-covered Mount Shasta to the north.

"We have come too far," Lingaard confessed. "We will have to turn back."

It became apparent to even his stanchest supporters that he was hopelessly confused and wandering back and forth. As faith in him began to crumble and rations grew short, the expedition broke up into factions. He was accused by many of having lied from the start, that his story of having found a lake where the shores were covered with gold was a hoax. Turning on him in their rage and disappointment, they threatened to hang him. The Downieville men, his original backers, came to his defense. They agreed that Lingaard was unable to find his lake, but they refused to doubt its existence or that he had deliberately deceived them.

This was exactly the experience Adams was to have when he attempted to lead a big party of gold seekers to Sno-ta-hay Canyon, in the spring of 1874. Miraculously, Adams escaped with his life. Although some commentators say that Adam Lingaard was not so fortunate, no evidence has ever been produced to substantiate the claim that he was hanged by his enraged followers. It has been said with equal authority that he was seen in Downieville that fall.

It wasn't only with dashed hopes that those who returned made their way out of the Sierras in August, 1851, and dragged themselves down the North Fork of the Yuba to the various camps; for men who knew little or nothing about the mountains, following Lingaard had been a harrowing experience. A few—no one can say how many—did not return. They belonged to the splinter groups that had broken away from the main party and were never seen again.

One interesting speculation remains: did Adam Lingaard ever find a mountain lake whose shores were lined with gold? Certainly it is not likely. Geologists say that no volcanic disturbance could account for it. But regarded as just a dream, it was one to quicken the pulse of any man. If it seems incredible that men of at least ordinary intelligence should have accepted Lingaard's tale at face value and risked their money and lives in pursuit of the promised bonanza, it is no more incredible than the scores of other fanciful tales of lost mines and buried treasure that have set hundreds of human beings to digging and following dim trails.

The little settlement of Genoa, Nevada, was almost denuded of its few trees on the strength of the yarn that beneath one of them stagecoach robbers had buried a wooden keg containing twenty thousand dollars in minted currency, though Wells Fargo never shipped coin in wooden kegs and never reported a robbery of that size within fifty miles of Genoa. To this day, men are digging in Oklahoma for the buried loot of the horseback outlaws, though it is an easily proved fact that the James boys, the Youngers, the Doolins, and the Daltons were penniless when death or the law ended their violent careers.

But any story will do, once one is bitten by the virus of lost mines and buried treasure. Along the Pecos River, in New Mexico, it is difficult to find an aged Mexican who can't tell you about some "lost" mine of the padres or where five or ten jack loads of silver were buried. These stories have been responsible for a great amount of digging over the years. They make it easier to understand why Sam Davis and his cronies succumbed to Adam Lingaard's tale.

They must have reevaluated it over the winter, for when spring came again, they made no second attempt to find the fabulous Lake of Gold.

8

The Lost Breyfogle

The three lost mines that have attracted the most attention and have been hunted the hardest are surely the Lost Dutchman of the Superstition Mountains in Arizona; the Lost Adams Diggings, somewhere in Apacheria, along the New Mexico–Arizona line; and the Lost Breyfogle in the Death Valley–Funeral Mountains region of California. All three have been steeped in tragedy, but the Lost Breyfogle, deep in the deadly wasteland of the Great Sink, has snuffed out the lives of more men than the Lost Dutchman and the Adams Diggings combined, and twice over.

The lore that surrounds it is as bewildering as it is extensive. Through it run conflicting tales that cannot be reconciled. There is a difference of opinion on almost everything concerning Breyfogle, but the real confrontation occurs between those who claim that the Lost Breyfogle has been found and that all it amounted to was a small pocket of fairly rich ore, and those (the majority) who insist that it is still "lost" and that there is bountiful evidence that the original discovery was of bonanza proportions.

Shorty Harris, the most famous of all Death Valley prospectors, saw some of Breyfogle's ore. "It was a chocolate quartz," he said. "I saw some of it at Phi Lee's place at Resting Spring Ranch. It was the richest ore I ever saw. Fifty pounds would yield up to five to six thousand dollars." Proof enough that Breyfogle's ore was not only rich, but that he actually had ore —which some reputable writers have doubted—for when he was sober Shorty Harris was a truthful man. At the time, about 1870, he had just begun what was to be a lifetime of searching for the Lost Breyfogle. Breyfogle himself had been dead a score of years.

With few exceptions the many chroniclers of the Lost Breyfogle story have devoted little time to Breyfogle. As a consequence, he remains a shadowy, almost unknown figure. He was of German origin, but for some reason he escaped being known as the "Dutchman." With his brothers Jacob and Joshua, he had come west in 1849 from Ohio in the great stampede to the gold diggings of California. His age is given as thirty. Each brother appears to have gone his own way thereafter, and with little success. A cousin, William O. Breyfogle, had proceeded them to San Francisco and established himself in business. What contact the brothers maintained was through him. Undoubtedly it was he who launched the Breyfogle of subsequent "Lost Mine" fame into local politics. His name was not Jacob, no matter how erroneously and frequently he is so called. He was Charles C. Breyfogle.

The official records of Alameda County, California, show that he served as county assessor from 1854 to 1857 and as county treasurer from 1857 to 1859. The confusing of Charles with his brother Jacob undoubtedly springs from the fact that in 1872, two years after the death of Charles Breyfogle, Jacob Breyfogle appeared at Pioche and persuaded Henry Welland, the prosperous proprietor of a general store, to grubstake him for a determined search for the Lost Breyfogle. Philip Johnston, a recognized Death Valley authority, says that Welland financed several expeditions and accompanied Jacob Breyfogle on at least one occasion. "They did not find the wealth for which they sought," says Johnston, "but, as it afterward developed, one of their camps was located within a rifle shot of the place where the first [Charles] Breyfogle found his marvelous specimens—a fact that is proved by an inscription cut in a perpendicular cliff: 'Hunting the Breyfogle. 1872.'"

The term Death Valley *country* or Death Valley *region* to signify not only the Great Sink but the thousands of square miles adjacent to it was never used by the old-time prospectors; to them it was all Death Valley, and the frowning Funeral Mountains to the east and the towering Panamints that keep watch from the west were an integral part of that great wasteland. Viewed in that inclusive sense, the mines of Death Valley have produced millions in gold and silver, owing in large part to a century of searching for the Lost Breyfogle, for it drew the attention of the mining west to Death Valley, located its springs and wells, and charted its trails.

Charles Breyfogle is often pictured as a confirmed, professional prospector, which he was not. Before entering politics, he had spent the greater part of ten years placering in the Mother Lode on his own account or working for others. When he left Alameda County (across the bay from San Francisco) in 1859, the rush to the Comstock was in full swing. He went to Virginia City, Nevada, as thousands were doing. The big silver camp was booming. He may have worked in the mines, but there is no evidence of it. Myron Angel, in his *History of Nevada*, published in 1881, has him dabbling in mining stocks. Apparently he was fairly successful, for in 1862 he is definitely established as the promoter of the new town of Geneva, Nevada, a few miles southeast of Austin, in the Big Smoky Valley, where Birch Creek flows down from the Toiyabe Mountains. He is credited with having had a hotel there. But "hotel" in those days could mean little or nothing, half a dozen rooms, perhaps.

In 1860, Dr. Darwin French had led his big expedition from Oroville in his unsuccessful search for the Lost Gunsight Mine. That minor excitement had no more than died down when Pony Bob Haslam, the celebrated Pony Express rider, accidentally discovered a ledge of silver as he was recovering from a fall on crossing Reese River, west of the town of Austin, Nevada. This discovery resulted in the famous Reese River rush that brought ten thousand people to sleepy little Austin. Its booming prosperity raised the expectations of Geneva.

Several outcrops of silver had been found in the foothills of the Toiyabe Mountains. News of this brought New York speculators to Geneva. With Nevada gone silver mad, it didn't take much persuasion to get the visitors to put up the money for exploration and development work. Breyfogle's hopes must have been high; but they were dashed when the showings failed to warrant further investment. Geneva began to fade, and it was soon on the way to becoming a ghost town.

It is from this point on that the comings and goings of Breyfogle and the great adventure that was to make him famous begin. If the Reese River excitement had any part in it—which on the documented facts appears impossible—he could have thrown some sort of an outfit together and been on the banks of that sluggish, shallow stream in two hours. But some have it that he wasn't in Geneva or anywhere near Austin, but five hundred miles or more away in Los Angeles. Even the late Frank Dobie, who was seldom wrong, was led astray by information furnished him by Donald F. MacCarthy, of Montrose, California.

According to his *Coronado's Children*, when the news broke of the silver discovery in the Reese River district near Austin, Nevada, three men, McLeod, O'Bannion, and Breyfogle, by name, were living in Los Angeles. Although they had neither financial backing nor means of transportation, they decided to head for the Reese River find. Instead of taking the stage route to Sacramento and then eastward, they determined to follow a much shorter beeline across one of the most barren and impassible regions of the entire West, truly in one area a Death Valley. Plodding blindly across the Mohave Desert, they eventually began their climb of the frightful Panamint Mountains. There, following a vague Indian trail, they discovered water and prepared to camp for the night. So jagged was the rocky surface that the three had difficulty in finding a place to sleep. According to Dobie, McLeod and O'Bannion bedded down near the water hole. Breyfogle slept some six hundred feet down the slope. This separation from his companions saved his life.

In the night Breyfogle was aroused by shouts and cries of pain and realized at once that a murderous band of Indians had discovered the other sleepers. Reaching for his shoes, he stole away through the blackness, incredibly making his way in his bare feet over rocks and thorny *grangeno* as he fled. By nature almost brutish in both mind and body, he was now completely mad with terror.

This sets the stage for the travail of Breyfogle as he gropes his way across Death Valley and wanders aimlessly through the Funerals, starving, maddened with thirst, his torn, swollen feet making it impossible for him to don his shoes, which he carries with him, using them as makeshift canteens whenever he finds a few ounces of slimy, green water. With his denim pants in shreds to the knees, hatless under a merciless sun, subsisting on roots, mesquite beans, toads, and lizards, his mind beginning to totter, he finally fancies he sees a spot of green. He makes his way to it and finds a mesquite tree and a bubbling spring. As he lowers himself to drink, his eye catches the glint of gold in an outcrop of blood-red quartz.

Sometimes the pricelessly rich quartz is blood-red, at other times pink, brown, chocolate, gray. Dobie calls it "grayish white." Breyfogle gathers some samples of float from the ledge and wraps them in a bandana. Dazed, growing weaker all the time, forced to travel by night with only the stars to guide him, he somehow manages always to course north. Eventually he reaches Baxter Springs, at the southern tip of the Toquima Mountains.

He is said to have recognized Baxter Springs and knew that ahead of him he had the Big Smoky Valley to lead him to Austin. The purveyors of this tale trip themselves here, for if Breyfogle recognized Baxter Springs and Big Smoky Valley it proves that he was backtracking over the route he had used in getting into Death Valley, which annihilates the argument that he had come in from Los Angeles and the south. But no matter! His sponsors take him up Big Smoky Valley, past Round Mountain, which a few years later was to produce more than $10,000,000 in gold.

As Dobie relates this part of the Breyfogle legend, a rancher named Wilson found Breyfogle in Smoky Valley, looking like a mad man, almost naked, his hair and beard matted with dirt. The rancher took Breyfogle to his home, gave him food and clothing, and later turned him over to a mining friend in Austin who found work for Breyfogle in a quartz mill. This friend was named Jake Gooding, the assessor who appears in many of the Breyfogle tales.

The foregoing is a hodgepodge of fact and fiction. With minor variations it has been presented by a score of writers. Dobie used it in his *Coronado's Children* in 1930. It had had prior circulation. Since it is one of the pegs on which much of the Lost Breyfogle lore hangs, perhaps it might be rewarding to sift the facts from the fiction.

First, there is nothing in the record to justify characterizing Charles C. Breyfogle as "very near the brute both physically and mentally." Having served for five years, first, as assessor, then as treasurer, of Alameda County suggests that he was a fairly well educated man. Nothing in his subsequent occupation as stock speculator and townsite promotor indicates a brutish man. Undoubtedly he was a dreamer and adventurer. But he was not a clod. If he was called a liar by many, it was only after his ordeal in Death Valley, which, admittedly, affected his mind and often robbed him of the power to recall.

The circumstances under which Breyfogle first found himself in Death Valley preclude the possibility that he was traveling north from Los Angeles with two companions. It is in what may be called, for purposes of identification, the Dobie account that the names of his two companions are given. They are otherwise unknown and their number is vaguely given as "several."

Breyfogle's little party was attacked by Indians, and only he escaped death, and in very much the way the Dobie version describes it. There is grave doubt, however, that the attack occurred in the Panamints. Most likely it took place at Stovepipe Wells or in the adjacent approaches to the Funeral Mountains. This conclusion is based on the fact that it was to country lying between Stovepipe Wells and Daylight Springs, on the eastern slope of the Funerals, that Breyfogle repeatedly led future expeditions in his attempts to relocate his mine.

The Indians who killed Breyfogle's companions and sent him fleeing for his life were Paiutes. Ethnically, the Indians living in the Panamints, who called themselves Panamints, were one with the Paiutes. Their combined number could not have been more than four or five hundred. They subsisted largely on roots, but "anything that crawled, flew or walked was food to them."

Hubert Howe Bancroft, the noted historian, says in his monumental treatise on the native races: "They are naturally pusillanimous, weak in development, sunk below the common baser passions of the savage, more improvident than birds, more beastly than beasts, it may be possible to conceive of a lower phase of humanity, but I confess my inability to do so."

Cowardly and treacherous though they were, they had one redeeming quality; they loved the harsh wasteland in which they lived and were ready to kill that they might keep it for their own. Incensed by the growing number of white men, ranchers, and miners moving into the Owens Lake region of California, they had attacked them in force and suffered a disastrous defeat. Thirsting for revenge, they murdered any white man they found. Only a few squawmen like Aaron Winters and Old Man Yundt were safe.

It was Aaron Winters who discovered borax on Furnace Creek. Rosie, his wife, was of Paiute and Mexican blood. Prior to the tidy fortune the sale of the borax claims brought them, they lived in a hovel at Ash Meadows on the western rim of the Amargosa Desert. Water and grass were there, and it was a favorite resting place for Death Valley wayfarers. Thirty-five miles south of Ash Meadows the Amargosa funneled into Pharump Valley. Blessed with money, the Winters moved there and bought the Pharump ranch. This made them neighbors of the Yundts.

If Old Man Yundt had another name one never comes across it. He and his Paiute wife had three sons, John, Lee, and Sam. They made the Yundt ranch, with its orchard and gardens, one of the show places of Death Valley; it appears on most maps. William Caruthers, in his *Loafing Along Death Valley Trails*, says that at Stump Springs, east of Shoshone, Winters and Yundt found Breyfogle more dead than alive. In his brief account there are some disclosures that will not be found elsewhere, as well as others that have been repeated many times. He credits Breyfogle with having discovered a rich mine, equips him with a burro, and has him in good health when he was attacked by Indians. This would rule out the attack made when Breyfogle's companions were killed. Breyfogle maintained that there were two attacks, the second one made after he had discovered the rich ledge of chocolate quartz. In the Dobie version there is only one.

Breyfogle, presumably coming from his mine, was accosted near Stovepipe Wells by Panamint Tom, Hungry Bill and a young buck related to them, known as Johnny. Hungry Bill, from habit, begged for food. Breyfogle refused, explaining that he had but a morsel and several days' journey before him. On his burro he had a small sack of ore. . . . Incited by Hungry Bill and possible loot, the Indians followed Breyfogle for three or four days across the range. . . . At Stump Springs east of Shoshone, Breyfogle was eating his dinner when the Indians sneaked out of the brush and scalped him, took what they wished of his possessions and left him for dead.

Ash Meadows Charlie, a chief of the Indians in that area, confided to Herman Jones that he had witnessed the assault. This happened on the Yundt Ranch, or as it is better known, the Manse Ranch. Yundt and Aaron Winters accidentally came upon Breyfogle unconscious on the ground. The scalp wound was fly-blown. They had a mule team and a light wagon and hurried to San Bernardino with the wounded man. The ore, a chocolate quartz, was thrown into the wagon.

Breyfogle recovered, but thereafter was regarded as slightly "off." He returned to Austin, Nevada, and the story (of his searching for his lost mine) followed.

Twenty-two years before the foregoing was published, Philip Johnston, in an article in *Touring Topics* (now *Westways*), said much the same thing, naming Stump Springs as the place where Breyfogle was found unconscious. He says the latter had suffered a severe head injury, but he does not make the error of saying he had been scalped. Men like Jake Gooding and Pony Duncan, good friends of Breyfogle, always ridiculed the story that he had been scalped. But Johnston errs in saying that Old Man Yundt put Breyfogle in his wagon and drove him all the way to Hawthorne, on Walker Lake, some three hundred miles, although in the other direction San Bernardino was less than half that far away.

It is easily established that Breyfogle was at Stump Springs on several occasions, but that was long after he had returned to Austin, regained his health, and as the leader of one expedition or another was trying to find the mine that had already attained some celebrity as the Lost Breyfogle. In a few years the name was to add a new word to our language. To say a man was breyfogling was synonymous with saying he was hunting a lost mine.

As the crow flies it is more than two hundred miles from the twenty-mile-square region in which Stovepipe Wells, Boundary Canyon, and Daylight Springs are located (presumably the area in which Breyfogle made his find) to Austin, Nevada. There is no reason to believe that a barefooted man, starving, thirst-mad, could have made such a journey, over rockfalls, volcanic tufa, and drifting sand, except that Breyfogle did. His trek becomes even more incredible when it is remembered that he was not in full possession of his faculties and that he had been clubbed into unconsciousness and left for dead by his Indian attackers before he began coursing for home.

His condition was so pitiable when he was brought to Austin as to preclude the possibility that Jake Gooding "put him to work in a quartz mill." As a matter of fact, weeks passed before he had sufficiently recovered to be able to go on to Salt Lake City, where he spent the rest of the summer in the home of his old friend Pony Duncan, a mining man of some prominence.

Although he regained his physical health and was once more as sound as ever, a wide variety of opinion exists as to his mental condition, running from permanently deranged to suffering from hallucinations. Actually, his trouble was that there were periods, sometimes of a few hours or days, when memory deserted him. Suddenly, his mind would come into focus again, and he could recall the minutest details of his terrible experience. He made a map of his wanderings and mailed it to his cousin William in San Francisco. After his death this map came into the hands of his brother Jacob and was used by him in 1872. It provides the strongest reason for believing that the Lost Breyfogle is in the Stovepipe Wells–Daylight Springs area.

Copies of this map got around. Shorty Harris saw one, a dozen years later. It convinced him. "Some folks says Breyfogle's ore came from around Daylight Springs," he said. "There was nothing on the map to indicate Daylight Springs, but it shows the buttes and the only buttes in Death Valley are those above Stovepipe Wells."

When Breyfogle was brought to Austin, he had specimens of very rich ore, either in the shoes he was carrying or tied up in a bandana. Without some visible evidence of the rich bonanza he had found, Jake Gooding and his cronies would never have accepted his story. Gooding was an assayer by profession, and certainly he made an assay of Breyfogle's ore. The test was so incredibly rich that he couldn't believe his eyes; the chocolate quartz was 50 percent pure gold! He took several of his cronies into his confidence, after swearing them to silence. When the heat of summer was over and Breyfogle was able to travel again, they would outfit an expedition and get him to lead them to his El Dorado. That they successfully smothered news of his find can be gathered from the fact that no account of it occurs in the columns of the *Reese River Reveille*, Austin's wide-awake newspaper, which, had it printed anything, would have served its own and the camp's self-interest by belittling Breyfogle's story.

Jake Gooding and his associates waited with growing impatience for Breyfogle's return to Austin. They took it for granted that Pony Duncan would come down from Salt Lake with him and would have to be cut in. That was all right; they already regarded themselves as millionaires. There would be enough for all.

9

Rainbow Gold

We know that Charles Breyfogle was in Death Valley and that by accident he discovered a marvelously rich deposit of surface gold, the extent of which no man can say. But how did he get there, and what impelled him, no better than a "jack-leg" prospector of sorts, to risk his life in that deadly wasteland? These are questions that can be answered with reasonable certainty.

In the spring of 1864 he had town lots for sale in Geneva that he couldn't give away. His hotel was empty and buildings were being torn down and carted away for the lumber. Geneva was finished and so was he. Working for wages in the Reese River mines seemed to be all that he had ahead of him.

He had plenty of time to think about it as he saw little groups of men striking out down Big Smoky Valley to prospect in the Toiyabe and Toquima ranges. He had something in common with them, for like himself they were losers—men whose dreams of fortune had not been realized on Reese River.

In California, Breyfogle had become acquainted with one of the survivors of the Jayhawker–Forty-Niner expedition and heard the tales of the Lost Gunsight—the mesa that was "black with silver." From the same source, presumably, he learned about the iron chest, containing $20,000 in currency, that the pioneers had buried on the little flat where they burned their wagons and killed their oxen. The bones would still be there to mark the spot, reasoned Breyfogle.

This story of the iron chest and its snug fortune has been widely accepted by the Lost Breyfogle commentators. The chest has been sought in vain for many years. Harold Weight, the Death Valley commentator, is convinced that Indians dug it up long ago.

Whatever fired Breyfogle with the notion that he, little better than an amateur prospector and unacquainted with the ways of the desert, could find one or both of those lost treasures is beyond knowing, although he later admitted to Pony Duncan and others that this was what he had in mind when he left Geneva and followed three men down the long corridor of Big Smoky Valley. They had stopped briefly in Geneva, and he had talked with them.

"They were outfitted for a long trip and had so little to say about their business that he [Breyfogle] got the idea that they were going into Death Valley to cut Darwin French's trail and hunt for the Lost Gunsight," Pony Duncan has been quoted as saying. "After they left Geneva, he loaded a burro and took off after them. He followed them for days, down past Round Mountain, Baxter Springs and Silver Peak, always keeping back a couple miles. He figured that when they got into Death Valley he would join them and talk them into taking him on as a partner."

The three men were not surprised when he put in an appearance. They had known for days that someone was following them. The surprise was on the other foot. Breyfogle was dumbfounded when they informed him that they were not looking for the Lost Gunsight or any other lost mine; that they were going south to cut the Old Spanish Trail and, by way of San

Bernardino, Yuma, and Old Mexico, reach Texas so that they could enlist in the Army of the Confederacy.

The great silver and gold camps of Tonopah, Goldfield, Beatty, and Rhyolite were as yet undreamed of. This was Death Valley and its environs in its raw state, the homeland of the lowly and murderous Paiute. White men had crossed it but without leaving any sign of their having passed.

Succeeding generations of breyfoglers, some who were not yet born, are sharply divided as to where Breyfogle's meeting with the Southerners took place, some saying it was at Ash Meadows, others at Mesquite Springs. (There are two Mesquite Springs. The reference here is to the Mesquite Springs thirty miles northwest of Stovepipe Wells.) Based on what evidence is available, it would seem that they met at the latter place, not at Ash Meadows. We know that they traveled together for several days, with Breyfogle bedding down at night several hundred yards apart from the others, which is understandable, for he was not a member of the party.

Soon after leaving Mesquite Springs they saw their first Indians, never more than two or three at a time; but their manner was hostile. Whether for safety's sake Breyfogle had decided to tag along with the others all the way to San Bernardino, where he did not want to go, or was still determined to strike off alone and pursue the business that had brought him to Death Valley, he does not say.

The last camp they made together was at, or near, Stovepipe Wells, where they were attacked and only Breyfogle escaped with his life, the details of which have been graphically described by Dobie and many other historians. When morning dawned, he was far from the scene of the massacre. He didn't know where he was, but he had done a lot of climbing and was sure he was somewhere in the Funeral Mountains, which he undoubtedly was. He found a watering place and drank. The water was so impregnated with sodium salts that it sickened him. But water of any kind was the difference between life and death. He bathed his swollen, torn feet but could no longer get into his shoes. They became the makeshift canteens that he carried for several hundred miles.

Whether it was the next day or two days later—he never could remember—he saw a spot of green on a mountain slope several miles away. Believing it meant water, he made his painful way to it, down a mountain meadow sparsely carpeted with bunch grass.

The green proved to be a bushy mesquite tree. There was no water (surface water, that is), but he gorged himself on the green mesquite beans; and as he was turning away his eye caught the glint of gold in an outcrop of chocolate quartz. There were pieces of float on the ground. He picked up one and its weight alone was enough to tell him it was rich with gold. He gathered several pieces and tied them in his bandana. He marked the spot well in his mind—the mesquite tree, the meadow and the Indian trails that crossed it, the middens of an old camp.

Sometime that day or the next, he found water at a seep spring. After drinking and resting, he crawled into the brush, built a low rock barricade around himself, lay down, and slept. It was there the Indians clubbed him into unconsciousness, stole most of his clothing, and left him for dead. No one found him, placed him in a wagon, and carried him to a doctor; he was on his own.

Without conscious direction, his staggering steps brought him to Coyote Holes that following day. The springs there were nameless to him, but he recognized the spot as one at which the Southerners whom he had been following had bivouacked. Several months later, his description of it enabled his friend Pony Duncan to identify the place as Coyote Holes. It is from there that Breyfogle's incredible trek out of Death Valley to within a few miles of Austin can be traced. He was an indomitable and tenacious man, and he needed to be, for from October, 1864, to his death in 1870, failure and disappointment were to be his lot.

An arrangement having been worked out by mail, Breyfogle and Duncan came down from Salt Lake late in September. Gooding and his partners had an outfit assembled, and they quietly slipped out of Austin and down Big Smoky Valley. Pony Duncan said many times that Breyfogle frankly admitted he didn't know how to get to Coyote Holes. "He wasn't in any condition to pay attention to landmarks and the like. He was lucky just to be able to keep on moving. But he was positive he would get his bearings, once we got to the Holes. 'Get me there and I'll show you the way to the gold' he told us."

Duncan had prospected the eastern slopes of the Funerals and anticipated no difficulty in reaching Coyote Holes. But they failed to get that far; on Sarcobatus Flats the Indians ran off their horses. After spending several days trying to recover the animals, they regretfully turned back to Austin.

They had been checkmated, but their expectations were still high, and before they reached town they agreed to go back for a second try as soon as the snow went off in the spring.

In April, 1865, they reached Coyote Holes without difficulty. Breyfogle studied the surrounding mountains with dismay and sickening consternation. Everything was as strange and new to him as though he had never seen it before. Blankly he stared about him, trying to find something that looked familiar. He had reached Coyote Holes just before dark and left during the night. In broad daylight everything looked different.

Pony Duncan, Gooding, and the three others knew about his lapses of memory. They were patient with him, but his mind remained a blank for hours. Coyote Holes was not so important, they told themselves; Breyfogle's golden ledge was not here; it was only *close* to where the Indians had clubbed him as he slept. If they went on, he very likely would see something he recognized and be able to find his way from there. The one landmark he repeatedly mentioned was the green mesquite tree on a reddish slope that could be seen for miles. At this season of the year it would be a dull tannish green; but as they went on, they studied every fresh vista that opened ahead of them for sight of the tree. Finally, they found it. They had been moving in a southerly direction for days. Conjecture has it that they had now reached Boundary Canyon, somewhere between Stovepipe Wells and Daylight (or Summit) Springs.

They crossed the canyon and climbed to the bush mesquite. They found ledges of chocolate quartz, but no indication of gold. In their bitter disappointment their faith in Breyfogle began to fade. They were saved from despair by the thought that perhaps this was not the *right* tree or the *right* slope. They began exploring up and down the canyon, looking for the spot where Breyfogle had been attacked by Indians. Finally they located it, and in the brush Breyfogle pointed out the rock barricade he had built before lying down to sleep. But there were no signs of a meadow, no ruins of an Indian camp, no trails crisscrossing. Duncan accounted for it by pointing out obvious signs that a summer cloudburst had torn down the canyon, sweeping away everything in its path.

He was convinced that it was from somewhere here in Boundary Canyon that Breyfogle's samples of rich ore had come. "We're either right on top of it or not far from it," he told the others. His enthusiasm was communicated to them, and for two weeks they explored Boundary Canyon from end to end. But it was in vain. With grub running out, there was nothing for them to do but get out of the mountains and head back to Austin.

It is said by some that Breyfogle was back in Death Valley again that fall. That is to be doubted; but in the spring of 1866, Pony Duncan assembled an expedition that was equipped to spend six to eight weeks in a determined search for the Lost

Breyfogle. What Captain Shaw was to be to Adams of the Adams Diggings, Pony Duncan was to Breyfogle. His faith in the man was absolute, and as late as 1887, long after Breyfogle's death, he was still searching for the ledge of chocolate-colored ore.

It was because Breyfogle was insisting in 1866 that his mine was in Death Valley proper that Duncan established the expedition's base camp on Furnace Creek, thirty-five miles south of Stovepipe Wells. From that point they prospected in all directions, which included the Black as well as the Funeral Mountains. It proved to be a busy spring in Death Valley. A party of men came in from Austin to seek the Lost Gunsight. They listened to the Breyfogle story and liked it, so they threw in with Duncan and the others. The valley was really getting crowded when Governor H. G. Blasdell, of Nevada, and a group of officials, with a dozen camp tenders and cooks to care for their comfort, moved in. Blasdell was trying to locate a serviceable, year-around road from Carson City to the booming Pahranagat Mining District in southeastern Nevada.

Duncan changed camps several times, trying to keep up with Breyfogle's changing whims. It was becoming apparent to the others, if not to the faithful Duncan, that Breyfogle was hopelessly bewildered and had not the slightest idea where his mine was located. One week he was certain it was in Death Valley, the next that it was in the Funerals. The situation came to a head when he said the place to look was in Amargosa Valley, east of the Funerals. It was June by now. Men who had left Austin in April had had enough. Duncan could not hold them. In a few days the whole party was filing north.

There are tales that Breyfogle refused to leave with them; that they gave him grub enough to last two weeks and deserted him. This is difficult to accept. J. Ross Browne, a much-quoted historian of that period, who was acquainted with Breyfogle and who was in Austin that year, quotes him as having said,

"I will continue alone. I have sworn to find the lost ledge or leave my bones there, and I intend to do it."

No matter what the others may have done, Pony Duncan would never have left Breyfogle alone to face the terrors of Death Valley. Yet out of this comes the story that Breyfogle, wandering by himself, was followed for days by two Paiutes, who overtook him at Stump Spring and gave him an almost fatal beating. The story goes on to say that travelers (?) found him and took him to Vegas ranch, from which he subsequently made his way up the Old Spanish Trail to Salt Lake City.

We are told that he had been scalped (which would have been for the second time) and his pockets "bulged" with specimens of tremendously rich golden ore. Presumably these were the same samples he had emptied from his bandana to show Jake Gooding in 1864. Or are we asked to believe that he had refound his lost mine and that these were fresh specimens?

Even in the often nebulous world of lost mines, some indisputable facts emerge, and one of the important functions they serve is to demolish such fanciful tales as the foregoing. There is positive evidence that Breyfogle and Pony Duncan were in Eureka, Nevada, sixty miles east of Austin that fall where deposits of silver and lead had been discovered. They were there again in 1866, when the district was booming. In the spring of 1867, they had headed another expedition to find the Lost Breyfogle. They were as unsuccessful as on previous occasions. Breyfogle's funds were exhausted, but he and his mine were so well known that someone was always ready to grubstake him. For the last time, he led a party into Death Valley in 1869. His health was failing. He went to Eureka and got employment as the secretary of the Secret Canyon Mining District Operators. He died at Eureka in the winter of 1869–70, confident to the end that the famous mine that bore his name would be found.

His passing left one question unanswered, and it remains

unanswered today: Is the Lost Breyfogle still lost? There is a sharp division of opinion among men familiar with the district. When George Montgomery, the well-known mining man, discovered the rich Chispa Mine and the Johnnie Mine, the story went the rounds that it was no longer any use to hunt for the Lost Breyfogle; that Montgomery had found it. The same thing was said about the Keane Wonder, the National at Rhyolite, the Round Mountain Mine, and other big producers. The Round Mountain ore closely matched Breyfogle's specimens. The big finds that were to be made at Goldfield, Beatty, and Bull Frog were all supposed to be, at one time or another, the Lost Breyfogle.

George Montgomery proved that he didn't believe either of his great mines was the Lost Breyfogle. In 1889, after spending a year in California, he put together the most complete and expensive expedition ever to move into Death Valley to search for the Lost Breyfogle. Montgomery had become acquainted with Pony Duncan and fallen under his persuasive personality. Duncan may have been with him on this scouting expedition. In any event, it failed to locate the Lost Breyfogle; pointing to the south, it got out of the valley by way of Wingate Pass and on to Mojave.

Of all the stories of the Lost Breyfogle's having been found, the most difficult to dismiss is the account given by W. C. Rice, who for years was the caretaker for a number of unworked claims in the California Hill district, which juts out into Amargosa Valley from the Chloride Cliffs, sixteen miles southeast of the ghost town of Rhyolite.

California Hill is in the heart of the region where Breyfogle so often searched for his lost mine. Viewed in some lights, morning particularly, it is reddish in hue. It is covered with loose surface quartz that can be described as reddish brown or chocolate. There are no trees, and no water.

One afternoon, as he was riding over the claims on an inspection trip, presumably to see if they were still there, he encountered two men who were searching for the Lost Breyfogle. They had a map, which they said had been given to them by Henry Welland, the Pioche merchant who had come into the country with Jacob Breyfogle. The survey stakes and monuments made it plain to them that the ground they were on belonged to Rice's company and was not open for location.

"But we had a long talk," Rice said when interviewed by Philip Johnston, the Nevada historian. "They asked me if I knew the location of a small meadow with trees, and an old Indian village at the base of a hill. I told them on the south side of California Hill were the ruins of an old Indian camp, that several trails joined there, but there was no meadow or green trees of any kind."

The meadow and an old Indian camp had been mentioned many times by Breyfogle, but the trees had been limited to one, a lone mesquite. Undoubtedly he mentioned such details to his cousin in San Francisco when he sent him the map.

"After we parted, I saw no more of them," Rice stated. "For amusement I began looking for the Lost Breyfogle mine. It was easy to recognize the Indian camp, the five trails, and the small hill covered with barren quartz; but try as I might, I could discover no trace of a meadow such as they had described, or any high grade ore on the small hill.

"One day, out on the flat below the point where the meadow should have appeared, I found a willow limb protruding from debris that had been carried down by floods. In a flash I could see it all—how a cloudburst had destroyed the meadow and the trees. I searched until I found other pieces of brush that confirmed my theory; I went back to the hill to dig a trench in order to see if there was another vein below the big ledge. . . . I found several pieces of red rock that horned coarse gold, and I kept following this lead up the hill until I opened a kidney-shaped lense of quartz about four inches wide and two feet long, with chunks of gold as large as wheat grains. At a depth of two feet it disappeared into a small seam . . . finding no more high grade, I quit.

"In my opinion, there is no doubt that this is where Breyfogle got his samples. If he had cleaned out the pocket, the world would have heard nothing more about the Lost Breyfogle Mine. Since that time many prospectors have lost their lives searching for the Lost Breyfogle—a mine that was only a small pocket."

Undoubtedly Rice found a small pocket of coarse gold on California Hill, as he says, but it is a wild presumption for him to liken it to Breyfogle's gold, samples of which he never could have seen. If he had, it would have taken metallographic tests to prove them identical. To find his pocket of ore, Rice had to do some digging; Breyfogle had not done any, nor could have done any, for he was without tools. His memory often failed him and he often contradicted himself, but on one thing he never altered his story—the appearance of the rich outcrop of gold ore and the pieces of float from it that he took for samples.

Shorty Harris, Frank Lambert, and other Death Valley prospectors dug out small pockets of coarse gold in the California Hill region; but they never deceived themselves with the notion that they had found the Lost Breyfogle. Some of them had been hunting it for thirty years and more. It's something to have a dream of that size handy when things are not going well. Perhaps little Shorty, who was something of a philosopher as well as a first-class human being and a man who "knew rock," secretly hoped it would never be found.

If so, he's had his wish; the Lost Breyfogle is still waiting to be found by some lucky man. A century and more have passed since Breyfogle beheld its glittering promise. In that time, hundreds of men have sought it. Death has been the reward of many. For years Senator George Hearst, the millionaire father of the publisher, kept two men in the field looking for it.

Today, one can whip across Death Valley on surfaced roads and find luxury at the renowned Furnace Creek Inn. But don't let such tokens of civilization, and the fact that Death Valley has been named a national monument, lead anyone to believe that that great wasteland of savage mountains and drifting desert sand has been tamed, or that Breyfogle and his gold are being forgotten.

COLORADO

10

Bandit Gold

There was almost $24,000 in the iron chest (an old-time express company strongbox) that was pulled up out of the shaft of the long-abandoned Black Prince Mine in Summit County, Colorado, where it had lain under eighty feet of water for a quarter of a century. Most of it was in gold, bearing the mark of the U.S. Denver Mint. Although one may doubt the many tales of buried or lost outlaw loot, the money recovered from the Black Prince was unquestionably the proceeds of several gang robberies.

The notorious Reynolds Gang, a favorite topic with Colorado folklorists, committed so many robberies and ranged so wide that the opinion has often been expressed that the money found at the Black Prince was Reynolds' loot. No evidence to support this contention has ever been produced. In fact, if the story of Stony Wilcox, who got the money in the end, is to be believed, Jim and John Reynolds never had their hands on it.

After the railroads succeeded in getting over, around, and through its mountains, Colorado had very few notable train holdups, but in stagecoach robberies it ranked second only to California. The majority of them were never solved and the guilty brought to, what, for want of a better word, was called justice. With Leadville and a dozen other camps booming, highway robbery was a lucrative business. All that was required was for three men or more to band together, make a sudden and unexpected strike, and then retire into respectability until they were ready to make another foray. The best of all alibis and cover-ups was for them to take possession of an apparently exhausted mine that the owners had abandoned and to which legal title could be had by the payment of back taxes, usually a matter of only several hundred dollars.

Summit County was plentifully supplied with such unpromising prospects. The Black Prince easily qualified; it had produced modestly for three or four years and might have continued to do so if the owners had not encountered water. Keeping the mine pumped out became too costly for the operation to continue.

It was under such circumstances that in 1881 three men, giving their names as Johnson, Davis, and Smith (obviously aliases), took legal possession of the Black Prince. They made a pretense of keeping the water level down and doing some work. They were unfriendly and discouraged the visiting that was a recognized part of the social life of a mining district in those free and easy days. They bought their supplies in Breckenridge or Alma, kept to themselves, asked no favors, and divulged no information about how things were going at the mine. In return, they were put down as unknowable, and dismissed.

To ward off any suspicion that mining might not be their real business, they had periodic assays made of carefully "salted" ore, the gold content of which came from the poke of a passenger in the holdup of the Idaho Springs–Georgetown stage. The assayer found sixty- to one-hundred-dollar values. Nothing startling, but certainly high enough to spread the feeling that reopening the old Black Prince was not as foolish as many had supposed.

They had better horses and more of them than were usually found at a mine. This should have aroused some speculation, but it failed to do so. Looking back, men wondered why they had not taken notice and drawn conclusions. All over the state more stagecoaches were stopped by masked highwaymen in the summer of 1884 than ever before. One such incident occurred twenty-five miles down the South Platte, below Alma, at Eleven Mile Canyon, in which a passenger was shot to death. It was a brutal, uncalled-for killing, and it aroused public feeling. The sheriff of Park County organized a posse and set out in pursuit of the bandits. He trailed them across the line into Summit County and refused to give up even though he was exceeding his jurisdiction. There the sheriff of Summit County joined forces with him. Two days later the circle they had thrown through the mountains began to contract. Finally, it centered on the Black Prince Mine.

It was obvious by now that the quarry was the three men who had made the Black Prince their headquarters for almost three years. The posse closed in on the mine, expecting the outlaws to put up a bitter fight. But there was no one there; the three men had fled.

A few months later, three masked men attempted to hold up a Wells Fargo treasure coach. Two of them were killed; the third man escaped. The sheriffs of Summit and Park counties identified the dead men as two of the three who had used the Black Prince for their hideout. They died unnamed.

The fate of their companion remained a mystery. There were rumors that he had succumbed to the wounds he had received during the holdup. It was also said that he had been seen in Santa Fe several years later. Whether or not there was any foundation for these tales, he disappeared and was not seen in

Colorado again—at least for a quarter of a century. By then the Cripple Creek mining district was loudly (and justifiably) calling itself the greatest gold camp in the world—which it was. After a bitter fight little Teller County had been formed by lopping off pieces of the adjoining counties, with Cripple Creek becoming the county seat. It had two railroads, the narrow-gauge Florence and Cripple Creek, and the standard-gauge Colorado Midland. To get there, roadbeds had been blasted out of mountainsides; spidery wooden trestles built over frightening canyons; curves, grades, switchbacks negotiated—all made possible by what Colorado had the most of—brains, brawn, money, and guts, the latter something more primitive and vital than today's prissy intestinal fortitude.

With the sky the limit and its millionaires becoming too numerous to be any longer a novelty, the Cripple Creek district's prosperity drained away interest in the older, long-established camps. Some faded out completely. Empty stores in the once booming Breckenridge-Alma district told the story of what was happening there. The big Orizaba Mine, employing over a hundred men, was still going strong, but many small, independent producers had closed down and hurried off to Cripple Creek.

All mining towns, in good times or bad, have an ever changing, drifting population. Very few people were left in Breckenridge, and fewer still in Alma, who could recall the time when the Black Prince Mine was used as a bandit hideout. To them it was just one of the several dozen abandoned shafts on the slope west of town, its only distinction being that it was flooded to a depth of eighty feet. That opinion was not held by a handful of old-timers, including little Stony Wilcox, who were already living in the past.

Stony had come over the Divide in the long ago and gone to work as a mucker in the Orizaba. The shoring in a drift tunnel had given away, crippling him for life. He had been an Orizaba pensioner ever since. Unable to work in the mine any longer, he pieced out his pension by doing odd jobs around town, such as swamping out Jim Brown's saloon or doing the porter work at the hotel. The ladies always found him obliging and ready, like Rip Van Winkle, to drop whatever he was doing and give them a hand, if a pane of glass had to be put in or a piece of furniture needed repairing. They particularly liked him because he was neat and clean. Cleanliness had a particular virtue in their eyes, and whenever it was necessary for one of them to walk out to his cabin, a short distance beyond town, they were delighted to see what a good housekeeper he was.

When Stony fell ill it provided the ladies of the Friday Afternoon Club, a select little group of do-gooders, directed by Mrs. Jim Petit, the wife of the superintendent of the Orizaba Mine, with an opportunity to demonstrate their high purpose. He became their pet project. They deluged him with delicacies he had not been able to afford; nursed him and tidied up his cabin and pestered him to death with their attentions and ceaseless chatter. But he was a cunning old coot and they often remarked among themselves how appreciative he was.

With life so easy, Stony stretched out the period of his convalescence. But if his "improvement" was so slow, it was eventually complete, and it was with something akin to regret that the members of the Friday Afternoon Club realized that he was fully recovered.

Summer was gone when an event occurred that was to change the course of his aimless existence. It was early in the evening when someone banged on his door. He opened it to find a stranger standing there, gasping for breath and obviously in agony. Stony helped him to the bed and dosed him with whisky, the only sure-fire medicine with which he was acquainted. Presently the man was resting easier. The two of them were about of the same age.

"I reckon this is my finish," the stranger said. "This is the third time it's happened."

"Who are you and where you from?" Stony asked.

"My name wouldn't mean anythin' to you, so we'll skip it. For the past two days I been up at the old Black Prince, tryin' to figger out how I could git my hands on what I came back for. There's no chance; that hole is full-up with water. There's a heap of money at the bottom of the shaft. It ain't goin' to do me any good; it may mean somethin' to you."

Of course, he was the surviving member of the bandit gang that had used the Black Prince for their hideout in the long ago. When the posse trailed them to the mine and they realized they could not escape with their loot, they had pitched the steel box into the shaft, hoping that they could recover it later.

Stony hurried into town for a doctor. The sheriff returned with them to find that the stranger had died. The sheriff asked some questions. Stony recounted how the man had banged on his door and he had done what he could for him. But that was all; the secret of the Black Prince was now his and his alone. He had no intention of divulging it to anyone.

To know where a fortune (he magnified the size of it no doubt) was located that he had no hope of claiming was something to live with day after day without taking anyone into his confidence. By scrimping and saving, he got enough money together in the course of a year to buy legal title to the Black Prince. Everybody was convinced that he was getting childish. No one was more infuriated than Jim Petit, the superintendent of the Orizaba. "Is that what we're paying him a pension for— to stick the money into a worthless hole in the ground? I hear he spends most of his time up there. He's put a couple planks across the open mouth of the shaft and sits there eating his lunch every day. I won't be surprised if he falls in. That'll be the end of him."

"Just to own a mine, even though it's worthless, means something to an old man who has never owned anything," his wife protested. "I've never known him to be so happy and cheerful."

There was a marked change in Stony. Hunters and fishermen often saw him puttering about his mine. Acquaintances, pretending to take him seriously, tried to draw him out about his plans for the Black Prince. He told them he was considering driving a tunnel into the mountain below the mine that would tap the shaft and draw off the water. It would take money, he acknowledged, but someone would come along who would be willing to take a gamble. That someone never arrived. It was no major disappointment to Stony, for he had never really figured that anyone would. In the meantime, he was weighing the possibilities of a scheme that had been born in his fertile mind. Shortly after spring came again and the snow went off, he made his move.

The first notice of it came when it was realized that no one had seen Stony for several days; it seemed that he had suddenly disappeared. He wasn't at his cabin, nor was there any sign that he had been recently. Mrs. Petit had her husband send a man up to the Black Prince. He found the remains of Stony's partly eaten lunch on the planks that spanned the mouth of the shaft, and ten feet below, floating on the water, a battered hat. This left little reason to doubt that he had fallen off the planks and been drowned, as Jim Petit had predicted was likely to happen. (This incident of the floating hat has appeared in so many pieces of short fiction that it has become a cliché. This is how it began.)

A special meeting of the Friday Afternoon Club was called, with Mrs. Petit presiding, at which it was unanimously agreed that they should march to Jim Petit's office and demand that the superintendent of the Orizaba send one of his portable gasoline engines and a high-pressure pump up to the Black Prince and recover Stony Wilcox's body.

In vain Petit protested that it would cost the mine a thou-

sand dollars to send a crew and heavy equipment to the Black
Prince. In the end, he gave in, knowing he would have no peace
at home if he did otherwise.

It took the men from the Orizaba the better part of a day to
get ready. Once the pump started, it did not stop. Morning
brought a crowd out to watch the operation. Late in the afternoon of the following day, with the job about finished, a cry
went up from the onlookers as they saw Stony limping briskly
down the trail. Jim Petit tore into him without regard for the
effect of the language he used on the ladies in the crowd. "You
crooked old skinflint," he roared, "you planned this whole
thing—leaving your lunch on the planks, tossing your hat on
the water and making yourself scarce. You damn well knew the
womenfolks would force me to move my stuff up here and
pump out your rat hole to get your rotten carcass to the surface."

Although it was a dozen or more years ago, I recall with what
gusto my old and valued friend Dinny Moran, who was present,
described that afternoon at the Black Prince.

"We'd never had reason to believe there was any fight in
Stony Wilcox," he said. "He took the tongue-lashing Petit gave
him, and then—great day in the morning!—he simply pulled the
rug out from under Petit. What a moment that was! He told
Jim he didn't have to ask anybody's permission if he wanted
to take a couple days off and go over the Divide to visit his
friends at the Three Brothers Mine. He also told him he hadn't
asked him to pump out his mine. 'As a matter of fact, you ain't
got no business being on my property.' he cried. 'You're tres-
passing, moving in with your men and machines. I'll hire me
a lawyer and sue you!'

"Petit realized that Stony had him up a tree. He tried to
placate him. 'The only way you can square things with me,'
Stony told him, 'is to keep on pumping and bring a windlass up

here and send a man down to fetch up the iron box that's at the bottom of the shaft.'

"This was the first any of us had heard about his iron box. We understood at once what all this trickery and scheming was about. He had repaid Mrs. Petit and the other ladies for their concern by betraying them shamelessly. Feeling against him began to run pretty high. I don't know what might have happened if the sheriff hadn't been there. But the hard talk bounced off Stony like rain off a duck's back.

"A windlass was put in position in the morning and one of the boys from the Orizaba was lowered in a bucket. Half an hour later a muck-covered chest was brought up. We crowded around to see it opened, but Stony had it placed in the wagon he had rented and drove off with it. We didn't know what was in it or how Stony knew it was down there under all that water. About the only thing we were sure of was that he hadn't dumped it into the old shaft. We took it for granted, of course, that it contained treasure of some sort—bullion or minted gold.

"There was no doubt about it when he cashed in his find at the bank for a little less than $24,000. He cleared out for Denver then to take things easy for the rest of his life. When we got our wits back, we figured the whole thing out. Somebody recalled the time when bandits had headquartered at the Black Prince, and the fight with the posse. That was before my time. I didn't know anything about it: but I remembered when the stranger had died at Stony Wilcox's cabin. We were sure he was the man who had escaped alive from the fight with the Wells Fargo guards, after the gang had been run out of this country."

The only time I ever saw Stony Wilcox was some years later as I sat with Dinny Moran in the famous circular lobby of the Brown Palace Hotel, in Denver, with its balconies on every floor all the way up to the roof. As he came out of the ground floor brokerage office, a neat, shriveled-up little man, still spry for all of his lameness, and sat down some distance away, Dinny pointed him out to me.

As I watched, several men stopped to exchange a word with him. I wondered if he were prosperous.

"He is. He dabbles in the market and is shrewd enough to do all right for himself. You'll find him here every day. He spends most of his time between the Brown Palace lobby and the New Albany."

"Well," I observed, "he looks innocent enough."

"He always did," Dinny laughed. "Looking at him, you wouldn't believe there was a deceitful bone in his body."

11

The Gold of Treasure Mountain

The San Juan country, in the southwestern corner of Colorado, has more than its share of lost mines and buried treasure—as it should have, for that region of awesome mountains along the spiny backbone of the Continental Divide has been mined intensively for almost a century, and the multiplied millions it has produced tax the imagination.

Between the little mountain town of Summitville, in Rio Grande County, and Wolf Creek Pass, ten miles to the northwest, there is a bald-faced peak on which the folklorists of Colorado have succeeded in fastening the name of Treasure Mountain. Many tellings and retellings have made its story the most popular of all Colorado tales of lost treasure. It is also the best. To measure its authenticity it is necessary to strip away the mythical exaggerations that have become a part of the tale and depend on some provable bits of history in the last years of French Louisiana.

At the close of the disastrous French-Indian War, France lost all of its territories east of the Mississippi to Great Britain. It would have lost Louisiana and its claims to all lands west of the Mississippi, had it not ceded them secretly to the Spanish Crown in 1762. For the next thirty-eight years Louisiana remained a Spanish colony, but largely in name only; New Orleans remained a French town; so did the fur-trading outpost of St. Louis, far up the Mississippi River. During that period many of the governors of the colony were Frenchmen, and they openly encouraged French exploration of the country between the Mississippi and the Rocky Mountains—all part of Louisiana.

That the French had some knowledge of the Rocky Mountain country and were openly competing with the Spanish for the Indian trade of that region is easily established. In 1722 Etienne Venyard, Sieur de Bourgmont, went up the Missouri River from St. Louis and built a stockade fort at the mouth of the Osage, which he named Fort Orleans. For two years he traded with the Kansa Indians and penetrated all the way to the Rocky Mountains. Shortly thereafter Manuel Lisa and Auguste and Pierre Chouteau, the fur traders, were sending their agents among the Plains Indians as far north as the Platte. Others were going up the Arkansas. It was from the tales that they brought back to St. Louis that the French got their first knowledge of the riches to be found in the Rockies.

Although at least a score of accounts of Treasure Mountain have appeared in print, they are surprisingly alike. The contradictions and disagreements which are a part of the lore of the Adams Diggings, the Lost Dutchman, the Lost Pegleg, and the Lost Breyfogle do not occur. Perhaps that is because the Treasure Mountain story is so venerable and widely accepted that its obvious errors and distortions have escaped comment. Without exception all Treasure Mountain stories begin by saying that in the early 1780's a French expedition came to America to investigate the mineral resources of Louisiana Territory. We are told that it was composed of three hundred men, "skilled miners, mechanics, geologists, and soldiers."

Of course, this latter is not true. At the time, France was in the throes of the violent political upheaval that was to cost Louis XVI his head. Its tottering Royalist government had lost all authority, and the feuding factions among the revolutionists were too engrossed with seizing power and avoiding the guillotine to be interested in exploring the mineral resources of a pseudo French colony half a world away. The conclusion is inescapable, therefore, that the expedition that came up the Mississippi to St. Louis, crossed today's Kansas and entered the Rocky Mountains, originated in New Orleans, and that the man who sponsored it was the Baron de Carondelet, the French governor of Spanish Louisiana.

Carondelet may have financed as well as sponsored it, for Charles E. A. Gayarre, the eminent Louisiana historian, has found nothing in the old and poorly kept records of the colony to indicate that funds were appropriated for such a purpose. It may be taken for granted that Baron de Carondelet had been advised of the terror that was stalking France and that looking ahead in his private capacity he would have had a personal interest in finding gold in the mountains of Colorado.

The many chroniclers of this expedition into the Rockies unanimously agree that it numbered three hundred men. It is to be doubted that among them were "skilled miners, mechanics, geologists, and soldiers," as is often stated. Certainly very few of them could have qualified as "skilled" miners. Very little, if any, mining had been done in Louisiana. That was equally true of all the French colonies from the Gulf of St. Lawrence to the Gulf of Mexico. The Frenchmen in America had followed other pursuits. They were brave, hardy adventurers, almost as much at home in the wilderness as the Indians. In the absence of any evidence to the contrary, it seems reasonable to presume that the Treasure Mountain Frenchmen were largely former *coureurs de bois* who had come down from French Canada. Used to hardship and life in the open, it would have been difficult to find their superiors for Carondelet's purpose.

The weakness, and often the charm, of folklore is that it prefers the implausible to the plausible, embellishing and enlarging details and multiplying the perils as it pleases. Asking us to believe that this expedition of Frenchmen to the Colorado mines numbered three hundred men is an excellent example of this perverseness. Three hundred men (and the five hundred horses they would have needed) is a preposterous figure. It is not known how many men came up the Mississippi to St. Louis, but it is known that the male population of that outpost of civilization did not number more than three hundred at the time; that the only way the adventurers could have come up the river was by canoe, keel boat, or pirogue—none of which could accommodate horses. Therefore, the necessary animals would have had to be acquired at St. Louis, which could not have supplied a third of that number. Perhaps fifty men at most came up from New Orleans, perhaps even fewer than that.

There is some difference of opinion about the route they followed across today's Missouri and Kansas to the mountains of Colorado. Some have it that they went by way of Bourgmont's old post at the mouth of the Osage River. Bourgmont's old Fort Orleans had been burned by the Kansa Indians, but a settlement had survived there. It is far more probable that the gold seekers followed the Osage Trace across Missouri to the Osage villages on the Neosho and from there cut southwest to the Arkansas and went up that river the remaining journey to the mountains.

The course they pursued in Colorado seems to have been carefully documented. It has them leaving the Arkansas at Pueblo and prospecting north as far as Denver, where they turned back up the South Platte to South Park, which they found to be a wilderness paradise, bountifully stocked with wild game—bear, elk, deer, antelope, and buffalo. They had estimated that the supplies with which they entered the mountains were sufficient to sustain them for a year, but with game so abundant it became apparent that they could remain much longer if necessary.

In many of the accounts of their wanderings in the Rockies, they are credited with having discovered gold in small quantities in several places before they moved on from South Park. Perry Eberhart, in his *Treasure Tales of the Rockies,* says they may have been the first men to mine gold at Cripple Creek, Summitville, and other areas that later became famous. It should be remembered that they were prospecting in a mountain wilderness that, save for an occasional trapper from Taos, was unknown to white men.

The leader of the expedition is variously known as Lebreau, Le Breu or Le Blanc. Very likely his name was Remy (Remi) Ledoux, for that was the name given by a Frenchman who appeared in Taos in 1842, claiming to be the grandson of the leader of the original French expedition.

Before reaching the Bayou Salado (South Park) they had become used to meeting hunting parties of Arapaho Indians, whose temporary goodwill they had purchased by making them presents of tobacco and beads. In the Bayou Salado the Frenchmen had as their neighbors a big village of Utes, who were accustomed to resorting there in strength not only to make meat but for their winter home. Maintaining their exclusive rights to that favored region, where there was game for themselves and grass for their pony herds, kept the Utes at war with their traditional enemies, the Arapaho. Naturally the Arapaho, fierce fighters that they were, were soon aware of the friendly relations existing between Ledoux's party and the Utes, and it has been suggested that their chief reason for attacking the French a year later and all but wiping them out was that they regarded them as allies of the Utes.

When Ledoux's party moved on, it recrossed the upper Arkansas. For several weeks it explored the Sangre de Cristo Range, without success, and then proceeded down San Luis

Valley and eventually saw the Rio Grande for the first time. To the west, they had the Continental Divide and the rugged San Juans ahead of them. Somewhere on the East Fork of the San Juan River, between present Summitville, in Rio Grande County, and Wolf Creek Pass, they struck bonanza.

If one could travel a straight line southeast from Wolf Creek Pass in the direction of Summitville, four horrendous mountain-miles would bring you to the snow-crowned sugarloaf peak that is Treasure Mountain. For the past century and a quarter it has been attacked with pick and shovel so often that its slopes are pocked with the futile efforts to locate its secret horde. Don Archuleta, the land and cattle baron of adjacent Archuleta County, and his son, Jose Manuel Archuleta, spent more than $50,000 in their efforts to find the treasure that Remy Ledoux and his Frenchmen left behind.

With winter approaching, that first year, Ledoux's party were into such rich ore that they had no thought of turning homeward. They had been told by the Utes that if they went down the Rio Grande far enough it would bring them to Spanish Taos, a journey of "ten sleeps," according to the Indians, which was an accurate estimate, the distance being about one hundred and twenty miles. This presented the Frenchmen with a problem. Whether or not they decided to risk wintering in Taos, they could not remain where they were. To survive, they would have to seek a much lower altitude before the snows came to make escape impossible. That they feared they might encounter difficulties in Taos could only have been, as some chroniclers have pointed out, because they knew, or at least surmised, that they were doing their mining on Spanish territory, taking Spanish gold out of Spanish ground. If this were true, and they were caught, it would mean a long term of imprisonment or possible death.

They had been smelting their ore and reducing it to gold bullion. The metal was then buried in three hidden caches some distance from the workings. Proof of this is found in a map, believed to have been made by Ledoux, which turned up in 1842.

Before they appeared at Taos, a story would have to be concocted to explain their presence in the country. The best they could do was to pass themselves off as a large surveying party sent out by the Spanish governor of Louisiana to map the boundary of the former French colony. Their story seems to have been accepted without too much questioning, for nominally Louisiana was then under the Spanish flag. They paid for what they bought with minted money. To have used bullion would have raised questions.

In Taos were warmth, food, strong liquor, and women. After wintering there with pleasure, they bought fresh supplies and headed back up the Rio Grande. Fortune had smiled on them until now. Suddenly it showed them its other face. Continuing below-zero temperatures and an almost hundred percent diet of meat brought on a pestilence that sapped the health of all, producing a languor that none escaped. The weakest took to their pallets and died. A French Canadian from the lower St. Lawrence recognized the malady. It was scurvy. He gathered the green leaves of the evergreens and brewed a tea as the Algonquins were known to have done to stay the disease. The bloated and disfigured men drank the decoction eagerly. Its curative powers were noticeable almost at once, but it came too late to save the lives of many. Before the relentless malady passed, half of the company had succumbed to its fearful malignity.

The frozen ground would not permit burying the dead. They were carried into a gulch and covered with snow. As soon as returning health would permit, the survivors cleared the concealed mine shafts and resumed bringing out ore. It was reduced to bullion and added to the store in the caches. By the time spring was well-advanced they realized that the veins they were working were pinching out and the mine had been exhausted. When operations stopped, they filled the shaft and obliterated all evidence of it so that no one might be attracted to the vicinity of the caches, which they realized would have to be left untouched until such time as they could return with an escort powerful enough to guarantee safe transportation of the bullion across the plains to St. Louis.

All estimates of its value are pure speculation. They run all the way from three to thirty million dollars. Whatever it was it could hardly have been less than a king's ransom. With the caches so carefully concealed that they were not likely to be discovered, Ledoux made a detailed map of the area, and to confuse anyone into whose hands it might fall, he indicated false landmarks and blazed trees to lead a searcher astray.

With his reduced company, which by now could hardly have numbered more than a score, he led the way out of the mountains. There can be little doubt that he struck off to the northeast and reached the Arkansas below the Royal Gorge. To follow it downstream across the plains of eastern Colorado and two thirds of the distance across Kansas, which he attempted to do, was the most practicable course he could have taken, with the likelihood of encountering roving war parties of Cheyennes, Kiowas, and Pawnees no greater than could be expected elsewhere.

To anyone acquainted with the Arkansas it is amusing to read that the Frenchmen went down the river by boat. Such an attempt would have been as senseless in their time as it would be today. With its wide bottoms, shallow channels, shoals, sandbars, and snags, the Arkansas does not lend itself to such a journey.

The returning expedition, now numbering seventeen, it is said, well-armed and plentifully supplied with ammunition, reached the future site of Bent's Fort without difficulty. Ten miles below, they bivouacked for the night opposite the mouth of the Purgatoire (the Picketwire of the mountain men), where they were attacked at dawn by a party of Kiowas, outnumbering them two to one. In the bitter fighting that lasted throughout most of the morning, they lost five men and most of their horses.

Limping along, traveling by night most of the time, they reached a large Cheyenne encampment where, many years later, the Santa Fe Trail was to cross the Arkansas. There they were well received by the Cheyennes, who were hunting buffalo. From them they recruited horses and traded for a quantity of smoked buffalo meat. Their difficulties were far from over, however. In the Big Bend of the Arkansas they were attacked by a small war party of Pawnees. When the fighting was over, only Ledoux and four others were left alive, and two of them had to proceed on foot. With their ammunition exhausted, starvation threatened them.

They must have abandoned the river when it began to swing to the south. That they struck off to the east, in the general direction of Topeka, Leavenworth, and the Missouri River, which was, of course, all prairie wilderness, uninhabited by white men, is certain. We know that two of the starving survivors of that trek of not less than three hundred miles, Ledoux and one other, were brought down the Missouri to St. Louis months later. Of the heroic journey across hundreds of miles of unbroken prairie, eluding hostile Indians and subsisting on roots and berries, we know nothing. Some fanciful commentators have said that the five men who left the Big Bend were reduced to cannibalism and drew lots to see which should survive. It is a tale, unsupported by evidence, that can safely be rejected.

Ledoux's companion died of natural causes in St. Louis, so in the end he was the only member of the expedition to make his way back to New Orleans. He had no one to corroborate his story of the great treasure the expedition had buried, no samples of gold to show—only the map he had made! That he

alone of fifty men was the only one to survive was as incredible as the rest of his tale. Carondelet and his associates refused
to believe him. Discredited and ignored, Remy Ledoux disappears from the narrative. Had he returned at another time he
very likely would have been received quite differently. But
there were strife and terror in France; Napoleon was on the
way to having himself named Emperor. The repercussions were
being felt in Louisiana. The future of the colony was in jeop-
ardy, for there were rumors that Spain was about to recede
Louisiana to France. Men in official positions, fearful that
change might sweep away their fortunes, even that their heads
might roll, were too engrossed with such real problems to be
concerned about what they felt was very likely a mythical pot
of gold in the mountains of Colorado.

The changes they feared were realized. Louisiana was ceded
back to France in 1800. Three years later it was sold to the
United States. Save for the two tiny islands of St. Pierre and
Miquelon, in the Gulf of St. Lawrence, the French flag disappeared from the North American continent. After much bicker-
ing, the long Red River and the Continental Divide became
the recognized boundary between the United States and the
Spanish possessions. Thus, everything south of the headwaters
of the Rio Grande (including Treasure Mountain) now belonged to Spain.

Other changes were to occur in rapid succession. Unquestionably they account for the fact that years were permitted to
slip away before any recorded attempt was made to find the
cached bullion on Treasure Mountain. In 1820, the Mexican
Revolution resulted in the independence of Mexico. A year
later, New Mexico became a province of the Mexican Republic.
Within a few months the Santa Fe Trail was opened, and the
wagon trains of the Americans began rolling into Taos and
Santa Fe.

To add to the colony's prosperity, gold placers were discovered in the *Cerillos* (Little Hills) within thirty miles of Santa Fe. Other discoveries were made, and in 1828 the first gold lode west of the Mississippi was found on the *Sierra de Oro* (Mountain of Gold) and became the famous Ortiz Mine.

No news travels as fast or as far as word of a gold strike. That stories of the discoveries being made north of Taos reached New Orleans can be believed. Fifty years had passed since Remy Ledoux had returned from that country with his incredible story of the fortune that had been buried on Treasure Mountain. He was dead and gone, but his grandsons were very much alive. One can imagine with what interest they studied the map he had left them. Now that it was being demonstrated that there was gold in the Rockies, it could not have been difficult to convince a number of men that the old map was a waybill to great wealth.

In the spring of 1842, an expedition of some forty men, following a trail north from San Antonio to the vicinity of Wichita Falls, then up the Red and Canadian rivers, arrived in Santa Fe. They spoke Spanish fluently, but they were Frenchmen from Louisiana. One of them was Ledoux's young grandson. Although the original, and now precious, map was in his possession, the leaders of the party had made copies of it.

It was a matter of the first importance for them to have an audience with the Mexican governor, crafty Manuel Armijo. They were prepared to give in to his demands, whatever they were, for once they had located the caches they would need a large *muletada* (herd of the mules) and *muletoros* (drivers) to get the gold out of the mountains. Armijo agreed to supply these. To save them the time of returning periodically to Taos for supplies, he engaged Bernardo Sanchez, who had done some prospecting and who was acquainted with the mountains, to accompany them as camp tender and when necessary make the trip back and forth between their base camp and Taos.

The expedition made camp beneath the pines in a sheltered

mountain meadow on the eastern, or Rio Grande, side of the Divide within two miles of Wolf Creek Pass. They were not long in learning that the map on which they had depended to lead them to the buried bullion was not going to be the Open Sesame they had expected. In a land of ten thousand nameless mountains, all looking very much alike, only a map drawn to scale could have been of any great help.

With dogged patience they moved from one place to another, hoping to find a spot that matched up with the landmarks depicted on the map. As the weeks wore away, they explored the country for miles around. Several times they were sure they had found what they were seeking; the surrounding peaks matched those on the map, the leaning pine, the slope of slide rock—all seemed to fall in place. Their pulses quickened when they saw, head high on a smooth outcrop of basalt, a fleur-de-lis that had been scratched on its smooth surface. Beneath it was an arrow. They followed the direction in which it pointed and began digging. For several days they toiled there before moving on, convinced that the caches were not to be found on that rocky slope.

Very likely the fleur-de-lis was one of the meaningless, misleading directions Remy Ledoux had incorporated in his map, and to which he alone held the key. They found a cairn of flat rocks that a snowslide had toppled over. It led them nowhere, for in fifty years the unchanging mountains had changed enough to present a blank page to those who sought their secrets.

Perhaps this second expedition of Frenchmen were as close to finding the caches of gold at this point as they were ever to be again. By the time summer was gone, they had explored all of that harsh country between Bennett Mountain and Wolf Creek Pass to no avail. Beaten, discouraged, they followed Bernardo Sanchez down the Rio Grande to the New Mexican settlements.

In some accounts they are said to have engaged in a disastrous battle with the Indians, from which few escaped alive. The Utes were no longer friendly—too many white men were moving into their homeland—but it seems that a major engagement would have been noted in official circles. In the exhaustive historical commentaries of New Mexico of that period no mention of it occurs. Nor is there any reason to believe that the treasure seekers spent a second year in the Colorado mountains.

Young Ledoux returned the following spring and spent most of his time around Pagosa Springs, in today's Archuleta County, where he became acquainted with the Archuletas and other ranchmen. While there, he was drowned in the San Juan River. The body was recovered by a struggling ranchman named William Yule. Yule reported that he found no papers or map on the young man's person. Heretofore, he had shown no interest in hunting for the lost gold of Treasure Mountain, but he suddenly became one of its most avid seekers. Without funds himself, he induced Don Archuleta to finance his operations. For a decade and more the wealthy Archuletas continued to pour money into his unsuccessful searching.

The long hunt for the Frenchmen's buried gold was just beginning. It really got under way when Asa Poor, the well-known and successful southern Colorado prospector, began looking for it. Up in Saguache County he had made two strikes that netted him upward of $75,000. He was a hardheaded man and he brushed aside the numerous tales of lost mines and buried treasure as fairy tales for halfwits. He made his headquarters in Pagosa Springs. It was a good place to hear the stories that were always going the rounds.

He was acquainted with William Yule. Yule was inclined to be talkative when he had taken on a few drinks. One night in a saloon in Pagosa Springs, Asa Poor heard him admit that he had a tracing of the original map to the gold caches on Treasure Mountain and that a grave at the foot of the mountain was the key to it. Yule was vague about how the tracing had come into his possession.

Poor did not press him for an explanation. With him Yule's vaporings were a case of in one ear and out the other. He knew that country thoroughly, and a year later was prospecting there again when he found a sunken grave. Recalling Yule's story, he began digging. He found the skeleton of a man that had laid there so long that it disintegrated when he tried to move it—but he did not find any gold.

Poor searched the grave carefully and was rewarded in finding a rust-encrusted poniard with a triangular blade. The leather hilt had long since rotted away. That the weapon was of French origin hardly admitted of question. Asa Poor's interest in Yule's map of the fabled lost caches of Treasure Mountain skyrocketed. Being a methodical man, he refilled the grave and started for Pagosa Springs.

The year was 1870. Yule had left Colorado. Poor set out to find him and ran him down in northern New Mexico, some say at Shiprock. What is important is that when he returned to Pagosa Springs, he had the map. He proposed to inaugurate an intelligent and exhaustive search for the buried bullion. He took in as partners Leon Montoy, the superintendent of the Little Annie Mine at Summitville, a recognized mining authority and as well acquainted with the region as Poor himself, and A. T. Stollsteimer, U.S. Indian Agent for the Southern Utes, for whom Stollsteimer Creek was named. Stollsteimer was brought into the partnership in the hope that he might be able to gather some information from the Indians. The Utes shook their heads and said no; if they knew anything, they weren't talking.

The intriguing story is told that Poor and Montoy found a notation on the old map that they were put to great pains to decipher. The instruction is alleged to have said: "Stand on the grave at the foot of the mountain, at six o'clock on a September morning, facing east, and where the shadow of your head falls, you will find the gold." This sounds like a page borrowed out of any one of a hundred lost mine tales of Old Mexico, where the devout and humble backcountry *peons* will solemnly offer you similar advice. If it is the fabulous lost silver lode of the Jesuits, somewhere in the wild Sierra Madre of Sonora, you are seeking, you will be told to climb to the crest of a certain *pioche* (peak) at sundown, and if God wills it, you will hear the angelus bells of Tayopa—ignoring the fact that no bell has rung there in over three hundred years.

Poor and Montoy pursued a more prosaic course. For two years they scoured the mountains in every direction from the grave that Poor had found. They went over it yard by yard. They discovered the sealed-up shaft of the Frenchmen's mine, opened it, and discovered the pinched out vein of gold—but they did not find the caches of bullion, and they understood why. Over the years, snowslides and avalanches had brought down untold tons of rock and changed the face of much of that country.

Montoy went back to the Little Annie Mine, which was a sure thing, and Asa Poor packed up his prospecting outfit and followed his burros through the San Juans into Mineral County and fell in with a miner by the name of Nicholas Creede, who was to drive his pick into an almost solid ledge of silver and give his name to the fabulous bonanza camp of Creede.

The searching for the lost gold of Treasure Mountain did not end with their departure. Countless other men moved in to continue it. It goes on, year after year. Today, the story of the buried gold bars is known to thousands. With a fortune of that size to set men to dreaming, its lure will never fade. Someday some lucky man may find it, if, as the Mexicans say, "God wills it."

12

The Lost Gold of the
Reynolds Gang

In the world of lost mines and buried treasure their comparative importance is measured, usually, by the amount of riches that can be expected. And yet the rich ones have seldom been sought by the greatest number of men and women. The Reynolds Gang gold and the hordes who have tried to find it is a case in point. If you live beyond the borders of Colorado you very likely have never heard of the buried gold of the Reynolds Gang. In fact, you may never have heard of Jim "The Bold" Reynolds and his desperadoes, for his career of crime was brief and distinctly minor league.

The legend of the buried gold and greenbacks of the Reynolds Gang began modestly, the estimates ranging from $3,000 to $7,000. But time took care of that. The figure was pushed higher and higher, and it now stands at a convenient, rounded $100,000, which is sufficient, even in these inflationary times, to make a summer weekend in the mountains highly profitable, if one is lucky. The most popular hunting ground lies between Shaffer's Crossing and Handcart Gulch, all within fifty miles of Denver. It is beautiful country, and over good roads it can be reached from Denver in an hour or better.

There was a time when the treasure seekers concentrated their searching on the headwaters of Deer and Elk creeks. Later, when instructions on how to find the cache, purportedly given by John Reynolds, turned up, the search shifted to Geneva Gulch and Geneva Creek. When a rusted knife, made from a file, was found buried in a tree on Vernon Crow's ranch on Handcart Creek, interest immediately centered there. The rusted knife, with the handle broken off, runs through all Reynolds Gang lore. Naturally, it was regarded as a red-hot clue. The knife was said to point to the grave of a member of the gang. Crow found the grave, and on opening it discovered the skeleton of a man, buried with his boots on and a bullet hole in his skull. This checked with numerous stories that one of the gang had been fatally wounded in a robbery and had been buried near their secret hideout.

Believing he was on a hot trail, Crow did some searching before saying anything. He found a little park in the aspens, above the grave, that could have been the outlaw camp, with the remains of a low barricade of rocks from which anyone coming up the gulch could have been seen and picked off. An enclosure of rocks and brush indicated a makeshift corral.

Undoubtedly Crow had found the Reynolds camp, but he did not find the cached treasure. When word of his discoveries got into circulation, Handcart Gulch received a going-over by an army of fortune hunters. They were back the following year and the next, again and again. Young and old, male and female, they keep on returning. Some interest remains in Elk, Deer, and Geneva creeks, but today the great majority of those who seek the Reynolds loot are convinced that it lies buried somewhere in Handcart Gulch. The natives of that country would like to see the last of these visitors. "They are sick unto death of all this treasure talk," says Perry Eberhart, as good an authority as you will find, in his *Treasure Tales of the Rockies*. "Fortune hunters have torn down fences and fence posts, trampled fields and dug holes up and down three gulches. They [the natives] wish they had never heard of 'The Bold' Reynolds and his infernal treasure."

Caroline Bancroft, able Colorado historian that she is, says, "That it was buried there—the loot of stagecoach robberies, perhaps amounting to $75,000 in gold, $100,000 in currency and diamonds and other jewelry—there is no reason to doubt." There is grave reason to question not only the figures she gives but that the Reynolds Gang ever buried any treasure. The first account saying that they had, appeared in (General) D. J. Cook's book, *Hands Up*, published in 1897. Cook was chief of government detectives in Colorado in 1864. He organized a posse at Fairplay that set out to capture the gang after they robbed the Fairplay-Denver coach near Kenosha Pass. Under Cook's direction, the thirty-man posse managed to keep out of the gang's way, which by all accounts wasn't easy. Being a detective and having "chased" the Reynolds Gang, he was accepted as something of an authority on the bandits. In his book he makes extravagant estimates of the loot they made off with, including several cans of gold amalgam, minted coin, and jewelry. Highly melodramatic articles in the infant *Rocky Mountain News* saying the gang had buried great wealth in several locations were accepted as fact by Cook, and he confirmed and enlarged on the buried treasure theme until it soon became a part of Colorado folklore.

Cook presented no evidence to document his conclusions. Nor has anyone else. Perhaps that isn't necessary or desired, for Eberhart shakes a scolding finger at what he calls "latter-day historians, who love to take the meat and bones off legend and leave it sick." There is nothing sickly about the legend of the lost Reynolds treasure. It has survived for over a hundred years; but in the absence of any documentation to the contrary it must be regarded as a hoax, however painful that may be.

It was not until 1863 that handsome Jim Reynolds began to attract some attention in the Bayou Salado (South Park) as a worthless young scamp, surrounded with three or four companions who shared his aversion to hard work. He had been in the Bayou Salado long enough to know the country as well as any man. Constantly on the move from one mining settlement to another, he and his friends were making a nuisance of themselves with their drinking and brawling. Though they never worked, they had good horses to ride and money to spend. It was not long before the undisclosed source of their income brought them under suspicion of being responsible for the rash of petty robberies that were plaguing South Park.

By the end of the summer there wasn't any doubt that they were the masked highwaymen who were stopping travelers and holding up stage stations. Their take was small, not over several thousand dollars, and with winter coming on to slow things down for months, they went out for bigger game. Not knowing that a posse from Fairplay was hard on their heels, they attempted to hold up a McClellen and Spotswood coach. They were caught in the act. The others got away, but Jim Reynolds was taken into custody. He was hustled off to Denver and lodged in jail. While awaiting trial, he and his cellmates, Charlie Harrison and Cap McKee, broke out and headed for parts unknown.

The War between the States was being waged with savage fury, and at the moment the fortunes of the Confederacy were brighter than they ever were to be again. But the treasury of the C.S.A. was becoming bare. Back in his native Texas, Reynolds is said to have suddenly burned patriotic and offered to organize and captain a guerrilla force that, in one way or another, would capture all the gold in Colorado and pour it into the empty coffers of the South.

It was a grandiose scheme that could hardly have won the

approval of any competent military man—not that the gold would have been unwelcome or that Reynolds had not demonstrated some talent for such an operation. No mention of Reynolds occurs in the papers of the commanding officer of Confederate forces in Texas. If he had ever been given a commission, as he claimed, it should be found in the departmental records. Had he made such a proposition to tough-minded General Henry McCulloch, ex-Texas Ranger, he would have been rebuffed in more violent terms than Confederate Secretary of War Seldon used on William Clarke Quantrill when that notorious, free-lance guerrilla journeyed all the way to Richmond seeking a commission in the Army of the South that would give his bloody marauding the quasi-dignity of a military operation.

Very likely Jim Reynolds saw himself as another, if minor, Quantrill. Unpromising clay sometimes burns noble, and it may be that when he headed north in the spring of 1864 with twenty-three hand-picked, so-called Rebel guerrillas, he honestly meant to turn over to the South the proceeds of his robbing and plundering. If so, he reckoned without the baser instincts of his followers, though they had been forced to take the following oath, a copy of which was found in Reynolds' notebook when he was killed:

I do solemnly swear or affirm that I will bear true allegiance to the Confederate States of America and the President and all officers appointed over me, so help me God. I further swear that I will aid or assist all true Southern men and their families wherever they may be at a reasonable risk of my life whether in the army or out of it. I furthermore swear that I will not reveal, divulge, or cause to be divulged, any of the grips, signs, passwords or proceedings of the order, except to those who have been regularly initiated or to whom it may by right belong, and if I should be so vile as to violate this my solemn oath or obligation I shall be taken and hung by the neck until I am dead, dead, dead, and my bones left on the plains to bleach as unworthy of burial.

It would be interesting to know where he got the foregoing. He copied it somewhere, for he didn't have the education to compose it. He had promoted himself to the rank of colonel—perhaps in imitation of Quantrill. The latter, after the burning of Lawrence, outfitted himself with the gray uniform of a colonel of the Confederacy. Reynolds' vanity did not take him that far.

Luck smiled on him and his followers at the first try. Moving up through New Mexico, they robbed a wagon train of, it was said, over $60,000. Thereupon they lost themselves in the region of the Spanish Peaks until the hue and cry died down. They were no sooner safe than an argument broke out over dividing the spoils. Reynolds insisted that the loot belonged to the South. The majority of his men were less patriotic and demanded their share of the money—mostly minted coin—at once. Reynolds gave it to them and ordered them to clear out. It left him with eight men: his younger brother John, Owen Singleterry, Jake Stowe, Tom Holliman, John Bobbitt, John Andrews, Jack Robinson, and Tom Knight. Whether they subsequently buried their share of the robbery is not known. More than likely they carried it with them. Splitting up into pairs to avoid suspicion, they arrived in South Park by way of Canon City on the Arkansas.

Two days later they joined ranks at Dolph Guiraud's ranch on Agate creek, a few miles above its confluence with the South Platte, and some twenty miles from Fairplay. Reynolds had a slight acquaintance with Guiraud and his wife from his former days in the Bayou Salado, and anticipated that the gang could find food and shelter there for a day or two.

The Guirauds had little choice about taking them in; but they were hospitable people and made them as comfortable as they could, although they knew Reynolds had escaped from the Denver jail and was wanted. He palmed himself and his followers off as Rebel guerrillas and boldly asserted that their mission in Colorado was to loot the Territorial Treasury for the South. A robbery of that scope was beyond the comprehension of such humble folk as the Guirauds, who were barely able to scratch a living out of their mountain ranch. As for the war that was being fought a thousand miles away, they knew so little about it that their sympathies were with neither one side or the other.

After leaving the Guirauds, Reynolds and his merrie men waylaid the superintendent of the rich Phillips Lode and relieved him of a few dollars, which was a disappointment, for he was reputed to carry big sums. Several small robberies followed, by way of practice for the big things ahead. At McLaughlin's Stage Station, ten miles north of Fairplay, about where today's Como stands, they turned serious. The station was on the main road to Denver and was used by the stages of McClellen and Spotswood.

Several persons were present. The gang disarmed them, concealed their horses and took possession of the station. Not a shot was fired. Indeed, these singular desperadoes were not bloodthirsty, and there is no record of their ever having killed a man. They had time to spare as they waited for the stage to arrive. The cook was ordered to set out a meal for them, and as they regaled themselves with food and drink, they made merry.

It is generally believed that they had been tipped off that the Denver-bound stage would be carrying treasure. When it arrived, they stepped out and quickly took possession of it, ordering Abe Williamson, the driver, and the passengers to step down, hands raised. They obliged, and this robbery at McLaughlin's Station was destined to become one of the most famous holdups in Colorado history. Here it was that the legend of the buried gold of the Reynolds Gang was born.

Nobody knows how much the bandits made off with. Name any figure from several thousand dollars to a hundred thousand

and someone will agree. In fact it was not long before anyone who was anybody in South Park—and some who weren't—claimed to have had money on that particular stage. Among the authentic losers was Billy McClellen, who chanced to be a passenger on his own coach. From him the desperadoes took three or four hundred dollars in cash and his gold watch. In addition to the strongbox, the mail was rifled and must have produced two or three thousand dollars. But the overall take could not have been more than ten thousand dollars—far too small a figure on which to found a worthwhile legend. The legendmakers soon took care of that.

One of the small losers was a well-known Fairplay prostitute who had mailed two hundred dollars to her mother at Springfield, Illinois. "It's too damn bad that a girl in my line of work can't send her ailing mother a couple hundred dollars without having it stolen by a bunch of blacklegs!" she screamed. "If the men of this town had any guts, they'd go after those bastards!"

She talked long and loud enough to produce some action. "General" Dave Cook organized a posse and took to the trail. They were cautious enough, however, not to get within shooting distance of their quarry, who had moved up the road a few miles to Kenosha Pass, where they were enjoying a hearty supper at the Kenosha House, after which they moved on to Omaha House for a good night's rest.

By now, news of the audacious robbery at McLaughlin's Station had gone winging across the mountains. Several posses were hot on the trail of the gang. A thirsty-man posse under Captain Maynard set out from Denver; another from Swan River, led by Jack Sparks, was hurrying south for the creeks that form the headwaters of the North Fork of the South Platte.

Reynolds evidently figured it was time to take to the hills. He was in country with which he was familiar. In view of the discoveries Vernon Crow was later to make—the rock barricade, the grave, the camp in the aspens—there can be little doubt that it was up Handcart Gulch that he led his band, and that if the loot was buried anywhere it was there.

Of course, this is widely disputed, many saying the treasure was buried at Shaffer's Crossing; others are positive that it was cached where the Webster Pass road crosses Elk Creek. As previously mentioned, Geneva Gulch has its adherents. Where it was buried—if it ever was—is not important; that country has had a methodical, even frenzied, going-over for years, and the money has never been found. What the general run of seekers of the Reynolds gold refuse to consider is that John Reynolds may have returned to Handcart Gulch sometime after his brother was killed and dug up whatever was buried there. Treasure hunters are peculiar that way, believing only what they want to believe.

Following their disappearance into the hills, the Reynolds Gang could not have taken up a defensive position in Handcart Gulch for more than two days, possibly three, when Jack Sparks and his Swan River posse reached the headwaters of Handcart Creek after dark and prepared to bivouac there for the night. They got their first intimation that they did not have the gulch to themselves when they caught the flickering light of a distant campfire through the trees. Thinking at first it might be another posse, they left their horses and proceeded warily on foot. In only a few minutes they realized that they had stumbled on the outlaw rendezvous. Sparks gave the word to surround the camp. Not a shot was to be fired until he gave the signal.

The possemen meant well, but one of them, overanxious, jumped the gun. The desperadoes scattered like quail, scurrying out of the light of the fire. One of them pitched to the ground as he started to run. A brief exchange of gunfire followed as the gang made for their horses at the far end of the little park. Once mounted, they quickly pulled away. The posse, on foot, was helpless to follow. But they returned to their horses and rode to the Kenosha House with news of the encounter. They spent the night there. At daylight they were back at the outlaw camp. There they found Owen Singleterry, Reynolds' right-hand man, stretched out on the grass, dead.

In their haste to get away the gang had left behind several rifles, blankets, bags of food, cooking utensils, and a can of gold amalgam. Among the possemen was Dr. George Cooper of Alma. He severed the head from Singleterry's body, and it was afterward placed on display in Alma for the edification of that hell-roaring community.

The gang scattered and never rode together again. John Reynolds, Jake Stowe, and John Andrews, after several brushes with a small posse, escaped through the mountains into New Mexico. Tom Holliman, riding alone, made his way to a house a short distance from Canon City, where he was given a bed. Exhausted, he fell asleep at once. But not for long. Directly behind were half a dozen members of the Swan River posse. They took him into custody without trouble and sent him back to Fairplay for safekeeping. That left only Jim Reynolds, John Bobbitt, Jack Robinson, and Tom Knight unaccounted for.

After two days of dodging pursuit, without food, they turned toward Fairplay in their desperation and took over a ranch house at the edge of town. Word of their presence became known, and their rashness was to cost them dear. A posse of no less than seventy-five men was hurriedly organized. No "General" Cook this time; a Captain Shoup was the leader, and he meant business. Reynolds and his companions learned what was afoot in time to flee. Undaunted, Shoup set out on their trail. With the posse rode the captured Tom Holliman, but for what purpose no one has ever been able to discover. It hardly could have been to act as guide, for he knew no more of the whereabouts of Reynolds and the others than Shoup did.

The big posse, accompanied by several supply wagons and

cooks, swept a wide slice of country. Keeping the quarry on the move began to pay off. Without food for four days, their horses giving out, Reynolds and his men were caught east of Canon City. They surrendered without resistance. Captain Shoup marched them, and Holliman as well, to Denver in triumph.

Seekers of the Reynolds gold never fail to point out that the bandits had very litle money on them when they were captured. They give this as positive proof that the proceeds of the robbery at McLaughlin's Station were buried somewhere.

The arrival of the prisoners in Denver presented the civilian authorities with a problem. Though the town's Southern sympathizers were decidedly in the minority, they were numerous enough to give rise to the fear that they might attempt to break into the jail and free the five self-proclaimed Rebel guerrillas. With this as an excuse, Reynolds and his fellow prisoners were turned over to the military. They were given a secret trial—the records of which were never made public—and sentenced to be hanged as conspirators against the United States. This military "tribunal," evidently fearing it had exceeded its authority, announced that the prisoners would be escorted to Fort Leavenworth, Kansas, for a review of their case and punishment.

A troop of the 3rd Colorado Cavalry, under Captain Cree, left Denver with the captives. Captain Cree and his troops returned to Denver the following day with the news that all five men had been shot near the old ghost town of Russelville while trying to escape. The truth was revealed when "Uncle" Dick Wooten, the famous scout, chanced to pass the scene and found the five men lashed to trees, riddled with bullets.

Along with the infamous Sand Creek Massacre, this shooting stands as one of the blackest pages in Colorado history. In the wave of revulsion that swept the Territory, Cree tried to excuse himself by claiming he had been given oral orders to shoot the prisoners at the first opportunity. It was the manner in which he died, not his robberies, that has kept the memory of Jim Reynolds green.

It was not until 1871 that John Reynolds was publicly reported to have returned to Colorado. There is no telling how long he had been back before he was identified, but certainly long enough for him to have reached Handcart Gulch and dug up any treasure that the gang had buried there. Likewise, he could have recovered the gold that had been cached in the Spanish Peaks. If he tried, he was apparently unsuccessful, for he and his companion, a two-bit outlaw named Brown, were reduced to stealing horses. In one such foray Reynolds was mortally wounded. Legend has it that as he was dying he told Brown about cached treasure in Handcart Gulch and drew a crude map of its location. Brown was later seen in Handcart Gulch. He certainly found no treasure, for he ended his days in Wyoming, a penniless drunk.

After the fight with the Swan River posse, in which Owen Singleterry was killed, the Reynolds Gang had scattered. John Reynolds, Jake Stowe, and John Andrews escaped into New Mexico. There are various accounts of what became of Stowe and Andrews. The most reliable say that Stowe never recovered from the wounds he received in the Handcart Gulch fight and died within the year, and that Andrews was killed in a saloon brawl in Texas.

That closes the books on the Reynolds Gang. Of the nine men who were going to rob Colorado of its gold for the Confederacy, all had met a violent death. As bandits, they were a bumbling, third-rate crew. It leaves only one question unanswered: what became of the money they stole—whether $10,000 or $100,000? For all of the "bone-picking" and scoffing, maybe it does lie buried somewhere on one of the nest of creeks that form the headwaters of the North Fork of the South Platte.

IDAHO

13

The Saga of Old Bill, the Burro

In all the lore and memorabilia of lost mines no instance occurs in which an animal, wild or domestic, is held responsible for man's inability to retrace his way to a discovery or to relocate previously buried treasure. On the other hand, animals are credited with being responsible, in one way or another, for a score and more of rich strikes. Needless to say, it was the burro and the mule that figured oftenest in such tales. And on several occasions it was a horse that led the way to fortune.

As Jim Priest, an experienced prospector, was riding down a canyon in the Bitterroot Mountains of Montana his mount suddenly went lame. Getting down to investigate, Priest found a nugget lodged in the frog of the animal's right foreleg. Removing the nugget, he turned back and explored the canyon floor. He found what he was looking for. His find led to the development of the Buckskin Mine that made him wealthy. Down in Arizona Henry Wickenburg shot a vulture on the wing, and where it fell on the banks of the Hassayampa River he discovered the Vulture Mine "which produced so mightily that by 1879 the eighty stamp mills he erected there were producing bullion worth $21,000 a week."

IDAHO

The story of Jim Butler and his straying burro is perhaps the most famous of all. In 1899, a vein of silver was found at a lonely spot in Nye County, Nevada. The discovery was promising enough to attract attention, and a tent camp took shape, named Southern Klondike. It was soon to become much better known as Tonopah (Paiute for little water).

Jim Butler had a small hay ranch up the state at Belmont. He was as much a prospector as rancher, and when he heard about the excitement at Southern Klondike, he decided to take a few days off from his haying and find out what it was all about. Packing some necessaries on a burro, he headed south. One morning, as he was camped in the vicinity of what was to become Tonopah, his burro strayed. To turn the animal back, he looked around for something to hurl at it. Chipping off a piece of rock from an outcrop, he was about to throw it, when he saw that it was heavily mineralized. He chipped off several other pieces. They showed the same formation. There was lead in it and possibly galena carbonite, the silver ore that had made Leadville the great bonanza camp of its day.

Butler dropped the samples into his canvas bag, and when he captured his burro, went on to the tent camp at Southern Klondike. It did not take him long to see that it was a washout. Turning around, he headed back to Belmont, where he showed his samples to his friend Tasker L. Oddie, the District Attorney of Nye County, a tall, gangling young politician.

The samples looked promising to Oddie, but like Butler he could not spare the cash for an assay. However, he knew Walter Gearheard, the superintendent of schools at Austin, who was also an assayer and might do the job on credit. The samples were sent to Austin. Several weeks passed before the head of the Austin schools got around to running an assay. When he did, the button of silver that resulted made him blink his eyes; he had never seen anything like it. A second assay proved to be just as rich. In a dither of excitement he hurried his report off by stage to his friend Oddie.

As evidence of the unpredictable nature of Jim Butler, with a fortune in sight, he insisted on getting in his hay before he took off for the south. When he was finally ready, he loaded his wagons with water, grub, and camping essentials, and accompanied by Oddie and Mrs. Butler, the latter going along to do the cooking and lend moral support, he set out for Tonopah, his assets amounting to twenty-five dollars. When he reached his destination, he and Oddie began staking off claims in every direction.

Word got around that he had found something. Southern Klondike, dying of boredom and sagging hopes, pulled up stakes and moved in. Overnight, Tonopah was born, and when Butler received a check for eight hundred dollars from the Austin smelter for the first ton of ore freighted out by mule team from the Mizpah Mine, Nevada went wild.

Having proved that Tonopah was the richest bonanza since the Comstock, Jim Butler sat back to take it easy and began leasing out his claims on shares, something that had never been done before. The millions rolled in on him. Out of his largess, he gave Tonopah a saloon that was as big and luxurious as Tex Rickard's Northern was to be several years later in the lush days of Goldfield, thirty-five miles away. Oddie, of course, was also to prosper outrageously; he became governor of Nevada and United States senator. There is no record of how Jim Butler's burro fared.

Although gold was discovered in the barren Columbia Mountains, south of Tonopah, without the aid or assistance of any animal, the birth of the camp had a distinct equine overtone. On July 4, 1903, it consisted of four tents and a total population of five men. Three of them had taken off to celebrate the day in Tonopah, leaving L. L. Patrick and J. D. Hubbard to hold the fort until they returned. These two had just settled down to enjoy a quiet evening with a bottle of Old Crow when a band of several hundred wild horses swarmed into camp, knocking down the tents and raising general hell as they attempted to stampede the picketed horses. Patrick and Hubbard were all night fighting them off. They were in worse shape than their partners when the celebrators got back from an equally riotous night in Tonopah.

But the prize tale of all comes from the Coeur d'Alenes of Idaho, and it concerns Old Bill, the burro, who, as a co-plaintiff, appeared in court and was awarded, along with his owners, the sum of $76,000 for the discovery he had made.

The story first appeared in print in *Outing*, around the turn of the century, when that famous slick-paper magazine, with its nationwide circulation, was the finest publication in its field. It has since been reprinted many times. The following is from the original article by F. G. Morehead and is the report of an interview he had with Jacob Goetz, at Murray, Idaho, in 1909.

Goetz, known all over the Coeur d'Alenes as Dutch Jake, was at the time the owner, with his partner Harry Baer, of the famous "saloon and music hall" at Murray, Idaho, the Bunker Hill. He had been roaming through the Coeur d'Alenes for over twenty-five years, having ventured into those mountains on snowshoes in 1883, with twenty feet of snow on the ground. He had helped to open up such camps as Murray, Mullan, Eagle City, Burke, Kellogg, and Wardner. He told Morehead:

"Dutch Jake was always pretty lucky. I was thirty years old in 1885 and had something like $25,000. It was easy come, easy go in those days. My partner, Harry Baer, and I had a saloon in Murray, a small place. We were partners in mining deals, too, and did a little grub-staking on the side. I fell in with Phil O'Roarke, an old Colorado miner, who was counted the best prospector in the Coeur d'Alenes in those days. Baer and I grub-staked him to prospect for us.

The Saga of Old Bill, the Burro

"O'Roarke and I had been out looking at some claims early in 1885, when we met N. S. Kellogg, who had been provided with a burro and $18.75 worth of provision by Cooper and Peck, the general merchandise outfit. They had told him to hunt around until he found color or never show his face in civilization again.

"The grub didn't last long, but the burro has gone down in history. It was this way—the burro did it; that's the God's truth. Kellogg had been plugging around in the mountains [Milo Gulch] and had not hit anything that looked good to him, until he was plum disgusted. He was getting back to the settlement where there was always whisky, women and something doing even if the grub-staking had not panned out. So, he made his last camp up in the Coeur d'Alenes, tied the burro, Old Bill, to a rock and hunted around for another slice of bacon that would make him think of home and mother.

"Bill smelt the bacon and thought of his own appetite. He knawed [sic] on the rope that held him but gave it up in disgust. He wanted something to eat just as Kellogg did. Finally he got so blooming mad that he snorted and rared around and pawed up all the loose gravel and boulders, then lit out with his heels as though he'd kicked the lining out of the sky. Kellogg gulped down his bacon and wandered over to see what ailed Bill. I guess Kellogg never did think to give that burro anything that night. He even forgot his own hunger, for Bill had uncovered a ledge of iron galena ore that certainly looked good to Kellogg. There it was, plenty of it, riches for everybody, but Bill the burro was just as hungry as ever.

"The next day Kellogg went down to the Coeur d'Alene River, crossed over to Murray, showed his specimens to his employers, Cooper and Peck. They showed them to John M. Burke, a respected assayer. Burke reported that it was only 'a smelting ore, not worth bothering with.' The merchants told Kellogg that if he could not find gold he could keep the rest of the small grubstake and get another job."

Kellogg evidently went out on his own, for it was then that Goetz and O'Roarke encountered him.

Goetz continues:

"He showed his samples to Phil O'Roarke. It did not take Phil but a moment to see that [they] gave promise of producing some galena or carbonite, like the ore that made Colorado famous. Phil called me to one side and said we couldn't do better than to go in cahoots with Kellogg in staking that ground. I agreed and turned over my cayuse and grub to Kellogg and Phil, and they started right off for the find.

"I guess they didn't let any grass grow under their feet. They wore out one pack horse and lost another. While old man Kellogg went in search of it Phil started up Milo Gulch to look for the place that Kellogg had described. At the head of the creek he found some galena float and although it was dreadful hard work to get through the brush and fallen timber he climbed up the hill about five hundred feet and there he stumbled upon the great Bunker Hill ledge [named for the Revolutionary battle] sticking right up out of the ground. There was nothing to it but glittering galena, and Phil knew he had found the greatest thing ever discovered in the Northwest. He was so excited that he sat right down, never said a word nor took his eyes off that galena for half an hour. Finally he rushed back and found Kellogg."

The next morning when they broke camp and started to go up Milo Gulch two miles to stake the claim, they found that their horses had strayed again. While searching for the animals they saw Old Bill, the burro, not far from the Bunker Hill Ledge. He was pawing the ground where he had made the big find. When Kellogg had quit Cooper and Peck, they had turned the burro loose. Since it did not belong to Kellogg, he had not bothered about the animal, and it had wandered back up the mountainside until Kellogg and O'Roarke found him.

"Sight of the samples the two men had set the camp crazy, but nobody knew where the lucky find was located. Phil took me off and advised me to locate the extension to the Bunker Hill. He thought I'd better take Con Sullivan along. Con was a sort of partner of Phil's. That night about ten o'clock we set out in a furious rain, without even a pack horse. We thought we could locate the mine by the directions O'Roarke gave us, but as it turned out he made a mistake in describing the location, and we took the wrong hog-back and had a dreadful time. We wandered around for four days and got completely lost, and had nothing to eat or drink for two days but some snow that had laid in a gully from the last winter.

"Sullivan was pretty well used up, his tongue was sticking out, and he could hardly move. You see, we were walking all the time, except for the little [when] we would sit down to get our breath. We finally came out on the south fork of the Coeur d'Alene, above Kingston. The Indians fed and watered us and we went back and located the extension."

Years later, a painting of the Bunker Mine and the Sullivan Extension, as they appeared in 1889, occupied a place of honor in Dutch Jake's "music hall" in Murray. Some wayfaring artist painted it from a sketch Goetz had drawn. As the world knows, the Bunker Hill and the Sullivan Extension became fabulous producers. They gained notoriety of another sort when in the early 1900's they were dynamited by Harry Orchard, the hatchet man for the Western Federation of Miners, whose career of murder and destruction ended with the assassination of Idaho's Governor Steunenberg, under whose front gate he had placed a bomb, for which he was sentenced to life imprisonment. In 1909 eight hundred men were being employed by the Bunker Hill–Sullivan Extension, and the dividends amounted to $180,000 a month. The mines were sold in 1891 for one and a half million dollars. Today they are valued at twenty million, and are not for sale.

Jake Goetz recalled:

"Naturally Cooper and Peck heard that their burro had been with Kellogg and O'Roarke, and although they hadn't cared enough about Old Bill to give him food, shelter or even a pleasant word, they figured a lawsuit could be based on his participation in the find. The case was tried in Murray before Judge Norman Burke and a jury. Peck and Cooper, suing on Old Bill's behalf, wanted a half interest in the whole find. The jury listened and brought in a verdict for the defense, disqualifying the burro entirely. But the judge shook his head and had the last word."

Here it is, copied from the court record:

"From the evidence of the witnesses this court is of the opinion that the Bunker Hill Mine was discovered by the jackass, Phil O'Roarke and N. S. Kellogg and the plaintiffs. They are entitled to half interest in the Bunker Hill and a quarter interest in the Sullivan."

Of course, the verdict was appealed, but the parties to the lawsuit finally got together and reached a settlement. Cooper and Peck received $76,000; Harry Baer and Jacob Goetz, $200,000 in cash; Phil O'Roarke got almost as much in stock and cash; Kellogg got $300,000 in cash and stock; Con Sullivan settled for $75,000 in cash. It was quite a juicy melon the boys divided.

"Old Bill wasn't overlooked," Jake Goetz told the author of the *Outing* article. "He got a square meal three times a day for six years. Kellogg bought Bill and paid a man at Forest Grove, Oregon, $50 a month to care for him. Bill lived in clover till he died, age 21 years, and his grave is marked with a stone today."

If Old Bill spent his remaining years in comfort and luxury, that is more than can be said for the men who shared in the windfall they owed to him. In a few years, all with the exception of Jake Goetz and his partner Harry Baer, were broke. They escaped the same fate only because the large office building in Spokane, into which they had put their money, had some insurance when it burned. Somewhat chastened, they returned to Murray and opened their famous saloon.

Travelers in that part of Idaho will find a few old-timers still alive who can add trimmings to the story of Old Bill, the burro that nobody wanted.

NEVADA

14

The Lost Blue Bucket Mine

Aside from his animalistic sex hunger, the three things that have most engrossed man since he was expelled from the Garden of Eden have been food, shelter, and treasure, and not necessarily in that order. In the main, his ingenuity has been sufficient to provide him with shelter against the elements. Finding food with which to sustain himself has always been more difficult, but though often driven to extremity, he has been able to survive. Over the centuries, the great incentive that has kept him going has been the hope of bettering his lot, an urge which, if reduced to its common denominator, invariably has meant being able to get his hands on more of this world's goods —treasure, if you like, and preferably gold. For that dream men have suffered and died.

Undoubtedly this explains why any tale of a "lost" mine or buried treasure fascinates so many of us, even though we may dismiss it with a skeptical smile as just another preposterous bit of folklore. But few of us find we can be done with it so easily, for we become obsessed by the recurring thought that maybe—*maybe*—there is such a hidden valley or canyon, with its fabulous riches, waiting for the lucky man to uncover.

It was from such an oblique angle that I became interested in the Lost Blue Bucket Mine. I first heard the story in Winnemucca, Nevada, in 1916. By then I had seen too much of the state's mountains and deserts, particularly Humboldt County, to take the tale seriously. It wasn't only what I felt were its obvious geographical errors that turned me away from it; I could not believe that a wagon train of hardy, California-bound pioneers, presumably of average intelligence, could have journeyed on for two hundred miles before realizing that the "pebbles" the children had tossed into a bucket hanging at the side of one of the wagons were gold nuggets. It was too late to turn back then; winter was at hand and the Sierras had to be crossed before snow closed the trail. The aftermath, as I heard it for years, was always the same—the frantic searching for the "wheel ruts of shiny brass" that were never found. If the minor details changed, that was the recognized prerogative of whoever was doing the talking.

"Late in October, 1845, a large wagon train bound for Oregon, split up at Garvelly Ford," I remember George Rose, editor of *The Silver State Journal* and later sheriff of Humboldt County, telling me. "Better than half continued on down the Humboldt for California; the rest—some forty wagons under the command of Captain Elisha Sowers—struck off to the northwest across the Black Rock country for Granite Springs and the Applegate Cut-Off, which would open the way to Oregon and the Willamette Valley. On their fourth day in the Black Rock, they were caught in a canyon so deep and narrow that ox teams had to be unhooked and doubled up to get one wagon through at a time. I've tried to find that canyon. But there's a hundred like it. I don't know whether I ever got close to the right one or not."

I knew he had done some prospecting. He was thoroughly acquainted with the country and described it in great detail.

"All across northern Nevada at that time, the Piutes [a localism for Paiute used by all men], enraged by the ever increasing number of white men passing through their country, were attacking wagon trains and massacring emigrants. Nowhere was the danger of attack greater than in the Black Rock. Captain Sowers was aware of it, and he and the other men worked feverishly to get out of the canyon, knowing that to be trapped there would be fatal. It was slow work. The children of the train, having no idea of their dangerous predicament, climbed up out of the way at the side of the canyon and, for amusement, began picking up pebbles and tossing them into the buckets that dangled at the side of the wagons. Their mothers let them play and paid no attention.

"After being stopped for hours the way was cleared and the wagons began to bounce and jolt down the rocky floor of the canyon, the heavy wheels leaving shiny tire marks in spots. Captain Sowers saw them; so did others. But the golden streaks meant nothing to them. Across open desert they continued on to the northwest, struck the Applegate Cut-Off without difficulty and, by way of Eagleville, entered California and settled down for the winter at Yreka, on the Klamath River.

"Almost from its founding the natives of that tiny hamlet, including Dr. Henry Dane, had been placering for gold on the streams of the region. Dane was called to the Sowers' camp in his professional capacity. The children had saved some of the 'pebbles' they had tossed into the blue bucket. When Dane saw them, he realized at once that they were nuggets of pure gold. Questioning Sowers and the others, he heard the story of the golden tire marks. It convinced him that the Sowers' party had discovered a bonanza out on the Black Rock. The camp was thrown into excitement and plans were made at once to return to the find in the spring. No one doubted that they could locate it.

"With the coming of spring, Dane and fourteen others, well armed, left Yreka for the Black Rock. East of Granite Creek they were attacked by Indians and all but two lost their lives. The survivors organized another party, and although they were harassed time after time by bands of Piutes, they scoured the Black Rock range for weeks. They were unable, however, to locate the canyon in which the children had found their 'pebbles' and the iron tires had left a golden trail.

"Several other attempts were made to find it, but without success. After gold was discovered in Sutter's millrace and the stampede to the Sacramento Valley began, the Blue Bucket was forgotten."

Thereafter, whenever I heard the story, it invariably concluded with the statement, "It's out there somewhere; no question about that. Somebody will stumble on it one of these days." But the Black Rock country remains the largely uninhabited wasteland it was fifty years ago, and no one has "stumbled" on the blue bucket up to this writing. In the meantime, however, my skepticism has been shaken by a number of things that have occurred.

Weatherwise, Humboldt County has changed drastically with the passing years. Jim Minor, the old-time cattleman, told me once that he could remember when the lower levels of the ranges stayed green until midsummer. Today, except for a few days in early spring, they are brown the year around. What was once rich cattle country has become primarily sheep country. A wagon train had to have grass for its oxen, and a man like Elisha Sowers would have followed the grass. In my time there has never been any grass in the Black Rock Range. That had always been a prime reason for my disbelief in the Lost Blue Bucket story.

"You can't discount it on that score," Minor objected. "Where you don't find grass today doesn't mean that it wasn't well grassed in Sowers' time. He was only followin' his nose—no trails, nothin' to guide him. If he got tangled up in the Black Rock, he most likely got there without leavin' grass. I've heard the story a hundred times, and I've always wondered if he ever got into the mountains. He could have swung around to the south of 'em. He would have had only ten miles of desert, with patches of deep sand, ahead of him, but he would have had no trouble gettin' through."

It was a viewpoint I had never heard expressed; always the Blue Bucket was placed in the Black Rock Mountains, and they had been gone over with a fine-tooth comb. Talking with Minor whipped up my flagging interest in the mine sufficiently to take me out to the Bank ranch, a few miles east of Winnemucca, to ask my friend Frank Button what he thought about Minor's observations. He was the manager of Bliss Brothers' string of ranches and known all over Humboldt County—a salty, dehydrated man, paper thin, with a face the color of an Indian's and a pair of eyes that had never lost their humorous twinkle. It was Sunday, and I reminded him of the fact.

"Too bad I didn't remember or I'd have given the boys the day off," he cackled.

I could see them at the far end of the yard, stacking hay.

"Jim's right about the grass not bein' what it was," Frank said, when I had repeated my conversation with Minor. "I know what's happened to it in my time, and that wagon train went through forty years before that. If that outfit ever found a canyon lined with gold, it couldn't have been the way that old yarn has it. Whoever put it together in the first place was careless about his facts."

"What makes you say that, Frank?" It wasn't always easy to get him to talk.

"Why, in the first place, what sort of sense does it make for a wagon train splittin' up at Beowawe if one half of it was bound for California and the other half for Oregon? Look at the map and you'll see what I mean. They'd have come down the Humboldt together and split up at Winnemucca."

From the first, the thing that had made me doubt the Blue

Bucket story was that senseless splitting up of the train at Beowawe, known as Gravelly Ford in those days, when it could have so easily come down the river for another hundred miles, with water and fair-to-good grass all the way, which would have brought them to where Winnemucca now stands. There was nothing there at the time, but the safe crossing was known to the trappers as Frenchman's Ford. The valley is fairly wide there, and wagons pointing for the northwest could have got away from the Humboldt with no more than a gentle climb of several hundred feet. In later years, that was the way the road went to Quinn River Crossing and Jungo. I have been over it many times.

"Of course, this story about the lost canyon of gold was concocted in California and didn't git back here much before 1868, when the stampede of miners from Virginia City spread out over the country," said Frank. "It was too late then to improve what you might call its geography. But there's another thing that has always kept me from puttin' much stock in the Lost Blue Bucket."

He reached for the coffeepot and filled our cups.

"It's this," he resumed. "The men with the Sowers party had sons, and I reckon they had sons. They'd be grown men by now. They musta lived with the story from the time they was boys. You'd figger they'd be interested. But in my time I ain't ever heard of one of 'em tryin' to find that jackpot."

It was a telling point, and I had to agree with him. And then I learned that two young Californians had appeared at Humboldt, bought burros, and outfitted themselves for a prospecting trip. Without disclosing their identity or destination, they set their course to the west of north and were not heard of again for weeks.

In Winnemucca, we always spoke of Humboldt as "Humboldt House." In those days that was about all that was there— the big general store and hotel. It lies about forty miles west of Winnemucca, and in the days about which I am writing it was a flag stop for local Southern Pacific trains. But it had had its moment in history.

After the rails of the Union Pacific and the Central Pacific met at Promontory Point and the thousands of Chinese laborers who had built the Central Pacific found themselves out of employment, they turned en masse to the mines for work. All across the state race riots flared as white miners drove the pigtailed Orientals out of one camp after another. At Unionville, ten miles south of Humboldt, and at the time the most important town between Virginia City and Salt Lake City, twenty-eight Chinese were ordered deported. An angry mob escorted them to Humboldt and the railroad. The west-bound train was late; unwilling to wait, the mob slaughtered the yellow men— a crime for which no one was ever brought to justice.

Trailing north by west from Humboldt it is not more than forty miles to the southern fringe of the Black Rock Desert, though in the 1920's there was no noticeable line of demarcation between the sandy, arid sagebrush plains that surround it and the true desert, as outlined on current maps. There are a few dependable springs, but no running water, other than the tiny streams in the Jackson Mountains and the Black Rock Range.

The secretive young Californians disappeared into the vastness of that inhospitable country for weeks on end. Their supplies exhausted, they found their way to the little desert hamlet of Jungo, which owed its existence to the Western Pacific Railroad. They were more talkative now. Subsequently, from the Jungo storekeeper, I learned that they had acknowledged being the grandsons of one of the members of the original Sowers party, and armed with an accurate waybill to the canyon of gold, prepared by their long-since-dead father, they had been searching for it in the Black Rock. They had failed to find it. They were exhausted, not discouraged or disillusioned.

They said they would try again. I don't believe they did. But other descendants of the pioneers who left a fortune of exposed gold in the Black Rock searched for it. It is evidence enough that men who had been suckled on their grandfathers' tales of the Lost Blue Bucket Mine had not lost faith in it.

Though I was weakening, I was still a doubter. A series of events were to happen, however, that were to make me a believer. Two of my novels dealing with Humboldt County and its Basques—a fine people, I found them to be—had been published with some success and I was roaming over the county, fishing, hunting, doing some amateur prospecting, and gathering material for a third book. And then it happened. Gold was discovered in the Black Rock Range—the first definite proof that the country was mineralized. Claims were staked and veins of metal found. Men flocked in and the excitement engendered was sufficient to bring Herbert Hoover out from the East to investigate and invest.

The claims soon petered out and the excitement was over, but I no longer doubted the existence of the Lost Blue Bucket. About that time my father-in-law, Tom Brandon, the mayor and leading attorney of Winnemucca, became obsessed with the idea that oil was to be found on the Black Rock. He obtained a prospecting permit and organized and financed a small company to find it. In the weeks that followed he was seldom home, for whenever he could tear himself away from his office, he joined the exploring party on the Black Rock. I went out with him, and they were wonderfully exciting days for me. I still have some of the fossils I picked up as we moved up and down and across the Black Rock. Several times we got as far north as King's River.

One morning, when I was several hundred yards ahead of our Model T, trying to discover a way to get through a stretch of deep sand, I stepped around a clump of tall sage, seven or eight feet high, always a sure sign of underground water, and came face to face with the biggest buck coyote I have ever seen. For a second or two, both of us were too startled to move. He was the first to recover his wits and bound away.

I knew in a vague way that in prehistoric times all of this country had been covered by the waters of Lake Lahontan, which accounted for the fossils we were finding. One evening, sitting around the campfire, I suggested that we have a try in the mountains west of Jungo. The geologist we had with us vetoed the suggestion at once. He had located several likely-looking spots for putting down a well, and according to him it would be folly to leave the flatlands.

With the bantering, good-natured smile that was part of the man, B. said (in the family we never called him Tom), "You've got the Lost Blue Bucket on your mind rather than oil. I think our chances are better than yours."

"For your sake, I hope so," I told him. "But you've agreed with me for years that the Lost Blue Bucket was not a fabrication. Have you changed your mind?"

"Not at all! I believe the children picked up the nuggets and that some of them were carried to California. Very likely the tire marks did reveal streaks of gold. But I'm just as positive that nobody's going to find that rich hoard. It's always been said that when Sowers' train came out of the mountains they were between two high peaks. No question but they were Division Peak to the north and Granite Peak to the south. In the twenty-one miles between the peaks, nine out of every ten men who ever tried to locate the Blue Bucket began their searching. With all that concentration, you can be sure there's not a draw or canyon that hasn't been examined. Undoubtedly men have trudged over the very spot where those children tossed their gold pebbles into the bucket. Time, nature—drifting sand, a rockfall, a cloudburst, no one can be sure what—has buried the Blue Bucket treasure where it will never be found."

Thirty years and more have passed since those words were

spoken. They appear to have been prophetic, for the Lost Blue Bucket remains a mystery. But what nature covers, it sometimes uncovers. I have wandered far away from northern Nevada, but I continue to read the mining news published in the *Humboldt Star,* and always with the expectation that someone at last has discovered the bonanza that lies buried in the Black Rock.

I always hoped Peter Organ would be the man to find it. He was so sure about it. For years he tramped the Black Rock, the Santa Rosas and Jackson Mountains. He was a loner, like Captain Cooney. He liked to get up high and have a lot of country spread out below him so he could "get his bearings." I shall never forget the morning that his son, the marshal, drove up to our place with him, in his battered Model T, and called me over to the fence.

"Are you the young fella that put me in a book?" old Peter asked.

I had to admit that I was, surmising that I was in for trouble and would be sued for invading the old man's privacy. But I was all wrong; old Peter was pleased.

"I wish you'd have come to me before you did yore writin'," he told me. "There's so much more I coulda told you. I know right where that gold is. I figger to git it next spring."

But he never did. He's been gone a long time now—and so are some of those old memories.

15

Dan Brennan's Grindstone

In the 1880's, when mining was the principal business of the West, most of the professional assayers of precious metals, gold, silver, and copper, were honest men. They had to be—or move on to another camp, where they might prosper until they were found out. Then it was move on again. However, even the most scrupulously honorable and sufficiently skilled in the science of metallurgy made mistakes. The brief "rush" to the Seven Troughs district in northern Nevada in 1914, or thereabouts, resulted from the carelessness of an assayer's schoolboy assistant.

Two miners, perhaps the Choate brothers, Ike and Eddie, or it may have been Eli Bradshaw and his partner, brought into Winnemucca, Nevada, some samples from Seven Troughs. The assay showed gold values running from twelve to fifteen dollars a ton. That meant that Seven Troughs' ore could be mined at a profit, especially since the district was less than forty miles from the railroad, and transportation costs to the smelter would be low.

Within a week, upward of a hundred men had pitched their tents at Seven Troughs. Caught up in the excitement he had caused the assayer was one of the first to arrive. Claims were staked and digging began. Ten days later, the Seven Troughs bubble burst; no one had found so much as a color. Back in his office on Bridge Street, the crestfallen assayer ran more tests. All were negative. And then one afternoon, as he happened to watch the boy who came in after school carelessly cleaning the crusher with a whiskbroom, he realized why he had found twelve- to fifteen-dollar values in the first samples from Seven Troughs. On the previous day he had run the monthly assay on high-grade ore from the fabulously rich National Mine. Enough dust had remained in the crusher to give the Seven Troughs samples values they did not possess.

But the strangest of all tales involving an assayer is the experience that befell young Jim Hewett, at Pioche, in eastern Nevada, hard against the Utah line, in the early 1880's. Silver had been discovered at Pioche in 1864. A dozen years passed before the camp began to boom.

Silver had come back strong with the passage, over President Hayes' veto, of the Bland Silver Bill, and by 1881 Pioche had a population of over two thousand. The town was isolated, far from a railroad, until it built its own little narrow-gauge Pioche and Pacific to connect with Senator Clark's San Pedro, Los Angeles, and Salt Lake line at Calienti. With its numerous saloons, gamblers, speculators, and prostitutes, it was tough. Perhaps it was the toughest of all Nevada mining camps, but the story that seventy-five men died violent deaths there before one died of natural causes can be dismissed as apocryphal. Likewise, there was far less claim-jumping in the Pioche district than the numerous tales would have one believe. There was some, however.

The most spectacular was the attempt of the Newlands brothers to "jump" a series of claims they held to have been "abandoned" by the Raymond and Ely Syndicate, owners of the Pioche Consolidated, the district's biggest producer. When the

Newlands moved in, they threw up a barricade about their glory hole and manned it with armed guards. Raymond and Ely sent up a party of men to drive them off. Considerable shooting followed, but the Newlands refused to give ground. Seeing that force of arms had failed, big John MacLeod, superintendent of the Pioche Consolidated, resorted to strategy of a different sort. He arranged with a Pioche saloonkeeper to deliver a case of whisky to the Newlands' camp, apparently by mistake. A few hours later the Newlands' miners and guards were helplessly drunk. MacLeod moved in with a contingent from the Pioche Consolidated and sent them staggering down the slope.

Because Pioche was a proved district, there was more than the usual speculation. Working mines, mines just coming into production, and claims that had not yet been opened up were bought, sold, and traded every day. This produced a great amount of work for Jim Hewett, the camp's leading assayer. Guided by the reports they got from him, the big plungers invariably made money out of their transactions. Men who sold their properties at prices based on the predicted value of Hewett's assays, and then found they had been undervalued, began saying that the assays were rigged in favor of the speculators. Of the disgruntled, little Dan Brennan was the most outspoken.

"I'll trip up the dirty skunk!" he told his drinking companions in the Index Saloon one evening. "He knew which side of the bread his butter was on when his report said I had no better than twenty-dollar ore in the Superba." Dan had sold his mine, the price he received being dictated by Hewett's appraisal of its worth.

Hewett knew he was being attacked. His honesty was his greatest asset. He had never accepted a bribe or written out a fraudulent report. But there was nothing he could do to stem the tide that had set in against him. When Brennan walked into his office two weeks later with some chunks of gray rock and left them to be assayed, Jim Hewett did not suspect a trick was being played on him that would make him the laughing-stock of the camp and drive him out of Pioche.

When the new owners of the Superba had driven Brennan's tunnel only several yards deeper into the slope of Mount Ely, the vein of silver they were following widened into bonanza. Dan Brennan had to be forcibly restrained from using his gun on the person of Assayer Hewett. He still owned a mine on the eastern slope of Mount Ely that he had worked intermittently for several years. No great riches could be expected from it, but it could be counted on to produce a living. He called it his grubstake. He had a cabin at the mine, and when he recovered from the forgetfulness of a heroic drunk, he repaired to it and sulked in private until he regained his wits. As he brooded over the injustice that he believed had been done him, a diabolic scheme of revenge occurred to him. Without wasting time, he started the wheels turning. Seizing a sledge, he demolished a discarded grindstone. Picking up some choice pieces, he shoved them into his pocket and headed for Pioche. The "samples" he hired Jim Hewett to assay were fragments of the old grind-stone. That evening he told his intimates what he had done. "Let's see what sorta values he finds in that stuff!" he roared.

His friends gave him no encouragement. A grindstone might be a conglomerate, but it was largely sandstone. Hewett was no fool; he would recognize it at once for what it was.

"God knows there's no mineral values in a grindstone," one told him.

"Of course there ain't!" Brennan agreed. "But I don't expect his report to say so. He knows I been stirrin' up trouble for him. To git me off his neck, I figger he'll find some silver values in that junk."

It happened as he predicted; Hewett reported that Bren-nan's "samples" were incredibly rich in silver. The grindstone story went the rounds of the saloons, and everyone agreed that

Jim Hewett was either a crook or a fool. There was some rash talk of giving him a coat of tar and feathers and riding him out of camp. Big Jim MacLeod, the superintendent of the Pioche Consolidated, stopped it. "It won't be necessary to go that far," he argued. "Just don't give him any more business and he'll have to pack up and leave Pioche."

Hewett began to feel the effects of the boycott at once. When he discovered what was behind it, he made another assay of Brennan's grindstone "samples." The second assay corroborated the first. Desperate by now, Hewett went to the Pioche Consolidated and talked to MacLeod.

"John, you can run as accurate an assay as any man. Will you get Brennan to bring you some pieces of his grindstone and see what you can find?"

MacLeod agreed reluctantly. Fifty-dollar ore in a grindstone! It was incredible. But that's what he found. He called Dan Brennan and told him what he had done.

"Where did you get that grindstone, Dan?"

"Why, I'm damned if I know where it come from—"

"Well, you better find out," MacLeod informed him. "There's fifty-dollar ore in the tunnel where it was cut."

Dan Brennan did a lot of thinking back. He knew he had never bought the stone. It had been lying out in the weeds near the cabin as long as he could remember. He had bought the claim from Vic Torrey, who had worked it for a time. Torrey would know about it. But Torrey had left Pioche and his whereabouts were unknown. Brennan buttonholed every man in camp without results. Others were asking questions, too, for the greatest grindstone hunt in history was under way.

Wherever there was a mine, there was a grindstone for sharpening drills. At the time, there were several hundred mines in eastern Nevada, at any one of which a searcher for the "lost grindstone" might pick up some useful information. From the little that was learned, it seemed that Vic Torrey had been a bird of passage; some men recalled having known him. But they hadn't seen him for years and didn't know where he was.

Dan Brennan quit working his claim and did his searching methodically, moving up through the Ely Range and the Schell Creek Mountains to the big camp at White Pine and as far west as the Eureka district, and back to fading Hamilton and its barren, mist-shrouded Treasure Hill, where once two miners had thrown up a rock windbreak around their tent that later proved to be nearly pure silver chloride, worth seventy-five thousand dollars. Always the trail led on to another camp. It was more discouraging than looking for a lost mine, for he had no *derreterro,* or waybill, to tell him in which direction to go.

After a year of wandering, he returned to Pioche and went back to work. Months passed. When the lost grindstone had ceased to be a topic of conversation, Dan Brennan received a letter from Vic Torrey. He was in the Los Angeles County Hospital, where he was recovering from a long illness. He wrote that he had heard that Brennan had been inquiring about him. "I don't know what you want, but if you'll write me I'll try to tell you what you want to know."

Brennan did not bother with the mails; he started for Los Angeles at once, in person. How little, or how much, did Vic Torrey know? It was a question he could not answer. He remembered him as a man of cunning. If Torrey knew that a mine with fifty-dollar ore was at stake, he wouldn't give anything away for nothing. Brennan realized that he would have to be very careful; but he no sooner mentioned the grindstone than he saw that he was trapped. The sick man regarded him with a shrewd, crafty smile.

"Dan, you tellin' me you come all the way out to California about a grindstone that I threw away because it was so hard and worthless it wouldn't sharpen a drill?"

"I know it's no good, Vic. It's laid out in the weeds above

the cabin for years. I never bothered to pick it up. Where did you git it—that's all I want to know."

"I made it," Torrey chuckled. "I found an outcroppin' of schist and split off a slab, rounded it out and punched a hole in it. I saw there was some feldspar in the sandstone, but I figgered I could use it. . . . You wouldn't hardly expect to find fifty-dollar silver ore in that kind of rock—would you?"

"So you know—" was all Brennan could say.

"Sure, I know! With all the talk there's been, how could I help knowin'? That's why I wrote you. I figgered you might make me a proposition. I need money."

Brennan did not hesitate. "All right, Vic; you've got a deal. I'll put up the money to get the mine into production and we'll split everythin' down the middle. Now where in God's name is that outcrop of schist located?"

"In that little draw about a hundred and fifty yards up the slope from your cabin—"

Dan Brennan had never needed a drink so desperately in all his life. "All the huntin' I did for it," he groaned, "and there it was—almost in spittin' distance all the time."

Incredible? Certainly. But no more incredible than the $400,000 their mine, the Silver King—named after the more famous Silver King of Arizona—produced before it was exhausted.

The dialogue is not authentic but the story is. It would be pleasant to report that when Dan Brennan died, he remembered Assayer Jim Hewett in his will; but there is nothing in the files of the *Pioche Record* to indicate that he did.

16

They Called It Rawhide

Candelaria was about as far south as Zach Carson ever got. He was well known in Bodie and Aurora and other mining camps, but Candelaria suited him best. The beer in McKissick's Saloon was the coldest served in Nevada, being stored until needed a hundred feet below ground in an abandoned mine shaft. If he craved a stronger stimulant, and he invariably did after a month out in the sun-baked gulches along the old Candelaria Trail, he could find it in a dozen congenial establishments.

Back in 1882, when the rails of Darius Ogden Mills' narrow-gauge Carson and Colorado Railroad hooked up Candelaria with the outside world, the camp hailed the event with a wild, week-long celebration. But the novelty of having two trains a day to Carson City and the north had meant very little to him then, and now, twenty-five years later, it was of even less consequence. He was not going anywhere a railroad could take him, for like redoubtable Shorty Harris of Death Valley fame, he was a "single blanket, jackass prospector" to whom the distant wailing of a locomotive whistle was only an unpleasant reminder that civilization was closing in on him.

(Years later, the little diamond-stack locomotive, with its

combine and coach, that everyone has seen being attacked by train robbers as it puffed around the bend is, or was, a relic of the old narrow-gauge Carson and Colorado Railroad, a stretch of track across the line in California, between Laws and Keeler, serving as an authentic "location scene" for numerous motion-picture Westerns.)

Zach Carson seldom got more than fifty miles from Candelaria, always coursing in a northern or northeasterly direction. He spent part of his time along the considerable eastern shore of Walker Lake, going there to wash out gold-bearing sand that he had dug up five to ten miles away. He had to cross the unballasted tracks of the Carson and Colorado to reach the water. It appears to have been his only direct contact with Mr. Mills' orphan railroad.

Zach Carson limited the time he spent placering to producing a living. Once that had been attended to, he was free to pursue his questing for the vein or outcrop of gold that would lead him to his fortune. In some blowout or gulch in that god-awful desert east of Walker Lake, where even a jackrabbit couldn't scratch a living, he was convinced that he would find gold if he searched long enough. He was in no hurry; the desert taught a man how to be patient. In his time, he chipped off hundreds of pieces of promising-looking rock and carried them back to Candelaria to be assayed. The results were invariably disappointing—values sometimes, but too low to justify further consideration.

In the fall of 1903, Carson came into Candelaria with his usual bag of samples. He numbered them and turned them over to an assayer. After a weekend carouse he came in for the assayer's report on Monday. To his amazement, sample number five showed values running to $300 a ton. The old man blinked his eyes and could not remember for the life of him where he had found Number 5. In the course of the trip from which he had just returned, he had covered an area of thirty square miles, all of it very much like the proverbial peas in a pod. He had found a valuable mine and lost it too!

Of course, Zach Carson didn't consider it lost; knowing the country he had been in, he was sure he could return to it without difficulty. It might take a little time to find the outcrop from which he had chipped off the rich fragment of rock. But the fracture would still be fresh. He was confident he could not miss it. After four weeks of fruitless searching his grub ran out, and he had to return to Candelaria. He went out again and again until white winter dropped its mantle over Nevada and brought his wandering to a temporary halt. He proved he was not discouraged by refusing to join the great rush southward to booming Goldfield, which was draining men away from all the northern camps.

Candelaria was feeling it. Being a long-established camp, with a number of top-grade producing mines, it had shaken off the effects of the big silver strike at Tonopah in 1900 without losing face. But when Goldfield (it began life as Grandpa), thirty-five miles south of Tonopah, blossomed into bonanza in 1903, the competition was felt all over the mining West.

Lucius Beebe and Charles Clegg, the ribald and always delightful commentators on the Nevada scene, who see no reason for writing history as though they were conducting a memorial service, unhesitatingly called the Tonopah-Goldfield-Rhyolite complex "The Last Bonanza." They may be right. But in a land as highly mineralized as Nevada, how can one be sure?

With millions being brought out of the ground a hundred miles away, Z. T. Carson must have been sorely tempted to try his luck in that direction. Undoubtedly he was an eccentric, as most solitary desert wanderers are. Perhaps finding a second time what he had once found and then lost held a challenge for him that he could not resist. When he went out in the spring of 1904, as soon as brown patches began to appear on the slopes where snow had lain for four months, the long search for his lost treasure was just beginning.

For three years, between periods of placering to keep him in grub, he crossed and recrossed the country between the Sinkvata Hills on the west to Gobbs Valley and Mount Anna on the east. An open winter permitted him to start early, and on February 15, 1907, the long search ended happily in the lee of an overhanging bluff on the eastern escarpment of the Sinkvatas. He not only found the outcrop from which he had taken a sample years back, but an hour's work revealed rich veins of plate gold.

Carson staked out three adjoining claims and put up the required monuments and deposited his "notices" in a bean can on the contents of which he had dined that noon. In the morning, he set out for Hawthorn to register his claims—Bluff, Mascot, and Mascot No. 1. When he returned, his friends Cal Deming and Jack Davis were with him. On March 1, they got into high-grade on Murray Hill, a short distance north of Carson's claims. As usual, news of the strike went winging across the barren wastes to other camps. From Eagleville, Reese River, and Buckskin, men headed for the Sinkvatas and Gobbs Valley. On July 4, the first shipment of gold ore was hauled out to Luning. The small shipment gave returns in five figures. There was no stopping the new camp after that.

Presently, Zach Carson could look down the gulch from his claims and count twenty tents. The camp had no name. Charley Holman took care of that. He was a buckaroo rather than miner, but he had been working in a shaft at Buckskin for Jack Bell, the well-known leaser. More in jest than anything else, he nailed a soap box to a post in front of Carson's tent and scrawled across it in pencil RAWHIDE. The name stuck, and before the year was out *The Rawhide Rustler* was claiming a population of 22,000 for the camp. This was a vastly exaggerated figure, which was in line with its ridiculous inflation of all news concerning Rawhide. The truth in this instance is that at its peak Rawhide's population was not over 8,000, in itself a truly remarkable figure, since it had only one truly rich producer, the Rawhide Consolidated.

The rest was all promotion, conceived and directed by Tex Rickard, the master entrepreneur; his tosspot companion, the wealthy actor Nat Goodwin, with his well-known predilection for beautiful women (Maxine Elliot, Edna Goodrich, among others); Riley Grannan, the "honest" gambler; and George Graham Rice, the Wall Street operator and notorious promoter of worthless stocks. Associated with them were several other choice spirits.

The great San Francisco earthquake and fire of 1906, which destroyed the city, had a disastrous effect on the headlong prosperity of Tonopah and Goldfield. Gold and silver were mined in Nevada, but it was San Francisco that dictated the flow of investment, the credit and stock values of the rich properties. The great fire swept away, at least temporarily, the financial structure that controlled Tonopah and Goldfield.

Rickard and his fellow conspirators had waxed rich in Goldfield. Rickard's reputation had become nationwide. When you mentioned Goldfield, you unconsciously mentioned his Great Northern Saloon—the second of that name. The first was in the Klondike; the third, and last, was to take shape in Rawhide.

In light of what followed, one can only conclude that Rickard felt that Goldfield had lost its edge and had given him all he could hope to get out of it. The reports reaching him of the richness of Rawhide Consolidated and the substantial showings of Carson's Bluff, Rawhide Queen, Grutt Hill, Hooligan and Burro Mountain, and half a dozen other mines must have convinced him that there was enough there on which, with supercharged exploitation, a second Goldfield could be built.

Certainly at his elbow he had in the person of George Graham Rice a master-hand in the nefarious art of bogus promotion.

For mellifluous oratory mixed with homespun pathos, he could depend on H. W. Knickerbocker, the ex-minister, to supply whatever was needed. In January, 1908, he made his first move by shocking Goldfield with the news that he had sold his Great Northern Saloon and was going to Rawhide. With a maximum of publicity, flamboyant Nat Goodwin and Riley Grannan, the big plunger, the two most popular men in Goldfield, announced a few days later that they were pulling up stakes and going with him.

Beebe and Clegg report that a banner with foot-high letters appeared on the façade of the Goldfield Methodist Church declaring "This Church is Closed; God has gone to Rawhide." A few days later *The Goldfield Review* turned traitor and published a "Rawhide Extra." As soon as snow disappeared from the flatlands, Rickard and his conspirators piled into their high-center Loziers and Haynes-Appersons, with their moneybags, and set out for unknown Rawhide, with only the haziest idea of where to find it.

They no sooner reached their destination than George Graham Rice paid Zach Carson $50,000 for his claims, which put him and his fellow Argonauts from Goldfield in on the ground floor of the gold-plated miracle they were to perform in the short space of a few months.

A main thoroughfare was staked off, running down the gulch, and christened Nevada Street. Tex Rickard and his associates scattered like quail then to buy the material and make the connections that were to transform this desolate stretch of sand and sagebrush into a thriving, populous mining metropolis. Hundreds of Western mining camps mushroomed into prominence. The pattern is well-known and need not be repeated. But Rawhide was different; it was contrived, arranged, made its rich manipulators richer, achieved a crude magnificence seldom, if ever, equaled by other camps—telephones, telegraph, four mining exchanges, four reduction mills, cold

storage plants, automobile stages to Carson City and Reno—
and for all of the hullabaloo produced a surprisingly small
amount of gold.

It witnessed the last of the old-time "Throw down the box!"
holdups of a Wells Fargo stage; it saw the passing of the great
desert caravans of twelve-, sixteen-, twenty-horse team freighters, and with them went the old burro pack trains. Rawhide
has no blood-and-thunder history. According to the record,
only one man was shot to death in its brief history.

But much more passed out of existence when it faded—the
diamond-studded gambler, the female dealers, the big concen-
trations of ladies of the evening, such as the eight hundred in
Stingaree Gulch, the saloon orchestra (Tex Rickard's Great
Northern, with its hundred-foot bar, was the only saloon in
Rawhide that didn't have one). In more ways than one, the
Old West died with Rawhide. It was the end of an era. There
may be other great strikes in the future, but there will never
be another Rawhide.

In a sense it was a canvas-tarpaper town on September 5,
1908, for it was less than a year old. A well-beaten road to
Schurz, a small station on the Carson and Colorado, twenty-five
miles to the west, had been carved out of the desert. Over it
came most of the supplies and material that made Rawhide.
New buildings went up every day. Town lots that had been
sold for ten dollars in April were bringing fifteen hundred by
September. Day and night promoters kept the hoists of twenty-
four mines barking away, giving the impression that the camp
was booming. Great claims, never substantiated, were made by
The Rawhide Rustler for the ore that was being brought up.
To further aid the deception and keep up the brisk market in
local mining issues, great chunks of horn silver from the Mascot and bags of gold ore from the Rawhide Consolidated and,
allegedly, from other mines were kept on display in the windows of saloons and stores.

Jack Bell was working one of the Grutt brothers' mines on lease and was in Rawhide on the fateful fifth of September, 1908. In an article published in 1926, he described what happened that morning. He was on his way for coffee and had stopped at Ross' Brown Palace Hotel on Nevada Street. The time was 8:45 A.M. To reach Young's coffeehouse was but a minute's walk from the hotel. It was situated just beyond Rickard's Northern Saloon. "I had just sat down and ordered coffee and cakes from Curly, the waiter," he recalled. "He placed it on the table and then, attracted to the door, turned and cried 'She's going!' There was a high wind—a gale. Before I could negotiate the door, fire was sweeping down Nevada Street in one immense blaze. Men, women and children took to the hills. Men in the mines were hoisted hastily. The three chemical wagons were destroyed before anyone could reach them. Powder was secured and blasting began blocks away to backfire. But the town was doomed, and was razed and smouldering in ruins in less than forty minutes."

According to Bell, the fire started in the Brown Palace Hotel. It actually began next door in Banfield's Drug Store and spread to the hotel in a few seconds.

Before the ashes were cold, telegraphic connection with Reno was restored. Geoge Graham Rice ordered tons of food to be rushed to Rawhide immediately. It began to arrive, via Schurz, in time to check the exodus that began the following morning. The "fair Cyprians" of Stingaree Gulch, few of whom were fair, left en masse, their occupation gone. With them went hundreds of male undesirables. Others, many of whom had lost everything, rallied to Rice's cry that the mines were still there, undamaged, and that a new Rawhide must rise from the ashes of the old. Breathing a semblance of life into an expiring corpse was a role the notorious purveyor of worthless stocks was often to play.

His energy and powers of persuasion were great, and in a

few weeks Rawhide began to come back. Of his fellow Goldfield magicians, Tex Rickard and Nat Goodwin had established themselves at the Riverside Hotel, in Reno, never to return; only Riley Grannan remained. He did nobly by the new Rawhide, erecting a saloon in the Rickard tradition, costing a reputed $40,000, in which religious services were held on Sunday, the camp being without a church. Before the year was out, Riley was to die of pneumonia and provide ex-Reverend Knickerbocker with an opportunity to deliver the melancholy, perfervid eulogy that made him famous. The reader is doubtless familiar with it, for it has been reprinted so often that it has become an authentic bit of Western lore. An opening sentence will suffice here: "He was born in the sunny Southland where brooks and rivers run musically through luxuriant soil; where magnolia grandiflora like white stars glow in a firmament of green; where crystal lakes dot the greensward and the softest summer breeze dimples the wave-lips into kisses for lillies on the shore; where the air is resonant with the perfume of many flowers."

Riley Grannan had come on such hard times that Nat Goodwin paid his funeral expenses and had the body shipped to Paris, Kentucky, in accordance with Riley's wishes. Rawhide was not doing well either. It had come back, but it was only a shadow of what it had been. On September 3, 1909, a year almost to the day after the big fire, a cloudburst sent a wall of water rushing down the gulch that devastated the camp for a second time. Several of the mines made a halfhearted attempt to continue production. But Rawhide was finished. This second calamity was too much for even George Graham Rice.

Shafts were filled with water, and no one had the money to pump them out. A few hardy individuals made a living by placering and picking up float. Now they are gone. "Where life teemed, dry sand and gulches abound," wrote Jack Bell. "Of Stingaree Gulch there is not a vestige. Today it is a desolate, faraway place. The nearest tree or green thing is forty miles distant. All around is desert; bleak, unkindly, beautiful, fascinating barrenness."

That was the way it was when Zach Carson first saw it. His kind are gone. So is Rawhide, and with it, to repeat, disappeared a big slice of what is popularly known as the Old West. But when Zach Carson found his lost mine it left the Lost Gunsight and many others still to be found.

Some of the old-timers believe that the day will come when mining will be resumed at Rawhide. No one doubts that gold can be found there, but the values are low, and in view of the ever increasing costs of production, it is not likely that the old camp will ever be reactivated.

NEW MEXICO

17

The Gold of Gaspar Valdez

Forty years ago, seated around the campfire of some wild horse hunters on the Owyhee Desert, I first heard the story of Gaspar Valdez's lost gold. I should like to tell it now, unchanged, as I heard it from the lips of Joe Montero, a lean, swarthy-skinned Mexican from the Lower Rio Grande who had drifted into northern Nevada. Hunting wild horses was an extracurricular activity with him, for by profession he was a bronc peeler, and a good one.

There is something about a campfire in the evening that loosens men's tongues and gives an agreeable flavor to what they have to say. The night was cool, as they invariably are on the Owyhee, and with the wind kicking up a bit, the windbreak of mountain mahogany brush at our back was appreciated. Far to the west Disaster Peak was faintly visible in the moonlight.

"I was young, very young, when Gaspar Valdez, the old *pastor* [shepherd] disappeared, but I remember him," said Joe. "My father and Gaspar Valdez worked together many years as *pastors* for Don Ignacio Puente. After my father got to be *vaciero* [boss herder who made the rounds of the camps by wagon and supplied them with grub] for Don Ignacio, he sometimes brought old Gaspar to our home in Las Palomas. We were all Mexicans in Las Palomas, all poor; no one any better than anybody else, except Nicosia Guzman, the banker."

Joe paused to whip a cigarette into shape and light it.

"I will tell you the story of Gaspar Valdez's gold as my father used to tell it to me. I know it is true."

Against the eastern bastion of New Mexico's Black Range, south of the San Mateo Mountains, Don Ignacio Puente ranged his sheep and goats on the thousands of acres to which his family had held title for two hundred years. Twice a year he came up from El Paso to inspect his vast holdings and get an accounting from his *capataz* (foreman). These inspection trips were so limited that he never visited some of the more remote camps, leaving it to the *capataz* to see that the *vacieros* kept them supplied with food and get an accounting of the loss to predators. When it was time to gather the wool clip Beltran Salazar, the *capataz*, brought the shearing crew to the harvesting grounds. Otherwise, the *pastors* at the distant camps saw no one.

It was at such a camp, in the shadow of the mountains, that Gaspar Valdez had been stationed for years, always with a young assistant. This assistant changed from time to time, but he remained a fixture at Dos Pinos Spring, at the mouth of a long, narrow canyon that threaded its way back into the mountains for several miles. If you went up the canyon far enough you could find a trickle of flowing water. Down below, it was dry, except when a cloudburst in the mountains brought down a roaring torrent of water for a few hours. Gaspar Valdez knew the water's ways and pitched his camp where it would not be affected by such infrequent displays of temper.

As all good *pastors* must be, he was a contented man. Three times a year the *capataz* took him to town to spend a day or two with his daughter and grandchildren. What little money he earned, he spent on them. He had no other interests in life.

When he was returned to Dos Pinos, he was happy to be back. His money was gone and he had to earn more. His wages were only fifteen dollars a month. It did not occur to him to ask Beltran Salazar for more; he knew that fifteen dollars was the standard wage for *pastors*. What he feared was that one day Beltran Salazar would say he was too old to be a good *pastor* and would dismiss him. Some young man like Pedro Ruiz, his present helper, would take his job.

Of all his helpers, Gaspar Valdez liked Pedro Ruiz best. He had taught the boy much of what he knew about sheep. Not all—that could come only with experience. On range that had not been overgrazed, such as this, the work was easy. The dogs did most of it.

As was the duty of the helper, Pedro Ruiz did the walking. After breakfast he and the old man would part for the day. With a bottle of water and a stack of tortillas in the bag that was swung over his shoulder, the boy would move out with the dogs. Gaspar Valdez would stand for some time watching the grazing sheep. When he was satisfied that all was well, he would spend a few minutes taking care of the camp chores. This left him free for the greater part of the day.

This morning was no different from hundreds of others that had preceded it. He had often explored the canyon behind him, though he had never reached the head of it. On the way up were several small grassy flats. On them he had set snares for rabbits and sagehens. Armed with a stout walking club, he set out to have a look at them.

A rabbit had stepped into one of the snares but a bobcat or coyote had found it, and all that was left were some scattered tufts of fur.

The morning was still young when Gaspar Valdez got as far as he had ever been before. He decided to go on. In the course of another mile, he found a trickle of flowing water. He saw

) 189 (

where it disappeared into the earth. This, he realized, was the underground source of the spring that supplied the camp.

He had sat down to rest for a few minutes when his ears caught the faint sound of splashing water. In the stillness of the canyon it was unmistakable. Water seemed to be falling from a great height. He was tired, but curiosity got the better of him and he went on. He did not have far to go. The canyon was narrowing rapidly, and where it pinched out completely, a tiny stream was pouring over the rock wall and dropping forty feet into a small pool. Far above, the tumbled ridges and peaks of the mountains pierced the sky. Down below, in this sheltered glen, vegetation had taken hold—shiny-leaved *manzanita* and thorned *granjeno*.

The rugged beauty of this rockbound cloister held Gaspar Valdez spellbound for a few moments. In the sand that edged the pool he saw the tracks of animals that came there to water. There was no human footprint. Surely, he thought, no man had been here before him. He had been at Dos Pinos for twenty years and more, and in all that time no one had ever mentioned this tiny *vallecico*.

He got down on hands and knees at the pool and, spreading his arms to brace himself, bent down to drink. Beneath his outstretched fingers, he felt pebbles pressing into his flesh. Brushing the sand aside, he examined them. His heart almost failed him when he saw that they were not rounded pebbles but nuggets of yellow gold. Everywhere he looked he found them, some as large as the egg of a canyon wren.

When he had overcome his first excitement, Gaspar Valdez realized that he had discovered a fortune. Now he would be able to give his daughter Juana and her children whatever they might desire. But he must be careful to tell no one about his treasure, lest they should try to take it away from him. A little at a time he would turn his gold into cash, so that no one would become suspicious. He filled his pockets with nuggets and when he returned to camp he placed them in a tin can and buried them.

Thereafter, whenever he felt it safe to go to the pool at the head of the canyon, he returned with gold and added it to his cache. When it came time for the *vaciero* to take him to town, Gaspar Valdez was waiting. He had secretly opened his cache and filled a small bag with gold. In Las Palomas, he sold his nuggets to Nicosia Guzman, the banker. Guzman pretended not to be interested in the source of Gaspar Valdez's sudden wealth, but when the old *pastor* paid him a second visit, he could restrain himself no longer.

"Gaspar, you have evidently uncovered some buried treasure," he said. "I must warn you that if it is on Don Ignacio's land, he can claim it. If Beltran Salazar, the *capataz*, hears of it, he will find a way to take it away from you."

"I have thought of those things," Gaspar Valdez told him. "No one but you knows I have found gold."

"Your secret is safe with me," Nicosia Guzman assured him. "You have brought me a few ounces of gold. Will there be more?"

"Si Señor Guzman, much more."

It was all that the banker needed to know. He waited for Pedro Ruiz, the old *pastor's* helper, to come to town. He called him in. "I have something to tell you in great secrecy, Pedro. Gaspar Valdez has been selling me gold. He has found a great treasure. Watch him. Discover where it is buried. It will make both of us rich."

The spying began. Several times Pedro Ruiz saw his *pastor* bring gold to the cache. He followed him one day and found the pool with the golden nuggets. He saw no reason why he should share his knowledge with Nicosia Guzman. In time, he would show him the cache to satisfy his greedy fingers; but he would say nothing about the source of the gold. That he would share with no one.

First, he would have to silence Gaspar Valdez. A plan occurred to him, but he waited and permitted weeks to slip away without doing anything about it. He knew that on a clear day the old *pastor* liked to make his way up the trail that led to the rim of the sheer cliff behind the camp, where he could see halfway across New Mexico, and sit there in dreamy contemplation of the world below for hours at a time. The summer was gone before Pedro Ruiz caught him up there one afternoon. Gaspar berated him for leaving the flock unattended. In the argument that followed, Pedro crashed into him and sent him plunging to his death.

Word of the accident was relayed from camp to camp until it reached ranch headquarters. Three days passed before Beltran Salazar, the *capataz,* and the sheriff of Sierra County came out to investigate. "I was afraid this would happen," Pedro Ruiz told them. "He was too old to climb so high."

Beltran Salazar agreed regretfully, wanting to make a good impression with the sheriff. "He was getting feeble. When the camps were opened this spring, I should not have let him go out. But I was sorry for him; he had worked for Don Ignacio so many years."

Nicosia Guzman was waiting for Pedro Ruiz when the young *pastor* came to town. "You have let a fortune slip through your fingers," he said angrily. "You will never find Gaspar Valdez's treasure now."

"But, *patron* [master], I have found it! It is here in this sack —much gold." Young Pedro Ruiz lifted the heavy sack and poured its contents on the table. Guzman rubbed his hands in his exultation.

"If you will weigh it, I will take my half now," Pedro Ruiz told him.

Everything had gone as he planned. He didn't have to be a humble *pastor* any more, doing Beltran Salazar's bidding. The gold in the canyon was his now, but he would have to wait a long time before he could touch it. He quit his job, and with the money he had received from Nicosia Guzman, he went by stage and train to El Paso. When he wanted amusement, he crossed the bridge to Juarez. He had planned to be gone a year, but when spring came he could remain away no longer.

Secrecy being important to him, he went to Silver City, instead of returning to Las Palomas. There, he bought mules and an outfit and picked his way back over the mountains to the little canyon at Dos Pinos. After several days of wandering, he found the stream for which he was looking. As he approached the falls, he caught the sound of voices—English voices—and the scraping of shovels biting into sand.

He reached a vantage point from which he could see the pool below, and he was overcome with consternation. Half a dozen men were working down there and evidently had been for some days.

There was no need for him to go any farther; the *Americanos* had found Gaspar Valdez's gold—for which he had schemed and killed. It was lost to him forever. The money he had received from Nicosia Guzman was gone; he was penniless again. The shock of it cost him his mind. Two prospectors found him a week later, a starving, gibbering idiot.

"Pedro Ruiz got what was coming to him," Joe Montero concluded, with a cynical shrug as he gazed about the fire. "They say the devil takes care of his own—maybe, but not always."

18

The Lost Adams Diggings

Until the Lost Tayopa of the Sierra Madre in Mexico became an obsession with him, it was the opinion of the late J. Frank Dobie, whose contributions to the literature of our lost mines has given him a deserved pre-eminence, that the story of the Lost Adams Diggings was the most fabulous of all tales of treasure lost. The diggings were more than a mine, a hole in the earth, or an outcropping of precious metal; they were a walled-in canyon, through which ran a little stream, its sands so rich that nuggets the size of acorns could be picked up wherever one looked.

For a century, men have sought that little walled-in canyon in vain, and this searching has lured ten times as many to their death as lost their lives in the Superstitions. Singly, in twos and threes, and in parties of twenty or more, they have fought their way into a land of merciless mountains, horrific chasms, in and out of rocky gulches, and across the lava-strewn malpais in between, to where the diggings were supposed to be.

To square off the region in which the Adams gold has been hunted is easily done. Get a map, and along the New Mexico–Arizona line, find a little town named Reserve, the seat of

Catron County, on the San Francisco River. In the old days before New Mexico began to feel the retchings of progress, the town's honest name was Milligan's Plaza, which seemed to suit most people. It was 125 miles from a railroad, and anyone who wanted law usually had to make it himself. Milligan's Plaza was the jumping-off place from which the great majority of the searchers for the Adams gold began their wayfaring.

From Reserve, draw a line sixty miles due east across the Mogollon Mountains to today's Cibola National Forest, with its stands of ponderosa pine on the lower levels, and above the ponderosas Douglas fir, and higher up magnificent spruce. Turning north, mark off a straight line all the way to the little railroad town of Grants, which is approximately where old Fort Wingate used to stand. This will take you across the plains of San Augustine and through the Datil Mountains. At Grants, head west to the Arizona line and back down to Reserve. Somewhere in this tremendous box lie the Adams Diggings.

On some maps a wide place in the road is marked Adams Diggings, between Pietown and Quemado. This is the work of some wag. One will not find gold there.

When one gazes at the tremendous area he has blocked off, he may feel that it is unnecessarily large—approximately forty-eight hundred square miles; that it never could have been gone over carefully by hundreds of mountain rats, jackass prospectors, and raw tenderfoots. If so, he is mistaken, for from the high country, where the piñon jays scream a warning to the denizens of the forest at man's approach and the snows come first, down to every outcropping on the vast Plains of San Augustine, there wasn't a square mile, no matter how unpromising, that didn't get a going over at one time or another. This resulted largely from the blind rambling of seasoned old-timers to whom hunting the Adams Diggings had become a way of life. After years of unsuccessful reliance on their intelligence to lead them in the right direction, they threw reason and experience away and began following their hunches, satisfied if they could look where no one had looked before. Old Captain Mike Cooney, a loner from way back, was one of the frustrated. Many a morning, it was said, he would turn to Black Pete, his burro, and say, "Which way today, Black Pete?" And whichever way the burro pointed his ears, that was the direction Captain Cooney took.

The only way to tell the story of the Lost Adams Diggings is to begin at the beginning, with Adams himself. It well may have been Captain Shaw, his most faithful disciple, from whom the information came that Adams hailed from Rochester, New York. But in nothing Captain Shaw ever wrote, nor in the countless magazine and newspaper articles about him, is he ever referred to as other than just plain Adams, or "Adams of the Diggings." To quote Dobie, "Like Adam, Adams seems to have had no 'front name.'"

The record is plain about some things. In the early 1860's, he was freighting between Los Angeles and Tucson. In August of 1864, he was returning empty from Tucson, his twelve-horse team pulling his big wagon and trailer. He was about thirty-five and prosperous. Under the seat he had about two thousand dollars. His destination for the night was Gila Bend, with its good grass and water. He was twenty-five miles below the villages of the friendly Pimas, a favorite camping ground for freighters. At Gila Bend, he turned his horses out to graze, keeping one tied to the wagon, and saddled, in the Western fashion. At daylight he was awakened by the shouting of half a dozen Indians, Apaches, running off his horses. He took after them, killed one and recovered the animals. On turning back to camp, he saw that his wagons had been set afire. All he could do was watch helplessly as they burned. Harness had been slashed to ribbons, his money stolen, and the food that was to take him to California destroyed. Obviously, the attempted theft of the horses was a ruse to lure him away from camp. Had they succeeded in making off with the animals, Adams would never have had any connection with the famous diggings that bear his name.

All he had left were his horses and rifle and pistol. Driving the *caballada* to the nearest Pima village, he was surprised to find a party of twenty Californians there, placering along the river and mildly excited over the few ounces of gold they had washed out. They listened to Adams' story and were eager to buy his horses, for they had lost some of their own since crossing the Colorado at Yuma.

While they were dickering, a young Mexican walked into camp. He also had great need of a horse, for he was coursing home to Sonora. The agricultural Pimas and Maricopas had no horses; but here were several. They interested him far more than the little store of flour gold the Californians had washed out. Gold meant nothing to him until one of the men showed him a fifty-dollar gold piece and told him what it would buy. To the amazement of his startled listeners, he said he could lead them to a little hidden, zigzag canyon, about ten sleeps to the northeast, in Apacheria, where such yellow stuff could be picked up in chunks (nuggets) larger than acorns and the sand glitered with flakes of it.

The young Mexican had a deformed, knotlike ear, for he was the famous Gotch Ear who threads his way through all the lore of the Lost Adams Diggings. According to the tale he told Adams and the other Californians, as young children he and his brother had been captured by a band of Apaches in one of their raids into Sonora and had been brought up among them as Indians. They were well treated by their captors and grew to like the life they were leading. All had gone well until an Apache, in a jealous rage, killed the brother. Gotch Ear had avenged that slaying and fled for his life.

The canyon of gold did not lie in the territory claimed by the band of Chiricahuas with whom he had grown to manhood.

But he had visited it with them. When asked if he was afraid to return to it, he said no—not if they would pay him well. They offered him a horse and saddle. He shook his head; he wanted two horses, a rifle and ammunition, and the gold coin he had been shown. In their eagerness to lay eyes on the treasure house of gold, Adams and the others would have given him anything he asked, especially when, in evidence of his good faith, Gotch Ear told them they didn't have to give him anything until he had shown them the gold, and that if he had lied, they could stand him up and shoot him.

It was mid-August when they started up the Gila, twenty-two men in all, counting the young Mexican. Where they left it to plunge into the unknown wilderness of mountains, mesas, and sandy plains to the northeast, nobody knows. The place names on today's maps are no help, for the pin pricks of civilization they identify were not in existence then. Undoubtedly they passed somewhere west of Fort Apache. The early fall rains had begun and they found water enough in the *charcos* to sustain them. In after years, Adams, who became notorious for his inability to orient himself, claimed that they crossed the San Francisco River. At other times he was just as certain that it was the Little Colorado.

John Brewer, who was with Adams and who never got the Lost Adams Diggings out of his blood, says they crossed two streams. One of them had to be Black River; the other very likely the headwaters of the Little Colorado. No men could have known less about the country through which they were passing than the original Adams party. When they toiled over or through one range of mountains, other mountains reared up ahead of them, for this is a land that never opens up, except down on the Plains of San Augustine.

Brewer tells how they came to a faint wagon road one day, which ran north and south, and how Gotch Ear told Adams to mark the road well; that when they needed supplies they could follow it north to the fort in the malpais. That had to be old Fort Wingate. As they continued on to the northeast, Gotch Ear pointed out two twin *piloncillos* (peaks) some distance ahead of them. "Those peaks," he said, "mark the canyon where we will see the gold."

In that mountainous land there are several dozen places where twin peaks pierce the skyline. Gotch Ear's *piloncillos* may have been as far east as the Detils or as far south as the Gallo Mountains. No one has ever been able to say for sure. Because of its vagueness, what otherwise might have been the key to unlock the secret of the Lost Adams Diggings is meaningless.

We know from Brewer's account that they bedded down on the floor of an unnamed canyon that night and that Gotch Ear showed them a flowing spring in a niche of the canyon. In the morning, being warned by the young Mexican that they would find no water that day, they filled their canteens and watered their horses. A day and a half later, he led them to a crack in a mountain wall that was concealed by a gigantic boulder, the opening it hid so narrow that they could reach out and touch the sides. Gotch Ear preceded them down this rocky defile to a little flat, where a primitive, broken-down irrigation ditch circled around a field of withered pumpkin vines. This was the famous "Pumpkin Patch" that Adams and those who believed in him tried so hard to find in the years that followed.

That afternoon as he, Brewer, and the other members of the party trailed down the almost impassable zigzagging path, they caught momentary glimpses of the tree-embroidered canyon, with its purling stream, ahead of them. At its far end, a twenty-foot-high waterfall cascaded over the rocks, filling the air with the music of its splashing.

The sun was still high. Leaping from the saddle, they ran to the stream. Excited cries broke from their lips at what they beheld. Here was gold beyond their dreaming. Some, not bothering to go back to their packs for picks, began digging in the sand with sticks and their fingers. Gold-crazed, they temporarily lost their caution, forgetting that they were deep in Apache country.

In the party was a young German, later identified by name as Emil Schaeffer—another "Dutchman." He got them quieted down. Gotch Ear had earned his hire. They settled with him, and he bade them adios and left at once. Some accounts say he didn't get far before the Apaches killed him. There is no proof of it; perhaps he made it home to Sonora and his people.

Adams, who subsequently proved himself no leader, on this occasion took command. He asked them to agree that they should share their wealth equally. The only dissenter was the Dutchman. There wasn't any argument; if he didn't want to pool his gold with the rest, that was his privilege.

They built a cabin, with a fireplace at one end. A hearth was constructed of pieces of rough flagging. Beneath the largest piece, so heavy that it took two men to lift it, they dug a hole in the earth, in which to cache their gold, using for a receptacle a leather saddle pack. When they went out to work, they left their rifles stacked at the cabin. In their feverish excitement it did not occur to them that they were being watched, and they were caught flatfooted when Chief Nana, Victoria's successor, and some thirty of his warriors appeared before them without warning.

Fortunately, the Apaches were not hostile. Nana, in Spanish, gave the miners his ultimatum: they could kill the game they needed, graze their horses on the canyon grass, and dig in the sands, but they were not to go above the falls. If they violated the agreement, they would be killed.

As spokesman, Adams was happy to accept Nana's terms. He told Nana no one would be permitted to go above the falls. When he asked if the canyon had a name, he was told that to Apaches it was known as Sno-ta-hay. Adams never forgot it, and in after years, though others referred to it as Zigzag Canyon, to him it was always Sno-ta-hay.

The work went on feverishly, ten, eleven hours a day. Every evening the gold that was washed out in the rockers they had made was brought to the cabin and added to the store in the cache. It was growing so rapidly that they gazed at it in amazement. But supplies began to run out, and it was decided that a party of six men should go back to the road they had crossed and try to find what Gotch Ear had called "the fort in the malpais." John Brewer was chosen leader of the party and given gold to buy enough ammunition and grub to last them a month. A month, it was agreed, was as long as they dared to remain in the canyon; the days were growing shorter and the deer, which were their principal subsistence, were moving down from the high places. Before long, snow would be blocking the passes and escape would be impossible.

When Brewer and his party left, the Dutchman went with them. No one had worked harder than he, and he had gathered a nest egg of between ten and twelve thousand dollars, it is variously estimated. He said he wouldn't be back. He admitted that he was afraid of the Apaches and was getting out before they got him. He begged Adams and the others to leave also. They refused to listen and went on adding to their growing hoard of gold.

As well as they were doing, it was not good enough for some. At night, lolling about the fireplace, the greedy speculated that if there was this much gold below the falls, the pickings must be much richer above them. Adams warned them never to cross the deadline Nana had set. But one evening, in turning back a straying horse, a man got above the falls before he rounded up the animal. A nodule of gold as large as a hen's egg caught his eye. He picked it up and that evening made Adams a present of it. Though the trespass had been made accidentally, Adams berated him for having broken their agreement with Nana.

But Adams kept the nugget and dropped it into his saddle pocket. It was, in time, to become the only visible evidence he could produce of the gold he had seen in Sno-ta-hay Canyon.

Having seen the nugget, another man, not to be denied, crept above the falls the following day and came back with a coffee-pot half-filled with gold. He was observed by a watching Apache, and it triggered what was to follow.

It has been said that Brewer estimated he would be gone eight days—four days going and four returning. It is a generally accepted fact that he was back at the "closed door," which hid the entrance to the Zigzag Canyon, in eight days. How the time he was away is divided is of little consequence, but surely he could not have given Adams any estimate of how long he expected to be gone, for he was setting out through country about which he knew nothing, and without any knowledge of how far it was to Fort Wingate.

When eight days, and then nine, passed without the return of the provisioning party, Adams' anxiety became such that he detailed an armed man to guard the cabin and, accompanied by Bill Davidson, he rode up the rocky trail, resolved to keep on going until he found out what was delaying Brewer and his party. He and Davidson didn't have to travel far. Within a few yards of the closed or secret door, they found the scalped and mutilated bodies of five men, their dead horses, flour, and other supplies scattered over the ground. Only Apaches killed that savagely.

Adams and Davidson hastily hid the bodies of their comrades in a crevice and covered them with rocks. Without trying to account for the missing sixth man, they turned back down the defile. When they had got as far as the Pumpkin Patch, wild yells and screeching from many throats smote their ears. Finding a vantage point, they saw in the distance below them several hundred Indians stomping and dancing in wild frenzy, holding aloft the dripping scalps of the gold seekers, none of whom had escaped their wrath. The cabin had been set afire. From it a great column of smoke was rising as the flames slowly consumed the green pine.

Adams and Davidson turned off the trail down a side gulch and hid their horses and themselves in high brush. Taking it for granted that the Apaches had counted noses before they attacked, they were certain to search for the two who were missing. All Adams and Davidson could do was to lie close and wait, their pistols ready. Several times during the long day they heard Indians beating the brush in their vicinity. At last, evening came on. The squirrels ceased their chattering and the quail stopped piping. In the stillness, Adams crawled to a point from which he could peer down into Sno-ta-hay. He was in time to see the Apaches toiling up the rocks at the far end of the canyon and disappearing above the falls.

Though knowing that the search for them would be resumed in the morning, he and Davidson were faced with necessity of going down to the stream to refill their canteens. And there was another reason: the gold in the cache, which by now must have amounted to more than a hundred thousand dollars' worth. Realizing that in the still air the slightest sound would travel far, they decided it would be safer to go down on foot. But their horses had to have water, too, if they were to be of any use to them.

They got into Sno-ta-hay without difficulty. When they approached the smoldering ruins of the cabin, they saw that they could not get to the cache. The roof had fallen in and a maze of smoldering timbers covered the hearth. Only one course was left them—to get away with ther lives, if possible, and return to Sno-ta-hay in the spring, with a sizable expedition of experienced men.

They passed through the closed door before dawn and struck off to the southwest. A howling gale was blowing down from the north, wiping out their tracks almost as soon as they were made.

But knowing it wasn't safe to travel by day, they hid out in the first cover they found. Three times that day, they saw small scouting parties of Apaches. Great trackers that they were, in the booming wind that had wiped the slate clean, they could find no sign to follow.

Hiding by day and traveling by night, circling around mountains and picking their way up and down defiles and through rocky canyons, the stars their only guide, Adams and his partner progressed only a few miles a day, sometimes not at all. They were without food and lived on acorns and piñon nuts. They welcomed a rain that filled the *charcos* (pits) in the rocks with water.

Soon their horses began to give out. They shot the animals, and risking a fire, cut out the loin straps and broiled them. Adams was continually looking for landmarks that he would recognize. The first he found was the road across which Gotch Ear had led them. He said afterward that he was at a loss to know which end to take, so he and Davidson took neither and kept on coursing to the southwest.

This is difficult to understand. Granted that they may have reached the road many miles south of where they had crossed it with Gotch Ear, it was still a road and led somewhere. It offered much easier going than the course they chose to pursue. John Brewer was no better acquainted with the country than they, and not a more experienced man on a trail, yet he had oriented himself without difficulty and struck north for Fort Wingate. (That he was at the fort and purchased supplies from the post sutler is a matter of record.) Why Adams did not follow the road is something that he was never able to explain. Though he was passing through a terrible ordeal, his companions butchered and a fortune lost, he was, presumably, in full possession of his wits, which was not the case in later years. When caught in his own contradictions, he used to shake his head and say, "The Apaches made me forget about that."

Their boots gave out and they cut off the tops and fashioned innersoles out of them. But they wore out, too. Their feet became so sore they could barely crawl along. Ill, starving, they no longer had the will to hide when they saw horsemen approaching. The riders proved to be a detachment of troopers from Fort Apache. Adams and Davidson, more dead than alive, were taken to the fort to recover from their harrowing experience. Twelve days, or maybe fourteen, had passed since they left the secret door to Sno-ta-hay. They couldn't remember. Perhaps, as Adams said, the Apaches had made them forget.

At Fort Apache the two human wrecks came under the care of Dr. Spurgeon, the post surgeon. Davidson was past fifty, a much older man than Adams. His condition was so critical that Dr. Spurgeon didn't expect him to recover. Actually, he never fully regained his health. He is said to have been at Fort Whipple two years later, telling the same story Adams was to repeat the rest of his life. He disappears from Lost Adams Diggings lore after that. But not Dr. Spurgeon.

Caring for the two men, talking with them day after day, examining the nugget Adams had salvaged from the disaster, Spurgeon was filled with a wild desire to organize an expedition and return to Sno-ta-hay at once. But there was no one to "organize" at Fort Apache. Never doubting the truth of the story Adams and Davidson told him, he resolved that one day he would risk life and fortune in an all-out attempt to find the Adams Diggings. It took him a long time to get around to it; but he kept the promise he had made himself. Shortly after he lost track of Adams and Davidson, he left Fort Apache and government service and returned to his home in Toledo, Ohio, where he established a medical practice that made him a wealthy man. Though he was far away from New Mexico, by correspondence and reading every word that was published about the Lost Adams Diggings, he kept himself informed; and finally, in the late summer of 1881, he arrived in Socorro, New

Mexico, as the leader of an expensively equipped expedition of forty men, greenhorns every one of them, who had had such a taste of roughing it on the way down from Las Vegas, then the end of track on the Santa Fe, that they were already disenchanted with searching for the canyon of gold.

Years before, at Fort Apache, Davidson and Adams had shared a tent with one of the scouts. The former was still bedridden; Adams was up and around but as jittery and dangerous as a trapped wolf. One day five Apaches walked past the tent. Thinking he recognized them from Sno-ta-hay, Adams drew his pistol and killed two of them before he could be stopped. If the Apaches had made him forget some things, they had made him remember others.

The incident came at an awkward time for the garrison, which was doing its best to keep peace with the Indians until it was relieved by volunteers from California. Adams was placed under arrest and confined to the guardhouse to await trial for murder. He escaped several nights later, undoubtedly with the connivance of his guards, for in the Southwest in 1864 Apaches were considered fair game, no matter what the circumstances. Helping himself to a horse, Adams got away safely. Shortly thereafter he appeared in Tucson and sold his precious nugget at Goldman's store, for, according to all accounts, ninety-three dollars—poor pay indeed for an enterprise that, it was afterward determined, had snuffed out the lives of eighteen men. But that nugget was to become famous. Whenever doubters of the Adams story appeared, the true believers always had it to point to as proof that he had had his hands on the gold in Sno-ta-hay Canyon.

After Tucson, Adams made his way back to Los Angeles and his family. But he was to return, not once but many times, for the legend of the Lost Adams Diggings had barely begun.

19

The Searchers

Ten years passed before Adams set out a second time to find Sno-ta-hay, the canyon of gold. It was a long interval to wait, knowing what fabulous riches were to be garnered there. There must have been times when the thought of it made his senses reel and he had to convince himself that he was not dreaming. During those ten years he must have constantly tortured himself with the fear that someone else would get there before he did.

It may have eased his mind some to know that all through Apacheria the principal tribes—the Chiricahua, Mescalero, Jicarilla, and Mimbreno—were raiding and attacking as never before, with the government throwing more and more seasoned troops into the field to subdue or crush them. As a consequence, Adams could rest assured that few gold seekers were getting into the mountains. But a difficulty of another kind kept him in Los Angeles. This was his chronic inability to make a success of the various businesses in which he engaged.

Even when he was almost penniless, Adams talked a great deal about his lodes without giving away any secrets, and there was always someone glad to listen. His secondhand furniture store on lower Main Street became a gathering place for desert rats and hardrock miners from Death Valley and the Panamints. It was there that he became acquainted with Captain C. A. Shaw, a brother Mason, who was to become almost as prominent in the search for the Lost Adams Diggings as Adams himself.

Shaw was a retired sea captain of some means. From the first, he seems to have had complete faith in Adams, and to the end of his days he never wavered in his allegiance to him. He knew nothing about mining, but he was physically fit for his years, and with Adams to lead the way to the diggings, he was convinced that he could hold up his end. He didn't ask much for himself. His dream was to have a ship of his own and sail across the Pacific to some island of his choosing, build a house to his liking, and spend the remainder of his life among the gentle Kanakas. The Adams Diggings could make that dream a reality.

So it was that in the spring of 1874, when the trails were drying out and the mountain canyons were free of snow, he and Adams and a company of fourteen men, financed either wholly or in part by Captain Shaw—and judging by the dissension that arose later, probably only in part (Adams contributed nothing) —came up the Gila and, striking off to the northeast, reached the San Francisco River about fifty miles north of old Milligan's Plaza.

For days Adams led them back and forth, trying to cut Gotch Ear's trail to Sno-ta-hay and looking for landmarks that he failed to find. He was searching in the wrong place, for he was many miles off course. He was only forty-five, but he had the appearance of a man of sixty. He was going to the bottle oftener and staying longer, as the old saying has it, but whisky did not jolt his memory into focus as he brushed the matted hair out of his eyes and gazed into the depths of a canyon for sight of something familiar.

The party broke up into two factions, one side—it must have been men who had put money into the venture—accusing him of deliberately misleading them, contending that he well enough knew the way to the canyon of gold. It was the first of several similar experiences that Adams was to have. Captain Shaw, the heaviest loser, ever loyal, put down the uprising, and the expedition straggled back to the Gila and broke up.

Two years later, in 1876, Adams raised another expedition, with Captain Shaw's help, and left San Bernardino, California, with twenty-four men. It was well provisioned and largely composed of men who had served an apprenticeship searching for the Lost Pegleg Mine. He got them as far as old Milligan's Plaza (Reserve), and for two months they searched the mountains to the north. Failure turned them sour and they began to revile Adams as a half-witted fool who never had any gold. Soon they were accusing him of being a liar and a cheat who had no intention of showing them the way to his secret canyon.

Again Captain Shaw refused to listen to their violent accusations. No matter what they said, he did not waver in his loyalty to Adams. He knew Adams was a good man. Perhaps he drank too much and got a bit befuddled at times, but they must remember what he had gone through. Give him time and he would lead them to Sno-ta-hay.

The expedition got back to Milligan's Plaza. In Milligan's saloon, the disgruntled men, inflamed by whisky, cornered Adams and told him they wanted action; if he knew where there was gold, the time had come for him to show it; if he refused, they threatened to hang him. Things were becoming serious when Wash Jones, the Star Route mailman, bundled Adams into the mail wagon and took him to Magdalena and the end of the spur railroad that ran to Socorro.

In Magdalena, Adams came under the protection of Bob Lewis, a man of parts, who had been searching for the Lost Adams Diggings for years. Lewis was delighted to be able to sit down and talk with the man for whom these diggings were named. What he learned from Adams has never been disclosed. But it couldn't have been discouraging, for Bob Lewis continued to search for the Adams' gold year after year until his legs became so "starched" with rheumatism that it ended his wanderings.

Once, in the western fringe of the Datils, he found a pile of human bones and rotted saddle gear stuffed into a crevice in the rocks, and nearby what he always believed to be the secret door to Sno-ta-hay. He followed a zigzag trail into a walled-in canyon, but it was not as Adams had described it so vividly—no pumpkin patch, no stream of running water, no trace of a ruined cabin. As for gold, Lewis couldn't find so much as a "color." Twenty years and more had passed since the original Adams party made its great discovery. If this was really Sno-ta-hay, everything had changed. He had often mentioned the level floor of the canyon. It now had a decided upward pitch from east to west, as though some mighty convulsion of the earth's crust had occurred, squeezing it out of shape.

It was too late to compare notes with Adams. Discouraged, penniless, and repudiated by all but Captain Shaw and a few others, he had suffered a heart attack and died in Los Angeles on September 21, 1886. Repeatedly he had tried to lead men back to his canyon of gold, and failed. Had Bob Lewis found it? Most likely, though at the time few among the army of seekers of the Lost Adams Diggings were of that opinion. The golden dream was too real to them to permit it to be dashed in that fashion. Of those who continued the search, none was more dedicated than Captain Shaw. When his own money was gone, he talked others into financing his hunting.

About 1888, Shaw became acquainted with W. H. Byerts, of El Paso, Texas, in whom he found a kindred soul whose enthusiasm for the Adams Diggings became as great as his own. Byerts had never met Adams, but through Captain Shaw he became well acquainted with him, seeing him as Shaw saw him, a sometimes confused but always honest man who invariably told the truth. The episode is told in the rare pamphlet Byerts published in the early 1920's, entitled *The Adams Gold Diggings.*

Byerts produced the money, and he and Captain Shaw prospected together. They never found any gold that could be weighed on a scale, but they made many friends, in the course of which they restored the faith of more than one man in Adams. Langford Johnston, one of the most noted of their converts, was quoted as saying, "They are noble men, too honorable ever to have put their faith in a scoundrel." For forty-three years, as soon as the spring work was over, Johnston left his cattle ranch north of Silver City, New Mexico, and took to the mountains to search for the diggings. With him, they were a religion, and to the day of his death he scoffed at the idea that Bob Lewis had found them and that they were worthless.

At last, too old and feeble to continue his questing, Captain Shaw retired to the Old Soldiers' Home at Sawtelle, California. There, on August 15, 1917, his dreams all behind him, he sailed away on that voyage from which no man has ever returned. But the hunt for the Adams Diggings continued.

Dr. Spurgeon, the post surgeon at Fort Apache at the time Adams and Davidson were brought there after the massacre in Sno-ta-hay Canyon, had appeared at Socorro in 1881 with a demoralized expedition. It is worth returning to because, if for no other reason, it brings into the story of the Lost Adams Diggings John F. Dowling, a mining man of high repute, and the partial corroboration he gave Adams' story.

When Dr. Spurgeon saw that it would be folly to try to proceed with the men he had brought to Socorro, he cast around for someone who was familiar with the country and who might be interested in trying to find the diggings on a partnership basis. He was directed to Dowling. After acquainting him with what he had learned from Adams and Davidson, many years before, he told Dowling he would put up the money for a small expedition if the latter would lead it. Very little of what he had to tell was new to Dowling. In fact, Dowling was better acquainted with the searching for the Lost Adams Diggings of the past fifteen years than Spurgeon was. But he was interested in the doctor's proposition. Negotiations hit a rock when Dr. Spurgeon informed him that one of the men who had come out from Toledo with him, a young fellow named Moore, would accompany Dowling's party to look out for his interests—he was returning to Toledo, himself—and keep him informed of the progress being made.

Dowling objected strongly to such an arangement. He had seen enough of Moore around Socorro to conclude that the man was a worthless, troublemaking braggart. He didn't propose to be slowed down by having such a character along. But Spurgeon insisted, and Dowling let him have it his way. After outfitting in Socorro, he proceeded to Magdalena. Accompanied by Moore and two young men who had worked for him in the mines at Silver City and measured up to what he wanted, he struck north, intending to course through the Datils and west as far as the headwaters of the Little Colorado.

Acrimonious dissension among the three men began almost at once. Moore refused to do his share of the work of the camp; when they were moving, he always lagged behind. Dowling became so exasperated with him that he would have turned him adrift if that hadn't been equivalent to sentencing the fool to death. But they went on. In the Datils, they came down the bed of a dry stream to where in other days it had plunged over rocks to a small canyon below. They entered it and Dowling looked for the ruins of a burned cabin, but could find no trace of it. On the slope, however, he saw a number of pine stumps. Undoubtedly, he conjectured, the trees had been cut down to build the cabin that was no longer there.

For several hours, he and the two boys from Silver City explored the sandy floor of the canyon, looking for gold, and though they found none, Dowling was satisfied that this was the place Adams and Davidson had described to Dr. Spurgeon. He knew enough about geophysics to understand that in seventeen years this mountain-tossed country could change. This was five years prior to the time that Bob Lewis found the rotted saddles and human bones in the crevice near the secret door.

Dowling led his party back to Socorro and wrote Dr. Spurgeon what he had found. With that letter the two of them disappear from Adams Diggings history.

Two of the members of the original Adams party were still very much alive. One of them was John Brewer, the man who had led the provisioning party from Sno-ta-hay to old Fort Wingate. No effort had ever been made to find him. Even Captain Shaw, who was something of a bloodhound on the trail (among his accomplishments he had located the post sutler who was at the fort in 1864, and who recalled that six men had come out of the malpais to the south that year and bought ammunition and supplies), believed—as Adams did—that Brewer had perished with the rest of his party at the entrance to the canyon of gold. But in the summer of 1888, a strange little caravan, consisting of two wagons, followed by a small herd of cows and several horses, pulled up at the Tenney ranch on the Little Colorado and asked and received permission to light long enough to have a look around and give their animals an opportunity to recuperate. The Ute Indian woman and the girl of fourteen who sat beside her on the second wagon were the wife and daughter of the lean, bearded man who did the talking. His name was John Brewer.

For almost a quarter of a century he had lived among the Utes in the San Juan country of Colorado, and was unaware that in his long absence the Lost Adams Diggings had become famous. But it was his memories of the diggings that had brought him back. He knew, as all Indians did, that with the surrender of Geronimo the harried Apaches were no longer a menace. It wasn't by chance that he had returned to the beautiful valley of the Little Colorado, where the mountains seemed to relent and move back so that a man could look about. He had had a long time to think about it, and he was sure it was the Little Colorado, not the San Francisco River, across which Gotch Ear had led them so long ago.

Unfortunately, Brewer discovered, as so many others have, that after a lapse of many years, memory is not a reliable guide. He looked long and hard for landmarks that he could not find. By the end of the summer, he despaired of finding the diggings and settled down to the somewhat more prosaic business of raising cattle. Why he did not go to Fort Wingate and backtrack from there to the place where the other members of his party had been killed has never been explained. But his return supplied the choniclers of the Lost Adams Diggings with some heretofore missing bits of evidence. His story of how the original expedition reached Sno-ta-hay and what happened there, up to the time of the massacre, fully corroborated Adams' story. As for what had occurred at the secret door to Sno-ta-hay, he alone could give evidence.

Of his escape, it has been said by some that he either "wrote" the account in his own hand or dictated it to young Ammon Tenney. When viewed critically, it becames obvious that it has been "doctored" by the hand of a professional writer.

He says the ambush came as a perfect surprise; that a bullet struck him in the calf of his left leg and that his horse, seriously wounded, bolted, and after running a few yards, pitched him into a patch of mountain mahogany brush, where he lay half-stunned for the rest of the day. He had lost his rifle and was without food or water.

The Indians would have been expected to work the brush, looking for him. He says they didn't. After dark, he made his way down the zigzag defile into the canyon, not knowing whether Adams and the others had been attacked, but expecting at the worst to find some of them alive and forted up in the cabin. He saw enough in the first minute or two to convince him that all were dead. He saw two figures "skulking" about the cabin and mistook them for Indians. The supposition is that they were Adams and Davidson.

Returning to the secret door, half-crazed with pain and fear, he alternately ran and walked for an hour. He could not recall in which direction he went. It was not until the moon came up that he saw he was crossing a wide mesa from west to east. For four days he continued in that direction, moving by night and hiding in the rocks by day. By the third day his condition was desperate. He came to the dry bed of a stream and dug feebly in the sand, trying to find a sip of water. To ease his nagging thirst, he filled his mouth with pebbles. His one hope, he says, was that if he could keep going long enough he would reach the Rio Grande and the *jacals* of some Mexicans.

Realizing that time was running out, he resolved to travel boldly by day. The sun was several hours high on the fourth day, when he spied a clump of high sage. There he found a seep spring and a small pool of water. He drank carefully. The water revived him and he went on. Several hours later, he came to a wagon road. To quote him:

"It is impossible to describe the relief that the sight of wagon tracks gave me. They looked to be a month old, but there were some fresh horse and burro tracks. Here was a route to civilized human beings—to food and warmth and water. But following the road, I soon saw moccasin tracks. This alarmed me . . . but safe or unsafe, I resolved to keep to the road.

"The road went down into a valley. A line of cottonwood trees told me there was a stream through the valley. . . . I saw a patch of ground that had been planted in corn. Just before I reached the little stream I saw two burros run across it. I lay down at the edge of the water to drink. No sooner had I swallowed than I felt deathly faint. When I opened my eyes, I saw three Indians standing over me."

They were friendly Indians. Brewer does not identify them beyond saying "they were one of the Pueblo tribes." They carried him to their village and nursed him back to health. When he was fit to travel, they showed him the way to the Rio Grande. He reached the river at a Mexican town, very likely Belen, though he does not say so, and there joined a pack train bound for Santa Fe. Later, he was in Missouri, and after several years, drifted back to Colorado, where, in his words he "took up with the Utes."

Whether or not Brewer wrote or dictated the foregoing statement, it must be accepted at its face value. There was another man who could throw additional light on the Adams Diggings, if he could be found, and he was the "Dutchman," Emil Schaeffer, by name.

If there is one thing on which all Adams commentators agree, it is that the Dutchman went to Fort Wingate with Brewer's provisioning party, carrying with him a quantity of gold, variously estimated to have been from twenty-five to thirty pounds, which would have been about all that a horse could carry in addition to conveying a portly man. From the fort in the malpais, his trail disappeared in a dozen different directions. Of course, the favorite tale was that the Apaches had attended to him. Others had it that he had returned to California and was ranching somewhere in the San Joaquin Valley. A few said that after he left Fort Wingate he had not stopped going until he was back in Germany. It remained for old Doc Young to locate him.

Of all the strange characters who roamed the mountains of western New Mexico, Doc Young was the strangest. He was a psychic, steeped in the mysteries of the occult, a believer in dreams and omens. Despite all his eccentricities, he was a first-class prospector and modestly successful. He wasn't looking for the Adams Diggings especially, but wherever he roamed he kept an eye open for them. He ranged over a great amount of territory. One time he might be encountered with his burros in the Datils, and the next time in the Mogollons. He had been seen as far north as the Sandia Mountains and the land of the Zuñi people.

In addition to his prospecting, he concocted a nostrum that he claimed would restore the vigor of youth to an old man, if taken regularly. In Socorro, or wherever the snows penned him up for the winter, he peddled his elixir. Sometimes, when he was flush, he left the country and spent the winter in southern California. Late one fall, in the early 1930's, he came into Reserve with a quantity of wire gold and cashed it. The next day, he was on his way to Los Angeles.

In those days a number of old-timers like Doc Young could be found seated on the park benches in Pershing Square, soaking up the sunshine. Most of the talk was about mining, and it was a pleasure to Doc to listen to them, reaching back through the fog of nicotine-tinted memory to the strikes they had made or narrowly missed. One day a man sat down beside him, and soon the Lost Adams Diggings came into the conversation. The stranger appeared to be well acquainted with them. He mentioned the Dutchman, and to Doc's amazement said, "He's alive, and I know where he is. I traced him back to Germany. His name is Emil Schaeffer, and he's living in Heidelberg. I've corresponded with him but have never been able to get much out of him."

This was enough for Doc Young. Surely it was a propitious omen, getting this information by chance! He got Schaeffer's address and several days later was on his way to Germany. He located his man without too much difficulty. Schaeffer readily admitted that he had returned to Germany with better than ten thousand dollars, enough to keep him comfortable for the rest of his life in his native land. Doc tried to induce him to return to New Mexico with him, but Schaeffer said no; he was well over eighty and intended to live out his days where he was. From some source he had learned about the fate of the Adams expedition, and he had no interest in trying to find the diggings. He told Doc what he knew, but after half a century and more, he was of necessity vague as to directions and landmarks.

Doc Young returned little the wiser to the mountains he loved—a lone man who was never lonesome. The Mexicans said he was *poco loco* (a little crazy). Maybe he was, but he said some very wise things. "There's no such thing as getting lonesome if you've got a mountain to look at," is the one remembered best.

Doc Young and Captain Cooney, another loner, were only two of the many who tramped the harsh mountains along the Arizona–New Mexico line until they could no longer get up from their blankets and died, to steal a line from Kipling, "without benefit of clergy."

But the search for the Lost Adams Diggings continues—by foot and by air. Perhaps the rich lode from which Emil Schaeffer took his gold will be discovered someday. It is there, somewhere—perhaps right where John Dowling and Bob Lewis thought it ought to be. Perhaps great machines may have to be brought in to uncover it. Perhaps someday water will flow again in Sno-ta-hay Canyon. Stranger things happen. But one thing will not change, at least in the time of men now living.

This was the home of the Apache, and he fought as few men have to to keep it. We humbled, dispossessed, and degraded him. The reservation Apache is harmless, but his forebears put their mark on this land. It is indelible and time can not efface it.

Time ticks away, and a hundred years have passed since Gotch Ear guided the original Adams adventurers to the glittering bonanza in the canyon of gold, somewhere in the heart of Apacheria. Today, jet airliners streak across its skies in almost the twinkling of an eye, and surfaced roads uncoil over its peaks and tawny mesas. But there are men who, regarding such things as an invasion of their privacy, continue to follow the dim trails of the past. They know about Adams. It is not likely that he soon will be forgotten.

20

The Rose Quartz of the Navajo

One morning in October, 1929, I was having breakfast with Mike Kirk, the Indian trader of Gallup and Manuelito, New Mexico. I put a question to him. "Mike, you and your brother John have spent a good part of your lives among the Hopi and the Navajo. Do you understand Indians?"

After a moment's hesitation, he said, "I don't know. I used to think so, but I've been sure for a long time that the way *not* to understand them is to get the idea that you're dealing with children. The best of them can outsmart a white man most of the time."

The previous evening Mike had brought Hoski Naswood, the young Navajo singer; Jules Verne Allen, the first of the cowboy singers to record the old range songs for Victor; and an old-time honky-tonk fiddler whose name I do not recall, to our house, for some music and good talk. I thought (and still do) that Hoski Naswood was the handsomest Indian I have ever seen. He was soft-spoken and had the manners of a gentleman. Over coffee the next morning, I asked Mike about him.

"You could call him an educated man. But in his heart he's still an Indian; he could revert to his old tribal way of life as easily as you could shed your overcoat. I've seen a lot of young Navajos, boys and girls, come back to the reservation after being away to school for a couple years, and in a few months you wouldn't know they'd been away. They don't bring back anything that's of any use to them. They've been taught how to speak English, but after they've been back a year or so, you wouldn't know it; they refuse to use it. The old men govern the tribe, keep the mysticism and customs alive; the young men have nothing to say about it.

"It's the same with Hopi. They have no written language, so a few headmen perpetuate themselves in power. If you want to do business with the Hopi, you've got to stand well with the House Chiefs. I had an experience with one of them, old Saladino Rojas, who was *juez de paz* [justice of the peace], two years ago that will give you an idea of what you're up against when you try to match wits with them.

"It happened in connection with the Snake Dance at Oraibi. As you know, several hundred well-to-do outsiders make the rounds of the fall ceremonials. They can do it in five days, ending up at Oraibi. I made a business of guiding parties. I had a big Packard into which I could pile six people for the trip to Oraibi, about a hundred and fifteen miles each way. I had a second car for a cook and a camp man and the camping outfit. I'd made the trip so often I had things worked out. I'd leave Gallup in the morning and be at the foot of the mesa in time to set things up and have supper that evening.

"It was possible in those days to get a car up to the top of the mesa. It wasn't a road, just a trail. After dark it didn't look as dangerous as it did in daylight. I had a doctor and his wife from Detroit and their three children on this trip. I got them up on top without too much trouble. I always arranged with an old Hopi woman named Maria to put on a little entertainment for my guests. She was all wrinkles. I don't know how old she was—maybe a hundred. You always get a big moon at

Oraibi at that time of the year. Maria would get settled on a rock, and gazing across the desert or up at the moon, she would begin chanting, praying. I pretended to translate, but I couldn't understand a word. The doctor and his family were impressed. He gave her a few dollars and we came back to camp."

We lit cheroots and called for more coffee.

"In the morning," Mike resumed, "several dozen Indians rode past, headed for the little government schoolhouse about half a mile away. There wasn't any school at that time of the year. I stopped a Hopi I knew and asked what they were up to. 'We going to have trial,' he told me. 'Yeh,' I said. 'Who are you going to try?' Without batting an eye, he looked at me and said, 'You. Last night, your car strike horse and push him off mesa. Kill him. Good horse. Worth fifty dollars.' "

"Had you struck a horse, Mike?" I asked.

"Of course not! This was a shakedown. Among all the Hopi horses there wasn't one worth fifty dollars. But I was doing business with the Hopis. I didn't want any bad feeling. I got in the car and rode over to the school. Old Saladino Rojas was sitting at the teacher's desk. The man who claimed his horse had been killed was telling the *juez de paz* how fine a horse it was. The room was full of witnesses, all ready to back him up.

"I finally got old Saladino's eye and suggested that we walk out to the pump and have a drink. He agreed at once, so I knew he was a party to shaking me down."

Mike paused for a moment and sipped his coffee.

"You know the Hopi (Moqui) don't have any silver. They're crazy for it. I had a ring that was a beauty. I took it off and slipped it into my pants pocket, along with my handkerchief. As we stood at the pump, I pulled out the handkerchief, making sure the ring was in it. I let the ring drop on the platform, pretending not to notice. Old Saladino saw it at once. He picked it up and, after admiring it, handed it to me. I pushed it away. 'No, Saladino,' I said, 'I remember promising you I'd bring you a ring someday for little Manuela. Give it to her—*una poco donacion* [a little gift] from me.'

"When the trial resumed, it took a different turn. Saladino called the owner of the horse to the stand and berated him for letting his horse run loose where it might have caused a serious accident. The charge against me was dismissed, and that was the end of it, I figured. But a couple weeks later I saw Nat Smith, who ran a trading post on the Chaco, deep in the Navajo Reservation, standing on the sidewalk in front of my place in Gallup, convulsed with laughter as he read the sign that extended across the front of the store. He read it aloud to me as I came out: '*Mike Kirk, the Honest Indian Trader.*'

" 'Honest, my foot!' he chuckled. 'You bribed Saladino Rojas, slipping him that ring. But if you think you got the best of him, you're mistaken. That horse had been dead for two days before you got to Oraibi.' "

When Mike was able to control his laughter, he said, "You ought to look up Nat Smith; he's living somewhere in southern California. If you can get him to talk, ask him to tell you about the ledge of gold-bearing rose quartz in Navajo land that almost cost him his life."

In the press of other matters, I made no attempt to locate Nat Smith, and then by accident, as such things usually happen, I found him running an Indian curio store, around the corner from the old Hollenbeck Hotel on Second Street in Los Angeles. The place looked dirty and down at the heel. So did the proprietor, a tall, stoop-shouldered man with a bearded face. I made a small purchase and mentioned Mike Kirk's name. He brightened momentarily as some old memory flashed across his mind. "I read that he's passed away," he said. "I was sorry to hear it. I suppose he told you about the trouble I had."

"Just enough to arouse my interest. He said if I ever located you and could get you to talk that you could tell me a story."

A woman had stopped at one of the windows and was looking over the curios on display. She seemed to be about to enter, and then changed her mind and walked on. Smith guided me to the rear of the store and, pointing to a chair, invited me to sit down. I mentioned my interest in lost mines and buried treasure.

"Then you know no Indian will show a mine to a white man, at least no Navajo or Apache. They've seen what mining does to their homeland—men rushing in by the thousand, tearing hell out of everything. That's part of why they won't talk; but the real reason goes back to what the Spaniards—padres as well as the military—did to the Indians who showed them rich mines of silver and gold. What they got out of it was slavery and worse. Don't think those tales haven't been handed down from one generation to the next. They don't talk about it to white men; but they know.

"The market for Navajo jewelry was booming, and the Dine [Navajo people] were bringing in more and more gold to the trading posts and exchanging it for one-ounce slugs of silver. I was damned fool enough to think if I played my cards right I could find out where they were getting the gold and persuade the government to denounce the property so that the mine could be worked on shares with the tribe."

A one-ounce silver slug is exactly what the name implies. For the past thirty years or more the government has made them available to licensed traders for sale or trade to the hundreds of Navajo silversmiths, who were, and still are, the best of all native artisans working malleable metal. The Navajo silver jewelry being produced today is still beautiful, but it has been commercialized and some of the work, especially the filing and buffing, is being done by machinery. The blow torch rather than charcoal is being used in the welding.

Year after year the demand for Navajo silver jewelry, ornamented with native turquoise, continues to increase. To meet it and give employment to young Navajo boys, at least three schools have been set up in New Mexico, where under the competent supervision of their elders, they are taught the art of silversmithing. But the product does not compare with the old "pawn" silver of the past, so called because the owners often pawned it with post traders for supplies.

Silversmithing with the Navajo was not an ancient tribal art. The best information says it does not go back further than 1864, when the tribe was confined at Bosque Redondo by the United States Army and the art was acquired from Spanish silversmiths. Such silver United States coins that came into the Indians' possession were quickly hammered into buttons of various sizes and ornate silver *conchas* (large ornamental belt buttons). When the silversmiths discovered that there was more silver in the Mexican *peso* than the American dollar, they began buying and trading for them. It was after that practice was stopped that the one-ounce silver slugs were made available to them.

To get back to Nat Smith. He told me he noticed there were fine grains of pink or rose quartz in the gold he was buying.

"That told me a lot," he said. "I knew there must be a ledge of that pink stuff somewhere. I didn't say anything; I knew the worst thing I could do would be to ask questions. A young Indian used to hang around the store a lot. He was smart. He'd been to a reservation school and done so well he was sent down to Riverside to get some higher education. When he came back after two years, he had added a Spanish handle to his Navajo name and called himself Tomas.

"I needed someone to help out in the store, so I gave him a job. It worked out fine. He was trustworthy. His father was a silversmith, one of the best. I was glad to buy whatever he brought me. The old man was never in any hurry to leave. After we had finished our business, he would sit in a corner for an hour, watching Tomas waiting on customers. He was proud of the boy and had a right to be.

"I had an enlarging glass, and I always examined the gold I bought, looking for those flakes of rose quartz. I never failed to find them. One morning Tomas caught me using the glass. He didn't say anything, but he must have figured out for himself what I was looking for. Shortly after that there was no more rose quartz. I realized that the ledge could be exhausted and that the gold I was buying was coming from another place. But it was the same coarse gold it always had been. More likely, I figured, Tomas had tipped off his father and it was being washed out more carefully to throw me off the track."

A boy came in to buy some arrowheads. He knew exactly what he wanted and took some time selecting several. Nat came back to me when he had finished waiting on him. "That kid knows more about arrowheads than I do," he grumbled as he sat down. "Well, as I was about to tell you," he went on as he filled his pipe, "my curiosity was getting the better of me. I hopped in my flivver one day and rode over to the Chaco Canyon National Monument and asked the geologist if he had ever seen any rose quartz in the canyon. He said no, and advised me to look down the Chaco River. I figured that was the most likely place to find it, but I knew how risky it would be to do any prospecting. I figured if I could get my hands on a chunk of ore, and it showed high values, that I could get some mining company to take over.

"I felt my best chance of getting what I wanted was through Tomas. I didn't say anything, but I was pretty sure he knew what was running through my head. I had a few good things in the store that I had picked up on my trips over the reservation. Of all of them, the one that Tomas wanted most—not for himself but for his father—was a striped chief's saddle blanket, a genuine Bayeta from the Two Grey Hills District. You could run your hand over it and the softness told you it was the kind of wool that came from the old-time sheep, no kinky ends as you get on modern sheep. That small saddle blanket was a collector's item. I knew the Kirks or the Hubbells [famous Indian traders] would gladly pay me three hundred dollars for it.

"One day Tomas' father came in and spent half an hour admiring the saddle blanket. That evening I told Tomas the blanket was his—to give it to his father. It almost bowled him over. I know it was outright bribery, but I was getting desperate; I had to find out about that rose quartz before winter locked things up for months. He rolled up the blanket and started out. At the door, he turned back. 'Mr. Nat, you better take back this blanket; I cannot show you the mine or tell you how to find it.' 'Tomas, I don't expect you to,' I told him. 'All I want is a piece of that beautiful quartz. You can get it for me.' After thinking it over a moment, he said, 'I will see. I will speak to my father.'

"Next morning, as I was opening the store, Tomas' father walked in, the blanket rolled up under his arm. He placed it on the counter. The boy was with him. You think an Indian don't know fear? If you do, you're dead wrong. Tomas was scared— right down to the marrow—though he did his best not to show it. I knew the headmen of his clan had sat in judgment on him and tortured him until they were sure he had not betrayed any secrets. 'Pay my son his wages,' the old man said. I counted out the money and they stalked out, not saying another word.

"I never saw Tomas again. I don't know what they did with him. Sent him some place where he would not be tempted again, I suppose. I should have stopped right there, but when a man gets gold on the brain, he'll do a lot of foolish things. I went out to locate that ledge of rose quartz. I was going down the Chaco at noon, and as I came through a thicket of mesquite, six bucks seemed to rise out of the ground and surround me. I was acquainted with every one of them, but there was no sign of recognition in their steely eyes. Words wouldn't have done any good. I just turned around and backtracked out of there, figuring I was lucky to be alive.

"I'd been doing a fair business, but suddenly I didn't have any customers—not one. It wasn't any ordinary boycott; the *shamans* [medicine men] had put a curse on me and my store. I'm sure if I'd offered to give everything on the shelves away free, no Navajo would have crossed the threshold to cart the stuff out. And that damned beating of the drums, all night long, was more than I could stand. I packed what things I could into the flivver and filled her up with gas. I had a little left. I tosed it on the floor and lit a match to the place. As I drove away there wasn't an Indian in sight."

"How long ago was that, Nat?" I asked.

"Going on ten years now."

"And you've never been tempted to go back?"

"Never! I wouldn't go back for a million dollars. I got no hankering for gold any more. The Navajos knocked that out of me."

TEXAS

21

The Lost San Saba Mine

The folklore of Texas is laced with innumerable accounts of lost mines and lost hoards of buried silver. Most of these accounts begin in antiquity, when Spain, and later the Mexican government, had sovereignty in the state. As a consequence they begin with solid historical fact, but the magnification of legend soon takes over and they are accepted as authentic folk tales, which need no documentation to be believable.

Of all the lost mines of Texas, none has engaged the attention of as many men, and been as avidly sought, as the Lost San Saba. It is not only a mine but a cave in which a fortune in molten silver bars lies buried. In Texas it is as equally well-known as the Lost Bowie Mine—or *La Mina de los Almagres* (ochre red hills), or *La Mina de las Amarillas*. In common usage they are regarded as the same, although it is sixty-five miles from the Almagres Hills to the Mission San Saba de la Santa Cruz, on the south bank of the San Saba River, the area in which the treasure seekers have long since come to agree the San Saba silver will be found.

To begin at the beginning, in February, 1756, Don Bernardo de Miranda, lieutenant-general of the province of Texas, accom-

panied by a small company of soldiers, five civilians of consequence, an interpreter, and peons to do the camp work, set out
from the small settlement of San Fernando (San Antonio)
"with orders from the governor to investigate thoroughly the
mineral riches so long rumored on the Llano River." Having
traveled eight days to the northwest, he reached the Arroyo
San Miguel, today's Honey Creek, a tributary of the Llano.
From his camp, the Cero des Almagre (Almagre or Red Hill)
was visible, less than a mile to the north.

A cave that opened into the mountain revealed traces of silver. He explored it thoroughly and prospected both cave and
mountain. With the unwarranted optimism that seems to have
been characteristic of the explorers of New Spain, he wrote the
Viceroy, at Mexico City, on his return to San Fernando three
weeks later:

"The mines which are in the Cerro del Almagres are so rich
that I guarantee to give to every settler in the province of Texas
a full claim. . . . The principal vein is more than two varas in
width and in its westward lead appears to be of immeasurable
thickness."

He pointed out that everything was at hand for conducting
mining operations—the good pasturage for livestock, the land
that could be put to crops, and an abundance of wood and
water. He recommended that a presidio of at least thirty men
be established there "to guarantee the protection of the miners
against Indians."

With his report, as evidence of his findings, he sent several
pounds of ore to be assayed. No response being forthcoming,
Miranda, after waiting two months, journeyed to Mexico City
and presented his petition in person to the Viceroy. His samples of ore had been assayed by Manuel de Aldaco, a wealthy
mine owner, and had proved of considerable value. But Aldaco
pointed out to the Viceroy that three pounds of hand-picked

ore was not proof of any extensive deposit. He suggested that thirty jack loads of ore be transported to the nearest smelter—which happened to be at Mazapil, in the province of Zacatecas, seven hundred miles away—and that the cost of transporting it there be borne by Miranda and his associates.

Miranda's associates were the five men who had accompanied him on the expedition to El Almagre. They came to Mexico City and with him protested that the cost of transporting forty mule loads of ore to Mazapil was beyond their means and that the assay should be undertaken at the expense of the Crown. In the end, they agreed to underwrite the operation themselves, and after twenty months of wrangling, on November 23, 1757, the Viceroy accepted their offer.

This was a typical piece of Spanish political double-dealing. The Viceroy had used his wealthy friend Aldaco to discourage Miranda, for he at no time had any intention of building a presidio (fort) at Honey Creek on the Llano River. At the very time that Miranda and his friends were cooling their heels in Mexico City, the Spanish government had, without their knowledge, established a presidio of one hundred troops, named San Luis de las Amarillas, on the north bank of the San Saba River, in the vicinity of today's Menard, Texas, sixty miles to the northwest, on June 30, 1757.

With hopes high, Miranda returned to Texas, only to be dispatched on urgent business to the eastern part of the province. With that mission, he disappears from the confusing story of the Lost San Saba Mine.

Captain Diego Ortiz de Parrilla, the commander at San Luis de las Amarillas, asked permission to remove his garrison to the Llano River. His request was refused, which makes one wonder if the highest authority in Mexico already had information about the great deposit of silver on the San Saba. This new fort is supposed by history to have been established as a buffer against the wild Comanche Indians. There is equal reason to believe it was placed there to protect an important mining operation.

Just prior to the establishing of the presidio on the San Saba, which was built by troops from the recently abandoned San Xavier Mission on the beautiful little San Gabriel River, to the east in Williamson County, all three missions on the San Gabriel were closed because of, in the words of the Church, "internal disorder" and were consolidated in a new mission on the San Saba, named Mission San Saba de la Santa Cruz, with Fray Alonso Giralde de Terreres as superior. This shifting of the missions from the San Gabriel to the San Saba hints of further intrigue. To save face, it was said that this removal was not authorized by the head of state, and as a result the vicar general of the College of Santa Cruz, in Mexico, in command of all missions, is said to have turned over to the government all mission property on the San Gabriel. However, the effects of the San Gabriel missions were turned over to Fray Alonso to be used in the new mission on the San Saba.

What was afoot becomes plain enough when history discloses that Pedro Romero de Terreres, a wealthy and experienced mining man from Mexico, and the cousin of Fray Alonso, was in charge of the removal and the building of the Mission San Saba de la Santa Cruz. It was located three miles below the presidio on the south side of the river. Later, a second mission was built on the south bank of the San Saba four miles below the first. Of course, the ostensible purpose of the missions was to convert the Apaches and such Comanches as could be brought into the fold. But this concentration of power in so small an area suggests that the government had another stake there that it meant to develop and protect. It was able to do neither, for after twelve years of almost incessant raids and warfare with the Plains Indians, it was forced to retire from the San Saba in 1769. The year after the second mission was finished, it had been attacked and destroyed by Comanche warriors. The few survivors made their way up the river to the original Mission San Saba de la Santa Cruz.

Three of the six Franciscans stationed on the San Saba were ordered to return to Mexico. This they did. The three who remained endeavored to till their irrigated fields with the help of their converts, but the Comanches attacked again and again. Captain Parrilla would appear with a troop of soldiers and drive them off. But after camping in the mission yard for a few days, he would return to the presidio. He would no sooner be gone, however, than the harassment of the mission was renewed. Fields were destroyed and livestock either killed or driven off.

Captain Parrilla was a thorn in the flesh of the priests. Recognizing his inability to protect the mission, he ordered them to close it and return to Mexico. Knowing he had no authority over them, they defied him. On March 16, 1758, the Comanches settled the dispute in his favor. An estimated two thousand warriors swooped down on the mission, burning it to the ground and slaughtering all but a handful of its inmates, who escaped to the presidio. Including soldiers and their families, laborers (miners), traders, and others, there were about four hundred people in the fort.

The Indians, made doubly ferocious by their success at the mission, attacked the presidio at once, swarming about the stockade, exposing themselves recklessly to the gunfire from the loopholes. They were cut down by the score. Before darkness intervened, their losses amounted to three hundred or more. During the night they removed their dead and wounded. The attack was renewed at dawn, but the fort put up such a stout defense that they were forced to retire.

Parrilla seized this opportunity to divest himself of the three Franciscans and sent them south to Mexico with a bullion train over a road that came to be called by Texans the Silver Trail.

It struck southward to the Llano River and on to the Frio and the Neuces. Signs of it were still visible half a century ago. It could have been worn so deep only by pack trains, and bullion receipts still on file in Mexico leave no doubt as to the nature of the cargo they carried.

The Comanches were more determined than ever to destroy the Presidio San Luis de las Amarillas. They had learned to their cost that attacking en masse was not the way to do it. Returning to their accustomed way of making war, constant surveillance, sniping, picking off a man or two at a time, making it impossible for the Spaniards to tend their crops, and running off any livestock that strayed beyond the guns of the men sent out to protect it, served their purpose better.

Understandably those wild rovers of the plains did not want a Spanish fort on lands they held to be theirs. But the Spaniards had made other encroachments elsewhere without whipping them to such fury. Certainly they were aware of the extent of the mining operations being conducted on the San Saba, of the silver ore that was being smelted and carried out of the country in the form of silver bars.

It has often been said that gold and silver meant nothing to Indians. Obviously it meant something to the Comanches. They were not a hunting tribe. They had no furs to barter for guns and ammunition; in peaceful times, when they traveled to San Antonio, the only article of exchange they offered was silver. And it was malleable silver that they hammered out to make their conchas and other ornaments, even bullets.

The decade that followed brought neither peace nor any sense of real security to the Presidio San Luis de las Amarillas. History has very little to say about Diego Ortiz Parrilla, but he must have been a determined, capable officer. After the expulsion of the three Franciscans, following the burning of the mission, the presidio is mentioned only as a purely military outpost, without a spiritual adviser. This is unbelievable. Knowing the power and authority of the Church, it is unthinkable that the vicar-general of missions would have permitted the three or four hundred souls living at San Luis de las Amarillas to be without a priest and father-confessor.

It may have been that the fiery Parrilla, no lover of priests, deliberately ignored the presence of the men of the cloth he was forced to accept. In this he could have been abetted by Don Pedro Romeo Terreres, the cousin of Fray Alonso, the founder of the Mission San Saba. Terreres was not only a mining expert but a businessman. He was there for one purpose. Even if the tales of the countless and fabulously rich *cargas* of silver that he dispatched to Mexico City, year after year, are discounted by 50 percent, he acquitted himself with distinction.

Throughout the spring and summer of 1768, the Presidio San Luis de las Amarillas was practically under siege. A lull came when the Comanches drew off to follow the buffalo herds and secure meat for the winter. Captain Parrilla seized the opportunity to send his entire horse herd across the Rio Grande into the province of Coahuila for safety. The surmise can be ventured that he knew he was going to have great need of the animals the following spring.

By the time the great *caballada* returned, preparations for the evacuation of Presidio San Luis de las Amarillas were complete. In April, 1769, it was abandoned and the long march back to the Rio Grande began. It marked the end of any Spanish connection with what was to become the famous Lost San Saba Mine and the cavern of buried silver bars. Whether the Spaniards had spent the winter months effectively concealing their mine or mines and the rich cache they were leaving behind, or whether it was done by the Comanches when they overran the old fort and destroyed it, no one can say with certainty. That the Indians may have done it to thwart any party of white men, Spanish, Mexican, or American, who might be attracted to the region hunting treasure is certainly a possibility, which only very few writers have accepted. J. Frank Dobie was not one of them.

In his *Coronado's Children* three old men in Menard claimed that as boys, playing in the water hole below the fort, they often stood on a cannon barrel beneath the surface. When the water was drained off in 1927, no cannon was found. Earlier than this, according to Dobie, a man named Burnum had lost $1500 in pumping dry a cave north of the old fort and had emptied a small lake above Menard with no better results. It seems obvious that the Spaniards, before leaving the area, had diverted the river and so had effectively concealed their mine.

If so, why didn't Burnum find some trace of the treasure he was seeking when he pumped the lake dry half a century later? It is not to be doubted that it was the Spaniards who diverted the little San Saba River—although it was not an undertaking that was beyond the capabilities of the Comanches, who were being supplied with whatever they needed by the Comancheros from New Mexico at the little *plazas* (trading posts) they had established in what we know as the Texas Panhandle. But it can be taken for granted that the Indians knew the exact location of the silver riches and would not have gone to the labor of puting land underwater where there was nothing to conceal.

Far more important than who erased all sign of the twelve years of mining at the Presidio San Luis de las Amarillas is the fact that it was done so thoroughly that the Lost San Saba remains a mystery, despite several hard-to-dismiss claims to the contrary. Naturally following the withdrawal of the Spaniards, the tales of the Old Spanish Mine had a wide circulation among the Spanish-speaking people of Texas. They were content to talk and dream about it, and it was not until the vanguard of American adventurers (to put a good name on them) appeared in Texas that definite efforts were made to find it.

This was in 1810–1812. What was left of the Presidio San

Luis de las Amarillas to guide them to the bonanza on the San Saba? The ruins of a rock wall enclosing an area of three to four acres, the rubble of the fort itself, pieces of silver slag and traces of a smelter outside the stockade, and an ancient irrigation ditch—that was all. It was more than most seekers of lost mines have to lead them to fortune. Of course, maps purporting to show the way to the Lost San Saba were for sale in the plazas of San Antonio. They were worthless fakes. The fools who bought them for a few pesos were not rash enough to attempt to put them to use.

It is generally agreed that the first American to set out on the trail of the Lost San Saba was Harp Perry. Perry had ridden into Texas as a member of Augustus Magee's little army of filibusters whose announced purpose was to free Texas from Spanish rule and establish an independent state. This was the second such attempt. The first, led by Philip Nolan in 1799–1801, being poorly supported, was crushed. The Magee expedition, aided by Mexican revolutionists under Bernardo Gutierrez, captured San Antonio and defeated the Royalists in several minor engagements, but were ultimately overpowered and dispersed, the surviving remnants seeking safety in what were then considered to be the wilds of the Colorado (Texas) River, a hundred miles north of San Antonio.

One such party, led by Harp Perry and another American (name unknown) and numbering thirty or more Mexicans, left the Colorado and struck west up the Llano River, their goal being the old presidio on the San Saba. They got as far as the Little Llano, where, according to Harp Perry's story, told fifty years later, they found evidence of previous mining (it could have been where Miranda made his discoveries in 1756). Giving up any thought of going on to the San Saba, they settled where they were and built what he calls a "furnace" in which to smelt the ore (silver and some gold) that they were taking out of the ground. Having no molds for the molten metal, they poured it into hollow canes (sotol). When it was cold they buried the canes.

In that fashion, Perry claimed, they buried over a thousand pounds of gold and silver before the expedition was slaughtered by the Comanches, only Perry and the other American escaping with their lives.

Perry's story of the years that followed is largely a blank. He claims to have made his way to Mexico and lived there through the Mexican Revolution, the Mexican-Texas struggle, the Mexican war with the United States, and our Civil War. Wherever he was—and there is some reason to believe he was in St. Louis for a long period—he was back in Texas in 1865, looking for the treasure he had helped to bury.

It was a long time to wait. Too long, he was to discover. Out on the Llano the Indians were still a menace. It was about the only thing that had not changed. Erosion and thickets of encroaching brush had altered the face of the country. After a year of being unable to orient himself, even with the help of the several frontiersmen he hired, he gave up. He was too old to continue. Catching on with a trail outfit at Belton that was pointing north for Kansas, he set out for his old home in St. Louis. He was never to reach it, for somewhere north of Red River Station the accidental discharge of his pistol killed him instantly.

Any man with such a story as Harp Perry told always finds disciples, believers, to carry on for him. A man named Medlin had heard it first hand and hired himself out to herd sheep in the Llano Hills that he might be able to sustain himself while he hunted for Harp Perry's furnace and his buried treasure. He searched for two years and found what may have been the old furnace and other artifacts. But he did not find the gold and silver canes.

If any serious attempts were made to find the mines in the

Los Almagres Hills or what was then referred to as the Old Spanish Mine on the San Saba following the massacre of the Harp Perry party, they have escaped written history. But the mines were not forgotten. On November 2, 1831, James Bowie was to anoint them with his fame and give them immortality in the legends and folklore of Texas.

22

The Lost Bowie Mine

If there is no good biography of James Bowie it is, perhaps, because one could not be written without severe damage to the popular image of the man. Much of the glamor that surrounds him would have to be put down as legend. No one ever saw him ride alligators, spear wild cattle, or fight his deadly duels in dark rooms with his fearful "bowie" knife. Nor could it be omitted that he and his brother Rezin trafficked illegally in slaves with Lafitte and other captains on Galveston Island and along the Gulf Coast. If he was pompous, vainglorious, ever ready to pit his life against a chance at great wealth (which never came his way), he was also a remarkable man, courageous and brave to the point of foolhardiness; and he died gloriously at the Alamo.

Both he and his brother were born in the Tennessee hills at Elliot Springs. They drifted together into Arkansas and down into Louisiana. They were frontiersmen before all else. On coming to west Texas in 1828–29, they prospected for gold and silver far beyond the last settlements on the upper Nueces and Frio rivers.

The numerous tales of how Jim Bowie ingratiated himself

with the chiefs of the Lipan Apaches are not supported by anything that appears in written history. That he lived with Chief Xolic's band of Lipans for a time can be substantiated. That he tried to bribe the old chief to show him the secret mine from which they took the silver bartered in San Antonio would not have been out of character. That he succeeded can be put down as doubtful. But from the Lipans he must have learned much about their enemies, the Comanches, and the Old Spanish Mine on the San Saba.

When Jim Bowie set out from San Antonio for the Indian country on November 2, 1831, it was with the publicly announced intention of finding this mine. His brother, Rezin Bowie, was with him, and they were accompanied by nine carefully chosen men. One of these was Cephas Ham, who was to contradict much of Bowie's account of the expedition, after Bowie's death in the Battle of the Alamo, and to hold forth for a decade as the repository of all knowledge connected with what came to be known as the Lost Bowie Mine.

Cephas Ham flatly denied the widely believed story that when Bowie was living with the Lipans they had shown him the cave in which the Spanish treasure was stored, with "silver bars piled so high that a man on horseback could not look over them." Instead, he claimed, it was he (Ham) who had been adopted by the Indians. They were Comanches of Chief Incorroy's band. He often heard them talking about the great Spanish treasure, but he had never seen it. "It was near the old fort," he said. "The only white man to see it was Rezin P. Bowie."

Always he insisted that Rezin Bowie had made a previous trip to the San Saba and not only had seen the storage of silver but had found the mine; that he had hacked off some samples of ore with his tomahawk and sent them to New Orleans to be assayed. The report that came back was so rich that, although it was late in the year, October, James Bowie organized his expedition and set out at once. Ham says Bowie got him to "cut loose" from the Indians and that he didn't know until he reached San Antonio that it was a trick on Bowie's part to get him to join the expedition.

There is some truth in the foregoing, but most of it runs contrary to the known facts. Nowhere is it of record that Rezin Bowie made a previous journey to the old Presidio San Luis de las Amarillas. Had he been there before, then the Bowie expedition knew where it was going when it left San Antonio. If so, it could have traveled the one hundred and fifty miles to the San Saba in a few days, yet in Bowie's own words, three weeks passed before they reached the old fort. He covers this by saying, "We were examining the nature of the country."

What it was they "examined" or where it was that they wandered for those three weeks, he does not say. Having a definite goal in mind, it follows that neither he nor his brother apparently knew how to reach it. When Ferdinand Roemer, the German scientist, visited the San Luis de las Amarillas in 1847, he found a number of names carved on the old stone gateposts of the fort. One of the carvings was: "Bowie Mine: 1829." Others say the date given was 1832. Both dates are incorrect. But all true believers in the Bowie legend are certain that Bowie himself left his name there. They don't explain his confusion as to the year, which certainly was 1831.

If we are to be guided by provable evidence, the nearest the Bowie party got to the old Spanish fort was Calf Creek, in today's McCulloch County, over twenty miles east of San Luis de las Amarillas. There, at dawn on November 19, their camp was attacked by several hundred screaming Comanches. They were not taken by surprise. For several days they had known that hostile Indians were closing in on them and they had selected the camp on Calf Creek for its defensive possibilities. They had a thicket in front of them, running down to the creek, and a cave in the hillside at their back, into which they drove their horses.

The fight lasted all day. The Indians lost heavily, most accounts putting the number at fifty. Several of Bowie's men were wounded. One, a man named Buchanan, was shot in the leg, the wound so painful that he could not ride. Waiting for him to mend, the party remained on Calf Creek for a week, and then made its way back to San Antonio no richer than when it left.

Some choniclers have it that Thomas McCaslin was killed in the Calf Creek fight and was buried in the cave. This springs from the fact that ex-Judge J. R. Norton and his partner, a former actress calling herself "Princess Wenonah," found his grave in the Silver Mine area, forty miles west of Calf Creek, and put up a marker saying he had fallen in the Bowie-Indian battle, which obviously was impossible.

After his return to San Antonio, Bowie claimed that he had found the cached silver of the Spaniards. He offered no proof of it, but his name was enough to enable him to put together a second expedition the next spring and head for the San Saba. He reached the ruins of San Luis de las Amarillas without difficulty, but rains or Indians or both had erased all signs of the cave he claimed to have found. His detractors say that he only "pretended" not to be able to find it; that he took his bearings and planned to return a third time with a small party so that there would be fewer with whom he would have to divide the spoils. When he returned empty-handed to San Antonio for the second time, the Texas War for Independence was at hand. The part he played in winning it is history.

It was only after the struggle was over and Texas was mourning its gallant dead that the site of the Bowie-Indian battle began to be questioned. Fire had burned off the thicket on Calf Creek, but the hill and the cave were there, and what appeared to be a hastily made breastwork. Ham said no; that the fight had taken place on a then unnamed little creek (Jackson's Creek today), six miles east of the old fort. To the surprise of many, Rezin Bowie agreed with him. On tiny Jackson's Creek, searchers found a spot that matched the site named in the original story, even to a crude fortification of rocks. Ham and Rezin Bowie may have been right, for if the party were coursing for San Luis de las Amarillas it can be argued that the battle would have taken place more logically six miles to the east rather than twenty or more eastward on Calf Creek.

One place will do as well as the other. What is important is that soon the whole area came to be regarded as the site of the Old Spanish Mine, and in popular usage it was given a new name. Referring to it as the Lost San Saba went out of fashion and it became the Lost Bowie Mine. It is hard to understand why, unless one is acquainted with the Texas temperament at the time.

Bowie's name was enough to keep interest alive in the lost treasure until the Comanches and Kiowas began to lose their hold on the country. Cattlemen were moving out on the upper Colorado and the Middle and North Concho rivers; Goodnight and Loving were pushing their herds out to Horsehead Crossing and up the Pecos. Even before the Indians ceased to be a menace on the San Saba, the search for the Lost Bowie began in earnest. Anything that looked like a walled-up cave was opened and explored. The man who found an ax buried in the trunk of a post oak, the handle rotted away, or picked up a piece of broken bit or stirrup was convinced that he was close to the great bonanza.

The stories multiplied and became more fantastic as the years passed. The small-town Texas press welcomed such tales and printed them as straight news. As a result, the Lost Bowie was repeatedly "found." Although these accounts invariably proved to be premature or without substance, the next one to pop up was solemnly accepted as the "true" discovery. A man from Lampasas claimed to have found a cave in which icicles of pure silver hung from the ceiling. He brought a sample out to prove his story. He was organizing a company to exploit his find when, very conveniently for legend, he was stricken ill and died. Of course, his neighbors, who were acquainted with his story, tried to find the cave of silver stalactites but never could locate it.

Some of the tales that sent a continuing and ever increasing number of treasure seekers into the San Saba Hills were the fabrications of entertaining old liars. But not all. A justice of the Texas supreme court, successful lawyers and ranchers, men of some means, took time off from their regular occupations to join the adventurers questing for the lost Spanish treasure.

There was Moses Grumble, an old Indian fighter, who was ranching on the San Saba River near the mouth of Brady Creek, in San Saba County, seventy-five miles below the old fort, which was not far enough away to keep him from having a lively intrest in the Bowie Mine. From some undisclosed source he learned that a Mexican woman, who had been a captive of the Comanches for years until a Comanchero had purchased her freedom, was living in San Antonio, married and getting along in years. He went down to learn what she could tell him about the source of the Comanche silver.

She talked freely, but she could not tell him where the silver was taken out of the ground. "It was very near the old presidio," she said. "We used to go there four or five times a year. The women would go to a certain place nearby on Los Moros Creek. There we would wait, while the men went on. They would not be gone long. When they returned they would be carrying silver, which we had to carry to camp."

Grumble was satisfied that if she could show him the place where the squaws had waited he could find the mine. He made an arrangement with her and her husband. The Mexicans put their effects in a wagon and Grumble rode ahead. When they reached the village of San Saba, a week later, he put up at the hotel and they made their own camp. In the morning, he stepped into the saloon for a drink and came face to face with an old and bitter enemy. Both men drew at once. Grumble slipped to the floor dead.

The Mexican woman took it as a warning that she had better do no more talking. She and her husband returned to San Antonio, and although other men offered to pay her well to show them the way to the creek that she knew as "Los Moros," she refused. She died a year later. With her passing was lost the best hope of finding the silver of San Luis de las Amarillas.

The clear little San Saba River is a godsend to the parched land through which it flows. After 1900, it began to attract amateur treasure seekers and the just "curious." They explored and dug everywhere and found nothing. But bit by bit they carried away what remained of the ruins of the old presidio until little was left to mark the spot.

Interest in the Lost San Saba or Lost Bowie, call it what you will, was not confined to Texas, as the following feature article by James Bee in the St. Louis, Missouri, *Globe Democrat* of October 15, 1896, attests. Here it is in considerably less than its entirety. It is headlined: "Finds Lost Mine."

These mines [the Lost San Saba and Lost Bowie] . . . are somewhere in Menard County, Texas. Being lost in fact and not in fiction, they are not so rich as other lost mines, because they yield only plebian silver, and not patrician gold. They were certainly worked for a number of years, and, even with the crude methods of reducing ores then in vogue, furnished a rich return. This is a fact as historically true as the battle of Waterloo, and the evidence is as readily obtainable.

For nearly one hundred and fifty years these mines have lain so effectively hidden that no man has been able to find them. They are still there, where they have always been, for in non-earthquake region mines have no power of locomotion. . . . The history of these riches, that keep so persistently hidden, can be told in a few lines.

Here follows the story of the building of the missions and the presidio on the San Saba, together with a completely erroneous account of what the writer calls the "Indian uprising" and the retirement of the Spaniards from the San Saba. To resume:

In a few years, however, the enterprising Anglo-Saxon began to drift down into Texas. He heard of the lost San Saba mines and forthwith proceeded to hunt them up.

He next mentions the two Bowie expeditions.

Since Texas became separate from Mexico, few years have passed that have not seen numbers of eager searchers in the San Saba hills, and their numbers are continually on the increase. So far but one of them has ever found these mines; and strange to say, his story of success is the hardest hard-luck story of them all. His name is Frank Hobson.

He needs no further description here than that he is a young man, not given to reflection before acting. Two years ago he came to San Antonio with no definite object in view. . . . It was not long before he heard of the lost San Saba mines. He had had some experience as a mineral prospector. He was determined to hunt those mines and to keep hunting them until he found them. This he did.

In these late days there was no danger from Indians; the valiant defenders of the treasure have long ago disappeared. The location of this old mission church [?] was well known. Its four thick stone walls still form a conspicuous landmark in the valley in spite of war and fire, vandalism and the wearing of the years.

Carefully collecting all the information he could get, Hobson set forth on a systematic search. His outfit was very simple, and from the way he harnessed his equipment to himself it was not so much trouble moving about as one would imagine. . . . Everything he could, he carried in three heavy canvas bags. He had a few pounds of cornmeal, salt in a tightly closed tin can, matches, candles, a coil of rope, a canteen, fishing tackle, ammunition, a shotgun compass and a prospector's hammer. When he craved bread he made Johnny Cake with the meal. As to meat, there was game in the mountains and fish in the streams. With a fishing line and ammunition no man in that country need worry about the larder.

From the ruins of the old mission [he is referring to the fort, of course] he described a circle in the country round about, going carefully and patiently over all the ground within its circumference. Then he described another, and many others, with constantly increasing orbits. Every two or three weeks he would appear at Menardville, tanned, unshaven, and in every respect looking decidedly tough, but the Menardvillians were accustomed to the peculiarities of treasure hunters and he caused no special comment. These appearances were for the purpose of replenishing his stock of meal and ammunition. The practical side of this method of search can be readily appreciated. It promised to reveal something, provided life and patience lasted.

All through the hot summer months he searched, and one day early in the fall he was walking up the bed of a little creek, seeking a prominent landmark from which to locate his next circle. There were narrow bottom lands on each side covered with a dense growth of shrub and prickly undergrowth. Beyond were high hills, strewn thickly with boulders and spotted with a scattered growth of mesquite and scrub oak. It was the dry season and the creek was but a succession of long reaches of gravel, relieved by far-apart water holes. Hobson had his head down looking for "float"—pieces of gravel containing mineral.

Turning a bend he suddenly heard a flutter and chirping sound just in front, and looked up in time to see a bunch of wild turkeys disappear in the brush. . . . Putting aside all thought of lost mines, Hobson proceeded to trail them, forcing his way through the thorny brush. He found a feather here, a track there, where there was sand or soil, and sundry droppings which furnished indications to encourage the hunter. Across this bottom he went and then into a steep walled draw . . . then along a rocky ridge, down into another little draw . . . and entered a jumble of rocks, scrub oak and cedar. In his eagerness he lost all idea of direction, and after wandering around in this maze he found he had lost the trail of his turkeys also.

. . . divesting himself of his equipment and packs, he sat down, with his back to a mesquite tree which grew at the base of a large boulder. He drank from his canteen and looked about him. . . . There was a crescent shaped hole at the foot of the big rock which at once obtruded itself upon his attention. It was barely large enough to admit an average man's head and shoulders, and had a dark, cavernous beyond. Hobson pushed his head and part of his body into this hole. . . . He found the place opened out within and his arms were free to move and feel around. Above was the hard bottom of the boulder. In front and below he swung his arms into empty space.

Further investigation disclosed that his chest was resting on the edge of a hole whose bottom might be just out of reach or hundreds of feet below. Judging from the contour of the rim as far as he could feel, it was a circular pit about four feet in diameter. A wild idea came into his brain. He backed out and began with feverish haste to claw away at the loose soil and sand at the entrance, so as to enlarge the opening. Then he looked in again and lit a candle. . . . He was bending over a round hole to which the feeble light showed no bottom. On its sides, however, were the certain marks of tools. Hobson's heart gave a bound so tremendous that he thought it almost leaping from his mouth. He drew out into sunlight again, uncoiled his rope and tied knots at intervals along the entire length. He fastened it securely around the mesquite, threw the other end into the pit's mouth . . . and began to descend. The sides of the shaft were so close together and so jagged and uneven that he could brace himself with his feet and shoulders, relieving his arms. Down he went until he came to the rope end. He swung out but his circling feet touched nothing.

His disappointment was so keen that he was almost tempted to let go and jump, but he did not. He braced himself, lit his candle and peered below. . . . There below him, not more than a dozen feet was the bottom, vague and indistinct, but certainly the bottom. He let himself loose and dropped like a plummet. The rush of the fall blew out the candle, and he lit feet first in a pile of something that crashed and crackled. A pungent dust arose and stung his nostrils. On relighting his candle he found he was standing nearly knee deep in a pile of bones and there were skulls among them. But bones had no terror for Hobson; to his quick mind it called for increased exultation. They were probably the remains of the old task masters [the Spaniards, killed by the Indians, according to the writer] thrown down and covered, a punishment in harmony with their crimes.

Two tunnels led away to right and left, high enough for a man to walk through with a little stooping. To the right he [Hobson] went for some fifty feet and found a solid face of mineral that glistened and glittered in the candlelight. On the floor a pile of it lay broken up like macadam. It needed but a glance to tell what it was. It was galena, rich with silver, the richest he had ever seen. What extravagances he committed down there in the dark hole can only be imagined. The lost mine was found! He would go up, get a sack and take away some of the ore as evidence and for the almost superfluous certainty of an assay.

But when he came to the foot of the shaft he made another discovery that changed all joy to despair. . . . There was the rope— out of his reach. He could not climb by bracing himself at the sides, for just where the rope ended the shaft widened out, forming a room with a vaulted roof. He sat down among the bones, too sick and weak to stand. How long would the candle last? How long until he too would be an addition to those very old bones? Millions were his, and yet he was poorer than the most wretched beggar. But Hobson was not a man to give up. He looked all around and walked unsteadily into the tunnel on the left, hoping against hope to find something that would enable him to get out, when he almost fell over a pile of half-decayed poles. They were fifteen to twenty feet long, with deep notches cut into them. They were the rude ladders, which furnished the old-time miners with means of getting out and coming in.

Hobson is not ashamed to admit that when he found the poles he sat down and cried with pure joy. When he reached the top he could not tell for the life of him over which he felt the best—his discovery or his welcome escape.

He took a bag of ore, covered up the entrance under the large boulder, marked the trees and figured his direction by compass, and headed for the outside. He could not retrace his own steps because over the rocky surface he had left little or no trail. He kept to the south as well as he knew, taking note of prominent features for marks to guide a return trip. This was rough country, and he was continually getting mixed up in directions, walking in a circle. He finally came to water courses and followed one of them to the San Saba River. It was late at night when he reached Menard.

When Hobson undertook to find his mine again he could not locate it, try as he did. He is in that country right now, searching. He has not been able to locate any of the old landmarks he marked so carefully. He confesses he might think it all a dream were it not for his sack of ore.

Adams of the Adams Diggings often said, "The Apaches made me forget." Perhaps the sight of all that silver made Hobson forget—if there ever was such a character. Inquiry among the old-timers of Menard elicits no memory of a treasure seeker who packed more equipment on his person than one of today's astronauts. "Hobson" existed most likely only in the fertile imagination of the *Globe Democrat* writer, who used his slight and often inaccurate acquaintance with Texas history to give his story the required verisimilitude. If it is presented at some length, this is because such tales have a wide circulation and are repeated over and over until they are believed. As a Sunday supplement feature they are as prevalent today as they were then. It isn't only the plausible old liar at the end of the bar who knows the secret of this or that lost mine and has a million dollars as good as in the bank who claims attention. No one believes him, but the very thought of a great jewelry store of ownerless wealth lying somewhere underground is a constant goad that few men can escape—and they listen, no matter who is doing the talking or the writing.

23

The Secret of the Guadalupes

The Guadalupe Mountains rise abruptly from the high plains of the Trans-Pecos country. Guadalupe Peak is the highest point in Texas, 9,500 feet above sea level. Its companion, Capitan Peak, has an elevation of 8,078 feet. That rugged, almost treeless region was, until the Comanches finally succeeded in pushing them west of the Pecos into New Mexico, the homeland of the Mescalero Apaches. Although it is the continuing belief of many Texans that the Guadalupes are richly mineralized (both gold and silver), the treasure for which they are famous is Old Ben Sublett's Lost Mine—his honest name was William Colum Sublett.

Sometime in the late 1860's, William Colum Sublett put his family in his wagon and left Missouri for the Rocky Mountains of Colorado to make his fortune. Despite the similarity of names, he was not related to the Sublettes, the pioneer fur traders and trail breakers. After ten years of bitter failure, he packed his family in the wagon again and left Colorado for Texas, coming down through the Guadalupes. When he reached the tracks of the new Texas Pacific Railroad, he called a halt and pitched his tent at the flag stop that was to become the town of Monahans. He was in rags, and his wife and children, two young girls and a boy, the youngest of the three, were near starvation.

Somehow they made out, the wife doing washing for the section hands and Sublett getting work of some sort with the railroad. A few months later he filed on a homestead south of the little settlement of nearby Odessa. Ector County records show that he proved up on it and lived there after his wife died. The oldest girl, only fifteen, brought in a few dollars from the washing she did. The rest of their living was supplied by the generosity of the neighbors. Ben brought in nothing. He did a little hauling with his rickety wagon and bony horse, but it was only to provide him with money for another of his incessant prospecting trips into the Guadalupes.

This went on for several years. He always came back empty-handed from his trips. The best anyone could get out of him was that he was "making progress." Odessa regarded him as a joke and put him down as worthless as he limped about town. He had a bullet lodged in his left leg, an old wound that he never chose to explain. The oldest girl begged him to give up his prospecting and get a job. Acquaintances, who had the children's welfare at heart, used stronger terms, and threatened to have the law on him for not supporting his family. It had no effect on old Ben; he was stubborn. He wanted something better than wages for his young ones.

And then one day he got down from his rig at the general store in Odessa and limped inside, carrying a heavy canvas bag. Half a dozen men were in the store. He called them over to the counter and, opening the draw-string of a tobacco sack, poured out on the counter as many nuggets as it would hold. It must have been a great moment for Ben Sublett as he faced the scoffers. "I been poor, but I ain't poor no more," he informed them.

Then, lifting the heavy canvas bag to the counter, he spilled out its contents—fifteen hundred dollars worth of gold ore! Ben Sublett, the crazy prospector, wasn't crazy any more. He laughed in their faces as they begged him to tell them where his mine was located.

"If anybody wants my mine, let him go and hunt for it like I did," said he, remembering the slights and slurs that had been heaped on him. "People have laughed at me and called me a fool. The plains of Pecos and the peaks of the Guadalupes have been my only friends. When I die, I want to be buried with the Guadalupes in sight of my grave and the Pecos on the other. I am going to carry this secret to the other world, so that for years people will remember me and talk about the rich gold mine that old man Sublett found, and I'll give them something to talk about."

He certainly did, and they are still talking. Sublett suddenly became as wily and cunning as a lobo wolf. He was watched, followed whenever he left town, but he always managed to slip away. Every three or four weeks he would take to the hills and return with an ample supply of gold. It was discovered that he was taking his rich ore to Midland, Texas, thirty miles east of Odessa, where he turned it into cash and kept his money in W. E. Connell's bank. It almost proved to be his undoing. Connell and his friend George Gray, a wealthy cattleman, offered Sublett ten thousand dollars if he would show them the source of his gold.

"Hell," Sublett laughed, "I can go out and dig up that much in a week's time!"

Stopped in that direction, Gray and Connell traitorously hired a cowpuncher named Jim Flannigan to follow Sublett and not let him out of sight. It was a full-time job for Flannigan. He made his headquarters in Odessa and waited. When the word was flashed to him that Ben Sublett was gone again, he was on his trail in an hour. Most accounts say that the old man was driving what they call a "hack," drawn by two burros, which would seem to have been not only an unusual means of transportation but one that was bound to leave a trail that could be easily followed across the sandy wastes. Flannigan followed it for fifty-odd miles west to the raw settlement of Pecos on the Pecos River and then north for twenty miles or more before losing it, which is not as incredible as it might seem, for in that open country, with its minimum of cover, he had to lie back for miles to keep Sublett from seeing that he was being trailed.

Flannigan was only one of many who tried to follow old Ben to his mine and failed. In that arid country the winds are always blowing, and in a few hours they erase the tracks of man and beast. Often when he returned from one of his trips into the Guadalupes he confounded men who had tried to trail him by naming them and mocking them for having "lost" him. He was suspicious of all men by then. It became a phobia with him, and he suspected every stranger who appeared in Odessa of being there to steal his mine. The only sound reason that can be advanced for his failure to develop his property is that he found no one whom he could trust.

There is nothing in the last ten years of his life to indicate that he entertained any illusions of grandeur or was interested in acquiring great wealth. No one knows how much gold he brought out of the Guadalupes. It certainly was considerable. He built a fine home for his children and tried to make up to them for the starvation years of their childhood. Many accounts picture him as holding forth in the saloons and enjoying his notoriety. These tales spring from a newspaper article reprinted in *Hunter's Magazine*, October, 1916. Its misinformation has been accepted as factual by some of the foremost chroniclers of the Lost Sublett Mine. We read how old Ben stomped into Abe Williams' saloon, poured his nuggets out on the bar and called up the boys and told them the drinks were on him. " 'My friends, have all the drinks you want,' he said, 'for I have at last found the richest gold mine in the world. I can buy Texas and make a backyard out of it for my children to play in.'" After that, the saloon became his forum, we are told.

The foregoing, although a favorite tale with Texas editors, must be regarded as no more than engaging folklore, for the records of Ector County show that the first licensed saloon in Odessa did not open its doors until 1893, a year after Ben Sublett's death.

The article reprinted in *Hunter's Magazine* includes a personal interview with F. H. Hardesty, an El Paso County (Texas) rancher, that may or may not shed some light on the source of Sublett's gold. He relates how a man named Lucius Arthur stopped at his place to get water for himself and a pack animal, and remained overnight. Growing confidential, Arthur told him he was trailing two Mexicans who had left Ysleta, on the Rio Grande, the previous night. He knew from having followed them once before that they were bound for the Guadalupes to get gold. He related how he had learned that once a year the two Mexicans crossed the Rio Grande and ten days later returned to Mexico with precious metal.

"According to Arthur's story," said Hardesty, "he had trailed the Mexicans and from a place of concealment watched them climb down a rope ladder into a chasm. He saw them haul up sacks of ore and of water for their horses, which were staked on the rim. But he himself had to depend on water so far away that he couldn't keep regular watch. After he had hung around several days, the Mexicans left and then he made a closer inspection. The chasm, from the way he described it, must have varied in width from forty to a hundred feet and was all of sixty feet deep. Down at the bottom he could see the entrance to a cave with freshly broken rock in front of it. He claimed he didn't go down into the chasm because he was short on rope for a ladder."

Hardesty goes on to say that he offered to provide Arthur

(Frenchy, he calls him) with a good outfit, and go in as partners with the man. "But Frenchy never returned to me," Hardesty concludes. "That's all I know about gold in the Guadalupes."

One can believe as much or as little of Hardesty's story as he pleases, but there is no denying the fact that the description of the mine tallies exactly with Ross Sublett's boyhood recollection of the physical features of it, the deep chasm and the shaft that had to be entered on a rope. He was only nine when old Ben, his father, took him to the mine, the only person positively known to have seen it. Also, there is some corroborative evidence in the fact that a man named "Frenchy Arthur" lived for a time at Roswell, New Mexico. He left without giving any indication of where he was going and there is no record of his subsequent whereabouts. That he followed the two Mexicans to the mine in the Guadalupes and killed them, and was in turn killed by a third party, is within the possibilities. Could that third party have been Ben Sublett? It was widely known that he never went armed. But a club or rock would have sufficed if he had caught "Frenchy" climbing out of the shaft. Such things have happened when a fortune in raw gold has been the stake.

But there is nothing in the evidence to suggest that Sublett came into possession of his secret mine by trickery or violence. He was an eccentric, an embittered man who had soured on the whole human race—and not without cause. He had vowed over and over again that he would take the secret of his mine to the grave with him. Once, and only once, he wavered in that determination. On his way into the Guadalupes, he met Cicero Stewart, who was guiding a party of Texas and Pacific Railroad officials on a deer hunt.

It was not a propitious time for such an adventure, for rumors were flying that a large party of Mescaleros had jumped their reservation and were back in the fastnesses of their old stomping grounds in the Guadalupes. The fact that Stewart had his son with him, a boy of five or six, is proof enough that he did not intend to lead the hunters into dangerous country. He was a jack of all trades, much as Sublett had been, and he had befriended Ben's family in the past. He had come out from Mason County, Texas, with a herd owned by Joe Hyatt that was being trailed to the Lower Penasco, in Eddy County, New Mexico. He drifted back to Odessa and was to become a persistent hunter of the Lost Sublett. Gratitude for past kindnesses is the only explanation that can be advanced for Sublett's sudden change of heart about revealing the location of his mine.

The hunting party was camped at water, well out from the southern tip of the mountains, sometimes called "the Point of the Guadalupes." Sublett was invited to spend the night with them, an invitation which he accepted. There was talk about the Mescaleros. Sublett brushed aside the warning that he was likely to run into trouble if he pushed on into the mountains. He had often said that he had nothing to fear from the Apaches. The unlikely story that he had once admitted that a White Mountain Mescalero had shown him his secret mine has led some commentators to suggest that the Apaches may have been the secret sharers of his gold.

After supper, according to Stewart, old Ben called him aside and told him he was making his last trip to his mine. "I've always declared that my secret would die with me, but all day as I been driving along I realized as never before how old I'm getting (he was over eighty) and meeting you here like this, I somehow want to take you with me and show you the mine."

It was the opportunity of a lifetime for Stewart, but he couldn't desert the men he was guiding or risk his boy's life in the mountains. He asked Sublett to describe the location and tell him how to get there. Old Ben shook his head. "It wouldn't do no good. If I told you where it was you'd never find it. You've got to see it."

They parted. The old man was back four days later with gold. It was the last time Stewart was to see him alive. Ben took to his bed in Odessa and was dead a few days later. He was buried there, a long distance from the Pecos.

Stewart was to spend a good part of his remaining life trying to find the Lost Sublett, as did Mike Wilson, who claimed to have actually seen the mine once and brought out some ore, on the proceeds of which he had embarked on a glorious spree, only to find when he sobered up that he couldn't remember how he had found his way to it. For years he lived in a stone hut in the southern foothills of the Guadalupes "just to be close to the mine."

Up to the time of his death, in 1953, the most persevering of all seekers of the Lost Sublett was the one person who is known to have actually seen the mine. That, of course, was Ross Sublett, old Ben's son. When his searching had impoverished him and he could no longer produce his own grubstakes, others were glad to outfit him, for the story of the Lost Sublett had become famous up and down the Pecos Valley.

When it appeared that old Ben's days were numbered, Ross, his eldest sister and her husband, Sid Pitts, hurried over to Odessa from Carlsbad, New Mexico, where they had been living for some time. Ross was then nineteen. He and his brother-in-law begged old Ben to tell them how to reach the mine in the Guadalupes. The old man shook his head. "It's too late. If I told you, you would never find it." That was what he had told Cicero Stewart. "Even if you did," he added, "they'd get it away from you." The "they" he had in mind was undoubtedly the "whole damn human race" that he had so often reviled.

Ross Sublett often told how his father had taken him to the mine when he was a boy of nine. His recollections were understandably hazy. He was sure, he said, that they had crossed the Pecos and that sometime later his father had concealed the wagon, placed him on the horse's back and proceeded the rest of the way to the mine. "It was down in a crevice, and the only way to get to it was by a rope ladder that my father removed as soon as he came up with the gold. I played around while he got the ore out of the cave. I remember that my father packed water from the spring down to the cave in canteens to wash the gold. Some of the gold was in big nuggets as large as bullets. Some pieces of gold were in plain sight in front of the cave. I was glad when father said we could go home. I am sure the mine is within a few miles of the spring in the Rustler Hills."

You do not cross the Pecos to get into the Rustler Hills in the Guadalupes. They are, in fact, some thirty miles or more east of the river. The Lost Sublett well may be in the Rustler Hills. But the contradiction in Ross Sublett's story casts doubt on other parts of it, and the feeling grew among the scores of searchers that he didn't know any more about the location of the mine than they.

His passing, at Carlsbad, had no perceptible effect on the hunt for the Lost Sublett. It continues today, as in the past. Those who seek it are no longer the old-timers; they are younger men, many of them with a college degree. Of course, Ben Sublett wouldn't recognize that country today with its surfaced highways, the forest of trees on the horizon that are not trees but oil derricks and the massacred Pecos, with its multiple dams and reclamation projects. But, as he promised, he left it something to talk about.

Bibliography

Angel, Myron, *History of Nevada*, San Francisco, 1881.

Bancroft, Caroline, with Nafziger, Agnes, *Colorado's Lost Gold Mines and Buried Treasure*, Boulder, Colorado, 1963.

Bancroft, Hubert Howe, *The History of Arizona and New Mexico*, San Francisco, 1889.

Bandelier, Adolph F. A., *The Gilded Man*, New York, 1900.

—— and Fanny Bandolier, *The Journey of Alvar Nunez Cabeza de Vaca and His Companions From Florida to the Pacific*, New York, 1905.

Beebe, Lucius, and Clegg, Charles, *U.S. West, the Saga of Wells Fargo*, New York, 1949.

Botkin, B. A., *Treasury of Western Folklore*, New York, 1951.

Browne, J. Ross, *Adventures in Apache Country*, New York, 1869.

Byerts, W. H., *The Adams Gold Diggings*, El Paso, Texas, 1915.

Caruthers, William, *Loafing Along Death Valley Trails*, Ontario, California, 1951.

Conroto, Eugene L., *Lost Desert Bonanzas*, Palm Desert, California, 1963.

Cook, John W., *Hands Up*, Denver, Colorado, 1897.

Cornelius, Temple H., *Sheepherders Gold*, Denver, 1964.

—— with Marshall, John B., *Golden Treasurers of the San Juans*, Denver, Colorado, 1962.

Coolidge, Dane, *Death Valley Prospector*, New York, 1937.

Dobie, J. Frank, *Apache Gold and Yaqui Silver*, Boston, 1939.

—— *Coronado's Children*, Dallas, Texas, 1930.

—— editor, *Legends of Texas*, Austin, Texas, 1924.

Eberhart, Perry, *Treasure Trails of the Rockies*, Denver, Colorado, 1961.

Ellenbecker, John G., *The Jayhawkers of Death Valley*, Marysville, Kansas, 1938.

Ellis, Amanda M., *Legends and Tales of the Rockies*, Colorado Springs, Colorado, 1954.

) 263 (

Bibliography

Ely, Sims, *The Lost Dutchman Mine*, New York, 1953.

Ferguson, Robert G., *Lost Treasure; the Search for Hidden Gold*, New York, 1957.

Finger, Charles J., *The Distant Prize*, New York, 1935.

Glassock, C. B., *Gold in Them Hills*, New York, 1914.

Hafen, LeRoy, and Hafen, Ann, *The Colorado Story*, Denver, Colorado, 1956.

Harolds Club, Reno, Nevada, *Pioneer Nevada*, Reno, Nevada, 1951.

Holley, Mary Austin, *Texas*, Lexington, Kentucky, 1836.

Lee, Bourke, *Death Valley*, New York, 1930.

Lovelace, Leland, *Lost Mines and Hidden Treasure*, San Antonio, Texas, 1956.

McKenney, J. Wilson, *On the Trail of Pegleg Smith's Lost Gold*, Palm Desert, California, 1957.

Manly, William L., *Death Valley in Forty-nine*, San Francisco and Chicago, 1892.

Penfield, Thomas, *Lost Treasure Trails*, New York, 1954.

Powell, Donald M., *The Peralta Grant*, Norman, Oklahoma, 1960.

Rascoe, Jesse Ed, *Western Treasures Lost and Found*, Toyahvale, Texas, 1961.

—— *More Western Treasures*, Toyahvale, Texas, 1962.

—— *The Golden Crescent, the Southwest Treasure Belt*, Toyahvale, Texas, 1962.

Ruxton, George F., *Life in the Far West*, edited by LeRoy Hafen, Norman, Oklahoma, 1951.

Storm, Barry, *Trail of the Lost Dutchman*, Tortilla Flat, Arizona, 1939.

—— *Thunder Gods Gold*, Tortilla Flat, Arizona, 1945.

Weight, Harold O., and Weight, Lucile, *Rhyolite, Death Valley's Ghost City of Golden Dreams*, Twentynine Palms, California, 1953.

Weight, Harold O., *Lost Mines of Death Valley*, Twentynine Palms, California, 1953.

—— *Twenty Mule Team Days in Death Valley*, Twentynine Palms, California, 1955.

—— *Lost Mines of Old Arizona*, Twentynine Palms, California, 1959.

Wolle, Muriel Sibell, *Stampede to Timberline*, Boulder, Colorado, 1957.

W.P.A. Guide, *Arizona, the Grand Canyon State*, New York, 1940.

W.P.A. Guide, *New Mexico, a Guide to the Colorful State*, New York, 1940.

Magazines: *Colorado Magazine*
Desert Magazine
Frontier Times
True West
Nevada Highways and Parks
Arizona Highways
Westways (formerly *Touring Topics*)
Southwestern Quarterly Review
New Mexico Quarterly Review

Bibliography

Newspapers

Many of the Nevada newspapers mentioned in this book are still being published, such as the *Humboldt Star, The Lovelock Miner-Review,* the *Nevada State Journal,* and others. The great majority, however, disappeared when the boom camps that gave them birth faded into obscurity. The files of many, including the incredible *Rawhide Rustler,* are carefully preserved in the archives of the Nevada State Historical Society in Reno.

NOTE: The paperback pamphlets *The Golden Crescent* and *Western Treasures Lost and Found,* by Jesse Ed Rascoe, are published by the Frontier Book Co., Toyahvale, Texas and copyrighted by Ed. Bartholomew.

Index

Index

Index

Index

Index

Index

Index

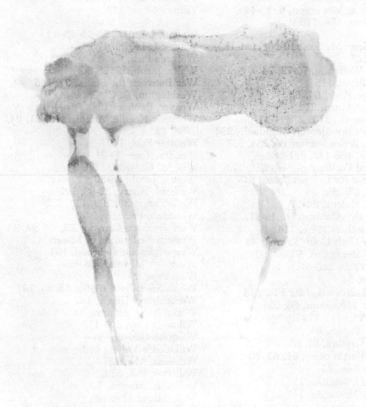